<u>S</u>cripture Politics

Selections from the writings of
William Steel <u>D</u>ickson
the most influential United Irishman of the North

Selected and Introduced by

Brendan Clifford

ATHOL BOOKS
10 Athol Street
Belfast
BT12 4GX

Also by Brendan Clifford

Published by Athol Books:
The Life And Poems Of Thomas Moore
Thomas Russell And Belfast
The Veto Controversy (including Thomas Moore's "A Letter To The Roman Catholics Of Dublin, 1810)
The Dubliner: The Lives, Times & Writings Of James Clarence Mangan
Thomas Russell And Belfast (A biography of "the man from God knows where", the Munster Soldier who was central to the social life of Belfast in the United Irish phase, and was executed for his part in Emmet's Rebellion)
Connolly: The Polish Aspect

Published by The Belfast Historical And Educational Society:
Belfast In The French Revolution
Derry And The Boyne: A Contemporary Account Of The Siege Of Derry, The Battle Of The Boyne and the General Condition of Ireland in The Jacobite War by Nicholas Plunket (Introduction: Brendan Clifford)

Scripture Politics
A Selection From The Writings Of The
Rev. William Steel Dickson,
The Most Influential United Irishman Of The North
Selected and Introduced by
Brendan Clifford
ISBN 0 85034 044 6

is published by

Athol Books,
10 Athol Street,
Belfast,
BT12 4GX.

BX
9225
.D5
A35
1991

© **Athol Books 1991**

Scripture Politics

Selections from the writings of
William Steel Dickson
the most influential United Irishman of the North

CONTENTS

Publisher's Note

This series of reprints of influential Presbyterian United Irish leaders—the Rev. W.S. Dickson, the Rev. J. Porter, and the Rev. T.L. Birch—was advertised as an intended project of the Belfast Historical and Educational Society. The BHES is a registered charitable company. It applied for grants to assist publication to a number of well known institutions, whose business it would seem to be to facilitate such publication. The BHES application was rejected out of hand by the Ireland Fund and the Central Community Relations Unit, Stormont, leaving the BHES out of pocket by the exercise—as applications cost.

Athol Books has therefore undertaken to publish this material. Athol Books has long understood that the extravagant system of subsidies in Northern Ireland is the preserve of well-connected coteries and is subjected to strict political supervision by the incompetent political authorities which exercise hegemony in Northern Ireland. Athol Books is entirely unsubsidised. It is made possible by the fact that all work, from writing to printing, is contributed free. It is therefore immune to the debilitating influence of the slush funds.

Why Steel Dickson Has Been Forgotten

William Steel Dickson was a Presbyterian clergyman, a political writer, and a man of action. He had a powerful mind, an enduring character, stubbornly held principles, and an elegantly forthright pen. He was the prime product of the culture of 18th century Ulster, and was a leading force in the events of the last twenty years of that century. And yet he has been almost entirely forgotten. He is not mentioned at all in most histories, and those which do mention him give no indication of his nature or of his weight in the affairs of his time.

Because of the way history has been written, mention of the United Irishmen evokes the name of Wolfe Tone before any other, and then perhaps the name of William Drennan. It would accord better with the actual course of events if the two best known names of the United Irish movement were the Rev William Steel Dickson and the Rev James Porter, Presbyterian ministers at Portaferry and Greyabbey respectively.

Porter wrote the most popular literature of the movement—the satire on Lord Londonderry and his agents called **Billy Bluff And The Squire.** And Dickson's **Scripture Politics** was the most influential straight political pamphlet of the time.

Other influential writers and leaders of the movement were Sinclare Kelburn and Thomas Ledlie Birch (Presbyterian ministers in Belfast and Saintfield respectively) and William Sampson, a Derry Anglican and the only Ulster barrister of any historical consequence. These too have been dropped out of history.

This great forgetfulness resulted from the Constitutional change of 1800 (the Act of Union) and the subsequent development of a Nationalist movement which, though different in kind from the United Irish movement, claimed to be a continuation of it. The great majority of the United Irish of the North became Unionists—not their children, as is often said, but the people themselves. There was no Nationalist movement of any consequence until 1830, and no Nationalist Republicanism until around 1850. Antrim and Down did not support either O'Connell's nationalism of the 1830's or the later Republican nationalism and were therefore accused of deserting the ideals and principles of their fathers.

The Republican Nationalists of the later 19th century knew little of the United Irish movement of the North beyond its military battles. All they knew of United Irish literature was Wolfe Tone's Journal, written in France. And as time went by they knew little even of that—a couple of paragraphs about separation from England were made well known by the Republican papers, but the Journal as a whole became unsuitable for a movement which was increasingly Roman Catholic in outlook because of the great satisfaction expressed by Tone at what he thought was the overthrow of the Papacy by France in 1798.

The change in the politics of Antrim and Down after 1798 resulted from the change in the Constitutional framework of politics and not from an abandonment of principle.

The United Irish movement was not a republican movement. I have read every issue of its twice-weekly newspaper, **The Northern Star** (1792-7), without finding a republican programme in it. Its aims were the reform of the Parliamentary franchise and the admission of Catholics into Parliamentary politics and the professions on the same basis as Protestants. The Irish Parliament set itself against these reforms, and from 1795 treated the demand for them as seditious. That was what brought about the rebellion of 1798.

The die-hards in the Irish Parliament imagined at first that the suppression of the rebellion would secure their position, and they prepared to subdue the country utterly by a regime of systematic terror. But the British Government decided at this juncture that the Irish Parliament was a public nuisance which should be got rid of. And, having placed an army in the country to suppress the rebellion, Westminster had considerable leverage against the Irish Parliament. The new Viceroy, Lord Cornwallis, made it clear at the outset that while he would suppress the rebellion he would do his utmost to prevent acts of terror against the populace. He quickly came to be seen as an enemy by those who had been the greatest enemies of the United Irish. And when he indicated that he considered them unfit to govern a country, and that their Parliament should be merged with the British, they were outraged.

The year beginning September 1798 was the moment of truth for the Ascendancy Parliament. That was the year when it showed what it was made of. And it *did* show what it was made of. I have read about fifty pamphlets against the Union published in Dublin that year. And the common charge made against the British Government was that it had adopted the programme of the Rebellion.

The Irish Parliament might have saved itself by reforming the franchise and completing Catholic Emancipation. But even in its ultimate crisis it could not bring itself to do these things. It was, in its own peculiar way, true to itself to the end. It defeated the first Union Bill early in 1799. While Pitt and Cornwallis prepared for a second attempt, it made spurious patriotic appeals to the country which a few months earlier it had demanded terrorist action against. Its appeals went unheeded by the country at large—Catholic and Presbyterian. Pitt and Cornwallis then produced their second Bill., having prepared the ground by judicious and extensive bribery of members of this corrupt Parliament, and the Union was carried.

Belfast was extraordinarily passive throughout the dispute over the Union. As far as I know it did not produce a single pamphlet on the subject, or even a newspaper editorial. The resistance bulletin of the Ascendancy, **The Anti-Union**, addressed itself "To The Electors Of Ulster" on January 19th, 1799. It said to them: *"When* *your causes of complaint were trifling, you rent the air with your cries. Now that you are about to be sacrificed on the altar of British aggrandisement, a single murmur does not escape your lips."* But Belfast stayed deaf to the appeals of the Protestant Ascendancy. It did not think its causes of complaint against the Ascendancy Parliament during the preceding century were trifling—and because it was not a participant in Ascendancy privilege it did not see that any of its vital interests would be "sacrificed" in the abolition of the Ascendancy Parliament.

The resistance to the Union was conservative at best and reactionary at worst, and the reactionaries were to the fore. The reactionary movement—being an instrument of the Ascendancy—had little weight in the life of Belfast. And the Belfast conservatives differed from conservatives in other parts of the country in being cautious supporters of gradual reform, rather than defenders of exclusive privilege. The leading conservatives during the 1790s were Dr. William Bruce, headmaster of Belfast Royal Academy, and Henry Joy of the **News Letter**. They were the tail-end of the popular movement, not the vanguard of privilege. And, by the late 1790s, they were aligned with Lord Castlereagh (Robert Stewart the younger), who was Pitt's organiser of the Unionist movement within the Irish House of Commons. They supported the Union as providing a better framework for gradual reform than the Ascendancy Irish Parliament.

Samuel Neilson, a businessman who owned and edited the United Irish paper, The Northern Star, and bankrupted himself in the process, heard of the proposed Union in prison and sent out a letter declaring his support for it. He might be excused if he had supported it only because his enemies, who had brought the country to chaos, opposed it. But in fact his letter is free of any such resentment. He declared for the Union because it offered the best prospect of advancing the causes of the United Irish movement—reform of the franchise and Catholic emancipation. He wrote: "I see a union is determined on between Great Britain and Ireland. I am glad of it. In a commercial point of view, it cannot be injurious; and I can see no injury the country will sustain from it politically... If I had possessed the means, I would have published my sentiments on this subject in a short, nervous pamphlet; so deeply am I impressed by its national utility" (Letter of 21st July, 1799, written from internment in Fort George, Scotland. It will be found in R.R. Madden's **The United Irishmen**. 4th Series, 2nd edition, 1860, pp105/6).

William Drennan is the only Northern United Irishman I know of who declared against the Union. He published a pamphlet against it. But he was at the time practising medicine in Dublin and seems to have been affected by the nationalistic hullabaloo set up by the Protestant Ascendancy there. Some time later he returned to Belfast and accepted the Union as the context of progressive politics.

The main opposition to the Union in the North came from Lord Downshire, who had been the most consistent and powerful opponent of Parliamentary reform and Catholic emancipation all through the 1790s. The Downshires of Hillsborough were the traditional aristocracy of County Down. In a series of county elections (culminating in that of 1790) they had been opposed by the Stewarts of Mountstewart representing the popular interest. Robert Stewart the elder became a minor peer in 1789 but shot up through the ranks of the peerage when he joined the reactionary interest in the mid-1790s. Between 1795 and 1798 the houses of Londonderry (as the Stewarts were now called) and Downshire joined forces and agreed to share the representation of the county between them. But they became antagonists again in 1799 when Downshire threw all his weight and influence against the Union and Londonderry supported it because his son, Lord Castlereagh (MP), was Pitt's chief agent in the Irish Parliament.

Although the United Irish who became Unionists betrayed no principle—and by 1832 could and did claim that their programme had been implemented by the Union Parliament—in later times they became vulnerable to Nationalist taunts on the matter. For lack of an adequate account of their own consistent development between the 1790s and the 1820s they became uneasy about their past. And, by the 1950s, even Unionist historians were agonising over the great "transformation" which occurred in the generation following 1800. The obvious fact that the Union Parliament was representative and progressive while the old Irish Parliament had been neither was somehow lost sight of. Because of this remarkable oversight, the formal change in activity which happened around 1800 became something to be forgotten about, or explained away, or to feel guilty about.

A groundless Unionist need to forget the 1790s and a Nationalist instinct not to look at the period too closely even while claiming continuity from it resulted in Dickson, Porter, Sampson and others being dropped out of history. At least I can think of no other reason why people of such calibre should be forgotten.

I have briefly outlined the Downshire/Londonderry relationship. That relationship also had far-reaching consequences for the development of politics in its particularity as distinct from general principle. Insofar as a major betrayal of principle played a part in things, that betrayal was the defection of the house of Londonderry from the cause of reform to the cause of reaction in 1795.

The Stewarts were, as far as I know, the first aristocratic family to emerge from Presbyterian Ulster. The dynasty was founded by Alexander Stewart, whom Steel Dickson greatly admired. I cannot say that Alexander did not merit Steel Dickson's praise. He was, as far as I can tell, a plain Presbyterian gentleman with a first-rate sense of social obligation. He was a diligent landlord, the founder of Newtownards as a town (as distinct from a pocket borough, whose chief purpose was to put two members in Parliament), and a Whig. His son, Robert, was bred to be a plain Presbyterian gentleman and was educated in Geneva. Dickson's account suggests that, for some time, breeding held nature in check, but that eventually nature had its way. That, too, corresponds with the facts so far as I know them.

The party politics of the 18th century was chiefly a matter of division between powerful families. Parties as organisations with mass membership and an independent apparatus did not begin until the 1832 Reform. The Stewart family was the hub of the popular interest in County Down and to a considerable extent in Belfast (which had no election of its own). The 1790 election in which the Stewarts took one one of the County Down seats from the Hills was the greatest event up to that point in the Parliamentary life of the county, the town and, indeed, of the province. The total defection of Mountstewart to the reactionary cause five years later, and its support for the Government of Lord Camden in 1795-8 (the worst Government Ireland has ever known), necessarily had a disruptive and disorientating effect on public life in the North. The threads which held the progressive elements together in an orderly evolutionary movement centred on Mountstewart, and they were therefore snapped when Mountstewart changed sides. And insult was added to injury by the fact that, in the same moment when Mountstewart defected to the die-hard Ascendancy, it also became the most important country house in Ireland. The new Viceroy, Camden, was Lord Londonderry's brother-in-law. His visits to Mountstewart were occasions of state, conducted with great pomp and circumstance—reactionary jamborees held in the midst of the most progressive tenantry and businessmen in the country. And when these tenant-farmers and businessmen would neither be coaxed into subservience by aristocratic displays at Mountstewart nor intimidated into it by threats from Mountstewart, Londonderry began demanding in 1796 that the Government make war on the County: and he would dearly have liked to see Belfast razed to the ground. (His letters to this effect can still be seen in Dublin Castle, where he sent them.)

Bad though the Camden Government was, a Londonderry Government would have been bedlam.

The political development of Belfast and Down was profoundly affected by the about-turn enacted by Robert Stewart the elder as he shot up through the ranks of aristocracy in 1795/6. And the lives of the great writers of the Ards Peninsula were affected by it in the most immediate way. James Porter, Presbyterian Minister in the adjacent village of Greyabbey, was a friend of "the family" at Mountstewart. (In correspondence of the time one often finds those Stewarts referred to simply as "the family".) He responded to the Stewart defection with the "Billy Bluff" satire and got himself hanged in June 1798 by Londonderry spite.

Steel Dickson was involved with Mountstewart even more closely than Porter, and over a longer period. He served it as an English reformer might have served one of the great Whig families. Though himself an utter republican of the intellect and spirit, he was not a doctrinaire republican in politics. He allowed that aristocratic distinction was a fair object of ambition, and was not disturbed when Robert Stewart the elder became Baron Londonderry in 1789. But when Mount Stewart defected he continued on the course he had set himself, and he replaced Mount Stewart as the centre of the reform movement in County Down.

Brendan Clifford
November, 1990.

A

NARRATIVE

OF THE

CONFINEMENT AND EXILE

OF

WILLIAM STEEL DICKSON, D. D.

FORMERLY

MINISTER OF THE PRESBYTERIAN CONGREGA-
TIONS OF BALLYHALBERT AND PORTAFERRY,
IN THE COUNTY OF DOWN, AND NOW OF
KEADY, IN THE COUNTY OF ARMAGH.

TO WHICH IS ANNEXED,

*An account of an Assault committed on the Author,
September 9th. 1811, on his return from the* CATHOLIC
MEETING *in the City of Armagh ; with a sketch of
proceedings consequent thereon.*

BY WILLIAM STEEL DICKSON. D. D.

Dublin :

Printed for the Author :

BY J. STOCKDALE. 71, ABBEY-STREET.

1812.

Chapter One

Autobiography To June 1798

[Introductory Note
Steel Dickson was born on Christmas Day, 1744. He was the son of John Dickson, a tenant farmer of Ballycraigy, Carnmoney, Co. Antrim. His mother was Jane Steel. It happened frequently amongst Ulster Presbyterians in those days that the wife's maiden name was combined with the husband's surname, either in the name or the husband, or in the names of the children. Two notable cases from the early 19th century are William Sharman Crawford, who was born a Sharman and married a Crawford, and James Emerson Tennent, who was born an Emerson and married a Tennent.

Glasgow University, the centre of the remarkable Scottish Enlightenment of the 18th century, was the College used by the Ulster Presbyterians throughout that century. Virtually all Presbyterian ministers and many others were educated there. The first major figure of the Enlightenment was Francis Hutcheson, son of a Presbyterian minister in Co. Down, who was Professor of Moral Philosophy in Glasgow in the 1730s and 1740s. Hutcheson's lectures were attended by Adam Smith, and Smith's **Wealth Of Nations** and **Theory Of Moral Sentiments** are a systematic working out of Hutcheson's basic ideas. Smith succeeded Hutcheson in the chair of Moral Philosophy, and his lectures were attended by Steel Dickson.

The Matriculation Albums Of The University Of Glasgow From 1728 To 1858 were published by the University in 1913, and Steel Dickson was given one of the larger entries. (He matriculated in 1763.) —

"2204. Gulielmus Dickson filius natu maximus Joannis Agricolae in comitatu de Antrim, Hibernia.
    Otherwise William Steel Dickson. Born 25th December, 1744. D.D. 1784. Irish Presbyterian Minister at (1) Glastry, 1771-80; (2) Port-a-ferry, 1780-99; (3) Second Keady, 1803-15. Moderator of the Synod of Ulster, 1783. Got deeply involved in the Irish Rebellion of 1798, and was for three years kept as a state prisoner at Fort-George, Scotland. Resident in Belfast, 1815-24, supported by charity. Died 27th December, 1824, and 'buried in a pauper's grave'."

Steel Dickson was licensed to preach in 1767 and called to Ballyhalbert (Glastry) in 1771.

The autobiography from which this chapter is extracted was written in self defence in the course of a dispute within the Synod of Ulster following his release from internment. It is 371 pages long, plus an Appendix of 118 pages. In the British Museum copy (which is from the library of Sir John Mackintosh, the Whig historian), there are the following handwritten notes:

"*Suppressed and very rare
See Note of Sir J. Mackin
tosh on the next leafing*"

And on the next leaf:

"*A prohibited Book
containing some very curious
Particulars of Irish History.
Anecdotes of Ld Castlereagh 17.21
& Appendix No.1.*"

The title page appears opposite.]

Rev. Dr. Dickson's Narrative

However painful it may be to a modest mind to obtrude itself, and its concerns, on the notice of the public—and still more painful to enter into details, which may excite a disagreeable sensation in any of the human kind—yet, circumstances, frequently occur, in life, from which such details become a duty to self, to society, to truth, justice, and honor. In such circumstances, for several years past, I have felt myself unfortunately placed. Had these ceased to operate, perhaps, I should never have taken up my pen to record them; most assuredly, I would never have exposed them to public animadversion. But, as this has not been the case, and even now is not, I flatter myself that I shall not be deemed unjustifiable, after a long forbearance, in presenting them to the eyes of my countrymen; and from past experience, I feel emboldened to confide in their candor, and hope for their indulgence.

As this detail will principally consist of grievances, severe in their pressure, extensive in their operation, and of long continuance, it will naturally be supposed that the criminality must have been great for which they have been inflicted, under a government, equally *celebrated* for justice and mercy; and aggravated by an ecclesiastical body, from which unmerited severity should never be suspected.

That the foundation of this supposition may be fairly estimated, I shall not confine myself to the *alleged* proximate causes of the grievances of which I complain. I shall briefly and fairly recite, so far as I can possibly recollect, every material occurrence of my life, and every part of my public conduct, previous to my long confinement and exile which can be supposed to have incurred the wrath of the Irish government, or those who exercised its powers, in 1798; and the *pious* and *loyal* severity of a small, but, latterly, a dominant party, among my rev. fathers and brethren of the synod of Ulster. This recital, I trust, will enable my readers to judge impartially between them and me; I have no doubt but their judgment will be founded in justice.

Of the early part of my life I shall say little. My boyish years were spent in the usual, and, I am sorry to add, almost useless routine of Irish country schools. Indeed, I might say, to me altogether useless had it not been for the paternal attention and valuable instructions of the rev. Robert White, then Presbyterian minister of Templepatrick, in the county of Antrim. To him I am indebted for my initiation into any thing approaching to knowledge of the elements and structure of the Latin and Greek languages—as also of logic, metaphysics, morals, and natural theology. In fact, he first taught me, not only to reason, but to think.

On my going to the college of Glasgow, in my seventeenth year, I was happy in the friendship, as well as in the instructions, of several of the professors, particularly Mr. Moorehead, professor of Latin, one of the most general scholars of his day; and Dr. Adam Smith, a man well known, and justly celebrated, in all the nations of Europe. To the latter I owed much—very much indeed—during the short time of his continuance in the University, after my entrance. To Mr. Moorhead I was indebted, not only for his instructions, and the care with which he was pleased to direct the course of my studies; but for an early introduction to the learned, liberal, and pious Dr. Leechman, principal of the University—A man, whose name will ever be truth, and unadulterated Christianity. In my intercourse with him, I enjoyed every advantage which a youthful mind, engaged in the pursuit of knowledge, could reasonably hope for: and such was his friendship, and that of Mr. Moorhead, that they honored me with their correspondence, as long as they lived.

Gratitude here obliges me to mention another name, which I must ever recollect with affectionate esteem. That is the name of Mr. John Millar, then professor of law, in the same university—a name too well known, in the literary and political world, to require encomium. To him I had the happiness of being introduced, rather as a friend than a student. And, by him was my attention first directed to jurisprudence, the principles of government, and the respective advantages and disadvantages of the different forms under which it may be constructed and administered.

What particular effects his instructions then had upon my mind, I cannot now pretend to say. This only I know, and this I acknowledge, that they, and a few books to which he directed my attention, produced a yet unaltered conviction that absolute monarchy is not the best possible government, except in the hands of absolute perfection—that aristocracy is, and ever must be, a bad government—that despotism, under the *masque* of limited monarchy, a mixed government, or a free state, is worse still—and, that a government, of whatever description, the administration of which is entirely submitted to a faction or sect—and particularly, to upstarts and underlings of such faction—subject to the influence, and liable to the control, of spies, informers, and mercenary clerks in office, is worst of all.

In regard to a republic, or a democracy, political theorists have presented nothing that could satisfy my mind. The states so called, whether antient or modern, are sources of information equally unsatisfactory. In no two of them

---

William Leechman (1708-1784) of Lanarkshire; Presbyterian minister; Moderator of General Assembly 1757; Principal of Glasgow University 1761-84; biographer of Francis Hutcheson, by whom he was taught; author of two popular sermons: **On The Character Of A Minister Of The Gospel** (1741) and **On The Nature, Reasonableness And Advantages Of Prayer** (1743). The latter was the subject of intense controversy.

John Millar (1735-1801) of Lanarkshire. Son of Presbyterian minister; intended for the ministry, but was uneasy about required declaration of faith; professor of law at Glasgow from 1761; supported Parliamentary reform and American independence; author of **The Origin Of The Distinction Of Ranks In Society** (1771) and **An Historical View Of The English Government From The Settlement Of The Saxons In Britain To The Revolution In 1688** (1787), both of which went through many editions.

has the constitution been the same. Their fate is the only thing in which they have been ever similar. In fact, rational republicanism, as it appears to me, has never had a fair trial. And, as the executive power, under every form of Government, seems to be necessarily entrusted to an individual; while the right of legislation is inherent in, and inseparable from, the people, whether that might be exercised in mass, or by representation, the difference between a limited monarchy and a well constituted republic is rather in name than reality, provided the chief magistrate be elected by the state, and amenable to the laws, under which he derives his authority. Whether he be denominated emperor, king, duke, stadtholder, consul, or president, is a matter of no importance.

This last paragraph I have inserted, that my readers may be enabled to form some general idea of my political creed, and the principles on which they are to judge of my political conduct. Let me request that their judgment may be guided by it, and it alone.

Soon after my final return from college, I was prevailed upon, by the flattering solicitations of my early and venerated friend Mr. White, to become a candidate for the office of a preacher of the gospel, much sooner than I intended, or ought, to have done; and, after passing through the usual trials, was licensed in March 1767.

During the four succeeding years, the frequent excursions which I was obliged to make to vacant congregations, some of which were many miles distant, not only extended my connexions, but gave me access to many families of rank and respectability, in the counties of Down and Antrim, of whose kind attentions I shall ever cherish a pleasing and grateful remembrance.

Among these I have the honour of mentioning that of the late Alexander Stewart Esq. father to the present earl of Londonderry, and grandfather to lord viscount Castlereagh. Him I mention particularly, not only in acknowledgment of many favours, which I owed to his kind attentions, but in expression of my sincere and unabated respect for his memory, as a man of polite and pleasing manners, a clear, and truly comprehensive understanding, and principles truly

---

Alexander Stewart of Donegal (died 1781), who purchased a number of estates in North Down in the 1740s and founded "the family" of Mount Stewart. He neglected to purchase the patronage of the pocket borough of Newtownards, assuming it would fall to him since the borough was surrounded by his estates. But the representation of Newtownards was acquired and held by one of the leading "Patriot" families of the Ascendancy, the Ponsonbys. Alexander Stewart was one of the better landlords and most public spirited gentlemen in the country. He developed Newtownards into a real town. The fact that the pocket borough remained in alien hands impelled the Stewarts into contesting the representation of Country Down (which had an extensive electorate) with the traditional patrons of the county, the Hills (Downshires) of Hillsborough.

Robert Stewart, the elder (1738-1821), Alexander's son, became Baron Londonderry in 1789, Viscount Castlereagh in 1795, Earl of Londonderry in 1789, Viscount Castlereagh in 1795, Earl of Londonderry in 1789, Viscount Castlereagh in 1795, Earl of Londonderry in 1796, and Marquis of Londonderry in 1816. His son, *Robert* (1769-1822), acquired the minor title of Viscount Castlereagh on the elevation of the father to an Earldom in 1796, but remained a commoner until the death of his father.

liberal, both in politics and religion. It is true, he had no small share of ambition; but it was ambition to raise his family to honour and Influence, in his country, for his country's good. Would to God, such ambition had continued to glow in the breast of his family, and that it glowed there still!

In the year 1771, I was ordained to the charge of the congregation of Ballyhalbert, in the barony of Ardes, and county of Down; and became an husband and a farmer.

Thus become stationary, I devoted myself, almost entirely, to my parochial and domestic duties, or the studies connected with them, till the commencement of the unnatural, impolitic, and unprincipled, war in America. Having paid considerable attention to jurisprudence, in the course of my studies, and read Locke, Montesquieu, Puffendorf, etc. etc. my mind instantly revolted against the mad crusade; and while I regretted its folly, I execrated its wickedness. Feeling as I did, and detesting the meanness, as much as the immorality, of dissimulation, I never concealed either my ideas, or sentiments, on the subject. Hence, my expressions gave great offence to all the dependants of government. The friends of the then secretary for the Northern department, who constituted a great portion of the landed interest of the country, were equally provoked to anger; and their anger was, afterwards, kindled into rage, by my preaching on the principles, object, tendency, and probable consequences, of the war, on two days, appointed as fasts, during the contest. A general outcry was raised against me, in which those, who never heard me preach, were very loud; and those, who had never seen me, were louder still. *"Traitor"*, *"Rebel"*, *"Trumpeter of sedition"* were levelled at my name, wherever a few of the "lives and fortune" men of the day got warm around their bottle; and all agreed that "I ought to be d——d, as hanging was too good for me". In fact, if God, in his justice and mercy, had not been as deaf to their imprecations against me, as he was to their prayers for success in the war, I might have been d——d to all eternity. However, I had my revenge in full. I published the two sermons, as they were preached, without the retraction, alteration, or addition, of a single word. They were read with avidity, found less pestilential than they had been represented, and, finally, justified, even in their conjectural parts, by events and the issue of the struggle.

About this time (1778) a new object presented itself, which strengthened my conviction of the *impolicy* of the war, aggravated my feelings, and roused the feeble energies of my mind in common with those of the great mass of my countrymen. The French espoused the cause of America; their fleets were riding triumphant in our seas, and insulting our coasts; our country was considered, by all, as in imminent danger; and government had declared its total inability to defend it. In this awful emergency, the desire of self-preservation gave birth to the general idea, and general resolution, of arming for self-defence. The city of Cork and town of Belfast took the lead in the execution. Other places soon followed their example. And, in a few weeks, a generous patriotic ardor, as if excited by a spark from Heaven, pervaded, animated, and actuated the great body of the Irish people. Every city, town and village, swarmed with volunteers. In the country, the plough, the loom, and every other implement of useful arts, lent their youth, strength, and vigor to the standard of the nation. Industry forewent a portion of its usual rest; whilst idleness betook itself to labour, and profligacy became sober; that they might be enabled, by their earnings, or their savings, to appear in arms, and in uniform, among their brethren, the idea of profession seemed to be obliterated. Physician, surgeon, and apothecary; lawyer and attorney—all were soldiers. Even the Presbyterian ministers were so fully inspired with the patriotism of the day, that, in several places, the rusty black was exchanged for the glowing scarlet, and the title of "Reverend" for that of "Captain". In a word, such was the prevailing spirit, that, in a short time, a self-created, self-arrayed, and self-supported, army presented itself, which strangers contemplated with wonder, enemies with fear, and friends with pride, exultation, and confidence.

Amidst the pleasing circumstances, which surrounded this institution, one equally shameful and impolitic, occurred. The Catholics, in great numbers, and with great zeal offered themselves as volunteers, in common with their Protestant and Presbyterian countrymen. Through the greatest part of Ulster, if not the whole, their offers were rejected, and, in some places, not without insult. In my own neighbourhood, this was universally the case. Hence jealousy and mistrust became prevalent, and in some instances, excited alarm. Impressed with a sense of the impolicy and danger of such conduct, and equally so with its injustice, I not only argued against and reprobated it, in conversation, but, in a sermon, preached before the Echlin Ville volunteers, March 1789, [sic, but clearly 1779 is meant—BC] expressed my opinions, on the subject, so clearly, as to offend all the Protestant and Presbyterian bigots in the country. This, once more, raised the cry of rebellion against me; and some were so liberal as to pronounce me "a Papist in my heart", for the very substantial reason, among others, that the maiden-name of the parish priest's mother was "Dickson". However, the general tenor of the sermon was so much approved, being calculated to promote the volunteer cause, that I was earnestly solicited, by a number of zealous friends to the institution, to publish it, *with a modification of the part respecting the admission of Catholics to the volunteer ranks*. To the publication I felt little objection: But, to the modification I submitted, with great reluctance, and merely from respect to, what I then thought, superior judgment, and, at least, an equal zeal in the public cause. However, I feel happy that I retained, *in print*, so much of the shadow of what I expressed, *in substance*, from the pulpit, as will give a faint idea of what then were, now are, and, I presume, ever will be, my opinions and feelings, on that important subject. The passage, as modified, is as follows:

"3dly. Ye ought to extend your views of doing good beyond the narrow limits of party, or outward profession, in matters civil, or religious. The names of party often excite jealousies; and these, again, are apt to resolve the most generous actions into

---

The address to the Echlin Ville Volunteers is given in Chapter 3.

the worst designs. This is, particularly, the case with us, in time of war. As our enemies are generally of the Popish religion, those of that denomination, among us, are apt to construe measures of public safety into private design, and attribute every armament to enmity against them. To remove such injurious suspicion is an object well deserving your attention, and your conduct ought to shew, that ye have not taken up arms, for this or the other denomination, but for your country—that it is not your purpose to spread alarm, terror or desolation, but to check them in their wild career—that it is only against the enemies of your country, liberty, and peace, be their religion what it may be, that your arms are pointed—and, that whoever is a friend of these, is your friend, and the object of your protection."

During some years after this, little occupied the public mind, or employed the public tongue, except volunteering and volunteers. The system was now become universal, with a very few exceptions. Many gentlemen of landed property, who, at first opposed, or barely tolerated, the measure; and even some who seemed to dread the armament of the people, as much as they detested American independence, or, horror-struck, anticipated a French debarkation, assumed the uniform of their country: some, as we supposed, merely to keep their tenantry under their own control, and others, because volunteering was become fashionable.

Be this as it may, in the year 1782, Ulster was so completely armed, that, at a review in Belfast, the number of patriotic soldiers was deemed little inferior to that of the spectators, capable of bearing arms.

In a sham-fight, on the day of this review, Robert Stewart now lord viscount Castlereagh, then only in his thirteenth year, commanded the light infantry of the Ards independents, of which his father was colonel. His company consisted mostly of boys, a few years older than himself. Their appearance attracted universal notice, and excited the most pleasing emotions, as it promised a succession of patriot soldiers, under whose banners Ireland would recline in safety. The conduct of young Stewart did more. The manner, in which he conducted his boyish band, through the variegated, and long-protracted engagement, displayed such germs of spirit, and judgment, as excited admiration, extorted applause, and laid the foundation of that popularity which he afterwards obtained.

One circumstance, of which I was a witness, had a most powerful effect on the public feeling. The sham-fight was a representation of an approach to, and attack on, the town of Belfast. The Ards independents, commanded by col. Stewart, now earl of Londonderry, formed the van of the invading army. By them the advanced guard of the defenders of their country was completely defeated. In their flight, they left a small party, with one piece of cannon, on a rising ground, to cover their retreat. To drive in this party, and take possession of the cannon, the younger Robert and his boyish band was dispatched, and the affair was so conducted on both sides, that some officers, who were present, declared that it bore the strongest resemblance to real action. That a great majority of our youthful heroes believed it to be such, I am fully convinced.

When the defendants gave way, and abandoned their gun, young Stewart rushed forward in the ardor of his soul, grasped it in his arms, then mounted its carriage, waved his cap, and, with tears of triumphs, huzzaed to the main body, and called them to come on.

This circumstance had a most powerful effect on the then ardent mind of the multitude present; and their account of it excited high expectations of, and warm attachment to, the rising Robert, through the whole country. From that day, many began to look forward to, and speak of him, as their future representative. "If such be the boy, what may we not expect of the man!" was to be heard in, almost every company; and I own that my own expectations were as extravagant, and my attachment as enthusiastic, as those of any other man living.

The continued effect, and importance, of this circumstance, were strongly marked in the year following. In that year, the first great contest for the representation of the country, took place, between the Hillsborough and Stewart family, or, as it was generally considered, between the court and country interests. At the commencement of the election, the success of Mr. Stewart was confidently spoken of. His conduct in parliament, during the preceding seven years, had fully justified his patriotic professions, satisfied the expectations and secured the support, of a numerous and powerful body in the country. Yet, even this well-earned popularity was weakened by a toadish coldness, and haughty distance of deportment, which disgusted and alienated many, who had been esteemed warm and steady friends to the independence of the county. The consequence was, that the contest, at the end of five weeks, became doubtful; and, a few days afterwards, notwithstanding every exertion of Mr. Stewart's friends, his conduct rendered it desperate, by a deriliction of Mr. Ward, with whom a junction had been formed and ratified, under the sanction of their *common* friends, for the *common* support of the *common* cause. This dereliction degraded him in the estimation of his warmest advocates; and his subsequent conduct in the house of commons, respecting a petition against the sheriffs return, and the committee which presented it, reduced him so low in the eyes of the county, that I believe all thoughts of attempting to reinstate him were totally abandoned. However, he avoided the disgrace of a public rejection, by taking shelter some time afterwards, under the shade of a peerage.

My attachment to, what I considered as the good of my country; and an attachment, scarcely subordinate, to the Stewart family, induced me to devote my time, my labor, and my purse, to their joint service, from beginning to end of this long and expensive contest. And as I had the *honour* of being a member of one of the committees, by which it was conducted, every public measure, and public character, came under my observation. Among the latter, that of the younger Robert Stewart already mentioned, was the most attractive and

---

Robert Stewart the elder won a County Down seat in the 1769 and 1776 elections and lost it in 1783. His son, Robert (Castlereagh) regained the seat in 1790.

interesting. He was every where, with every body, and his mild manners, unremitting attention, fascinating address, and manlike conversation, revived the impressions of the preceding year, and gave strength to the prejudices conceived in his favor.

Among the many instances of this which occurred, during the election, I hope I shall be excused for mention of one. A few days before its close, I brought forward about forty freeholders, whom I had formerly engaged to wait for my call, and of a description which would have done honour to any country. These were all wealthy farmers, and remarkably well mounted; and, as volunteering had given them some idea of order, I brought them in, in Indian file, and after *proudly* parading the town drew them up, two deep, before Mr. Stewart's lodgings. This was the unfortunate morning, though I did not know it, on which Mr. Stewart had abandoned Mr. Ward; and with him, as some maliciously said afterwards, *"honour and honesty"*, the mother of their junction. Ere my arrival, the sheriff and his deputy had been some time in court, and Mr. Stewart could not make up his first tally. On seeing me, therefore, the expressions of joy were considerable. The young Robert rushed into the street, and, throwing his arms round my horse's neck, exclaimed: 'O Mr. Dickson, are *all* these for my father?" "Yes, my dear boy", said I. On this, he darted into the house, and in an instant, returned, crying: "See! See! father! See what Mr. Dickson has brought! I would rather be at the head of such a yeomanry, than be the first lord ever a king created". The multitude, who crowded the street around us, seemed delighted with his spirit, and my corps was not less so with the compliment. Their language to each other was; "this is our noble young captain—he's a sweet boy—*he'll* be our man yet, if he lives".

During the succeeding seven years which were devoted to his education, his popularity not only continued, but encreased; and that he justly deserved it, I can personally testify, as the greater part of that time he spent in my neighbourhood, and almost under my eye. He was then the pupil of Mr. Sturrock, Chancellor of Portaferry, now Dr. Sturrock, Archdeacon of Armagh—a man, whose sweetness of temper, gentleness of manners, and correctness of morals, were as well calculated to conciliate the heart to virtue, as his judgment, taste, and literary attainments were to enrich the understanding with the principles of knowledge. Under the Doctor's tuition, his pupil's attention was unremitting, and his progress rapid. The knowledge of this being circulated, added to his reputation, and the hopes of his friends; and his going to the university under the auspices of the late Lord Camden, whose memory will ever be revered by the real friends,

---

Lord Camden: The reference here is to the 1st Earl Camden, **Charles Pratt** (1714-94)—barrister, judge and Lord Chancellor. He was one of the leading libertarians of his day. As judge he supported John Wilkes in his conflicts with the Crown. And in each of his three capacities he helped with the reform of the draconian libel law of the 18th century. **John Jeffreys Pratt** (1759-1840), son of the above, the 2nd Earl, was a political incompetent, and was described as "useless lumber" by Canning. He governed Ireland from 1795 to June 1798, when Lord Cornwallis came to clear up the mess he made of it. His sister became the second wife of Robert Stewart the elder. The

of the British empire, and of liberty; the full benefits of his Lordship's instructions and example; with the additional advantage of prosecuting his studies, under the special tuition of the celebrated Dr. Watson; led to the belief that he would enter upon the theatre of public life, not only as a profound scholar, but an accomplished statesman, a zealous friend to civil and religious liberty, and an honest advocate of the independence of the Irish legislature, and a radical reform in the representation of the Irish people.

This belief was more than confirmed, if possible, on his first appearance in the county, previous to his election in 1790. On his canvass, he was received, with marked cordiality, and expressive joy; and these were kindled into enthusiasm, by his strong expressions of attachment to the liberty of his country, of ardour for reform, and solemn declarations that, if returned to parliament, he would use all his efforts to obtain it. Nay, as some averred, by expressions of patriotism much stronger.

The effect of such addresses, added to his former popularity, in such a county as Down then was, may be easily conceived. In fact it was such, that, I am fully convinced, had the freeholders been left an unbiassed choice, nine tenths of their number would have voted in his favor.

The contrary, however, was the case. His popularity was met by an opposition as formidable as power, interest, or personal favor, could excite. The influence of this government, thro' its dependents and expectants; that of a peer of the first property in the county; amiable in his private character; unrivalled as a landlord; who had brought under obligations a great proportion of the gentlemen of smaller fortune, by providing for their sons, in the army, navy, revenue, and church; to whom many others looked up for preferment; and, who had two boroughs at his disposal; with all their dependents and de-dependents were marshalled against him.

To meet, and counteract, this opposition, every friend to the youthful candidate, and the cause to which he had pledged himself, set out to canvass in his favour. In the enthusiasm of the day, my mind was not witholden. For several weeks, previous to the election, and the three months, during which it continued, I was on horseback, almost every day; and seldom left in my own house, at night. In fact, I rode one horse, nearly to death, reduced another to half his value, and expended above 50l. part of which I was obliged to borrow: Nor can I now say, whether I was most actuated by affectionate esteem for the youthful candidate, confidence in his professions, or zeal for the interests of my country, in my quixotical excursions. Under the joint influence of the whole, I canvassed, far and wide, regardless of interest, influence, and connexions; and succeeded so far as to provoke some of my best friends, by voting their tenants for Mr. Stewart, contrary to their orders, and in their presence. Of that success,

---

connection between the first Londonderry and the second Camden was a general Irish tragedy and a very particular tragedy for public life in County Down. The Camden Dynasty is not much remembered: but there is a Pratt Street in Camden Town, which was, until its recent Yuppification, the Irish quarter in London.

whatever it was, I was proud, at the time: tho', God knows, frequently have regretted it, since, in the bitterness of my heart, not only on account of my country, but real pity for the successful candidate. Even now, I cannot repress the thought that, had he been happily rejected, on that occasion, he would never have reached the pinnacle from which he hath fallen, at least unpitied—that Ireland would yet have been the independent, proud, powerful, and affectionate sister of Britain—her Presbyterian church unfettered, and its extension unchecked.*

Be this as it may, our favourite was returned to parliament, though under age, at the time of the election, and, for a short time, retained his popularity, by some speeches in the house, and attendance on patriotic societies.

In the year 1791, the Whig Club in Dublin was warm, loud, and diffuse, in the cause of reform. A Northern Whig Club was formed, in Belfast, on the same principles. Of this the Stewart family were prominent members. About the same time a third Society was instituted, under the auspices of the Duke of Leinster, and other characters, then, highly respectable. Whilst the two former, by speeches and toasts, roused and animated the spirit of reform, the other zealously recommended the institution of Societies, *all over Ireland*, that the great body of the people might unite, and forward petitions to the throne, and to parliament, for its attainment. Pamphlets, were, every where, circulated, for the same purpose. Landlords, in many places, are said to have distributed them among their tenants. And, from the Agent's office of Mr. S——, if report spoke truth, they were issued in multitudes.

* Of my success on that occasion, lord C. retained a much higher opinion than I ever expressed, if a judgment may be formed after the following anecdote. A short time after my arrest, a particular friend of mine, alarmed by the dreadful reports industriously and artfully circulated of my criminality and consequent danger, asked his lordship, "what was to be done with me?" His answer was, "I do not know. Every thing possible has been done to procure evidence against him; but we cannot obtain a single sentence, *tho' we* know he is guilty?" "My God": exclaimed the gentlemen, "if that be the case, why keep him in confinement? Do you mean to destroy both him and his family?" "O sir" replied his lordship, "from his popularity in the year 90, I know he would be a very dangerous person to leave at liberty now."

His lordship might likewise have recollected 83. Even in that year I enjoyed some share of popularity, as appears in a preceeding page. And, whatever that share may have been, his father and he enjoyed exclusively the benefit of its exertions.

The Northern Whig Club had for its Secretary Dr. Alexander Haliday, friend of Lord Charlemont, and among its members were the younger Robert Stewart (the later Castlereagh), Alexander Stewart, and Henry Joy, owner of the News Letter. The Whigs became inactive as it became clear that the Government was intent on resisting reform at all costs, and many of them went into the service of the Government. The Northern Star on April 3rd, 1797, published a list of the members of the Northern Whig Club five years earlier, and showed that the Northern Whig aims were virtually identical with the United Irish aims.

S - presumably is Stewart.

Thus sanctioned and stimulated, the people formed themselves into societies in every town, village and parish throughout Ulster, and soon extended themselves over the kingdom. From the importance of its object, a test was drawn up, and initiation into these societies became regular and solemn. Under the strongest impressions of this importance, I took the test, so early as December 1791, in presence of "The first society of United Irishmen in Belfast", three of whom were members of the "Northern Whig Club".

In this society, I do not know that my name was ever enrolled, as a member, but this I can positively assert, that, so far as I can recollect, I never was present at any succeeding meeting of them as a society, in Belfast or elsewhere, where any member was admitted, or other business peculiar to United

---

Steel Dickson's statement that he cannot recall attending a meeting of a United Irish Society may strike the reader as evasive, but that is only because the history of the United Irish movement has heretofore been written from a Dublin viewpoint. In Dublin there were clubs; in Belfast there was a movement of society. When I began reading The Northern Star I expected to find reports of meetings of the Belfast United Irish Societies and United Irish declarations, such as was the case in Dublin. I soon realised that the United Irish Societies were of little consequence in Belfast, at least until the Camden/Londonderry terror began in 1795. **The Northern Star** was a general newspaper of the society at large, different in kind from the United Irish papers in the South—the **Cork Gazette** of 1795 and **The Press** (published in Dublin in 1797/8). It outstripped the circulation of the **Belfast News Letter**. The News Letter became the organ of the more cautious, gradual and deferential reformers, and it was these, rather than the United Irish, who had the character of a faction in the North.

Steel Dickson had been advocating what became known as the United Irish policy for thirteen years before the first United Irish Society was formed. After 1791 he accepted the new name for the policy, and played a leading part in the progressive movement of the society at large, while taking little notice of the Societies. And it is clear from the way the notices of the Societies are published in The Northern Star that their meetings were very much a fringe activity to the general reform movement.

The idea of a close conspiracy of elite progressives was elaborated by William Drennan in correspondence with William Bruce in the 1780s. Drennan, Bruce and Joseph Pollock saw themselves as the vanguard of a radical intelligentsia around 1780, and Pollock, author of a pamphlet called **The Letters Of Owen Roe O'Niall** was the most radical of the three. Pollock, a barrister, gradually distanced himself from the radical movement in 1797 became a judge under Lord Downshire's patronage. During the 1780s Drennan was a doctor of medicine in Newry and Bruce a Presbyterian minister in Dublin. Drennan (putting one in mind of Lenin around 1900) explained to Bruce his scheme for a progressive conspiracy which would manipulate spontaneous social movements for its own purposes. The undeclared final end of the conspiracy would be separation of Ireland from Britain. Bruce moved to Belfast in 1790 to become head, and virtual founder, of Belfast Royal Academy. In 1792 he turned decisively away from radical reform politics, and probably interpreted events through the filter of the scheme for a conspiracy in which Drennan had tried to involve him.

In fact the United Irish movement in Antrim and Down from 1791 to 1795 was the converse of a conspiracy. It was a public state of mind. Drennan had taken part in devising the United Irish Clubs, but the social movement was immensely wider than the Clubs and was not manipulated by them. In his letters to Bruce, Drennan had described his scheme as a sort of Freemasonry. But the actual organisation of the Freemasons played a much greater part in organising the reform society around Ulster, and stiffening it in moments of crisis, than the United Irish Clubs did.

I have no problem at all with the statement by Steel Dickson, United Irishman, that he cannot recall attending a meeting of a United Irish Society.

ERRATUM, p22, footnote, line 7: "under" should read "until"

Irishmen was transacted. It is true, when in Belfast,where I frequently was, I found myself surrounded by United Irishmen; and the union of Irishmen was , on every occasion, the common topic of conversation. In these conversations I always took a decided part, as it was well known from the year 1778, that parliamentary reform,and Catholic emancipation, without which reform was only an empty name, were objects near and dear to my heart. Nay in all conversations of the kind, for some years afterwards, I used all my powers and influence to elucidate the principles, prove the necessity, and diffuse the spirit of union, with a view to attain them: and this I did, in the full conviction, not only, that I was labouring to insure the security of his Majesty's throne, and independence of Ireland, but discharging a most important, moral and religious duty. In these efforts I felt a flattering encouragement from the resolutions, etc, with which the public papers teemed in the spring of 1792 : and the enthusiasm, with which all ranks looked forward, in the beginning of that summer, to the Volunteer reunions, and the celebration of the French revolution, tempted me to hope that the government would see the wisdom, and feel the necessity, of conceding the measures in question, to the public will.

This hope, as far as it related to Catholic emancipation, was soon checked by an artful manoeuvre. This was the holding up of a prospect of concession, not "total and immediate", but "gradual and progressive". The reasons assigned to this delusive measure were, the profound ignorance of the Catholics, and consequent incapacity, not only of enjoying, but *bearing* liberty. These reasons, or rather *shameless pretexts,* though equally *unfounded, insulting,* and *blasphemous,* imposed on a few, and gave others an excuse for opposing the public will, and public wish.

To my astonishment this delusion operated on a small party in the enlightened town of Belfast; and displayed itself on the 14th of July, after a public review. In a discussion, before the volunteer body there assembled, gradual emancipation was introduced, and pleaded for, on the ground of Catholic ignorance and incapacity: and the language in which the impolicy, danger , and folly of total and immediate enfranchisement was expressed excited disquiet and indignation in the minds of the people. Several gentlemen ably rejected, and warmly reprobated the assertions made, and sentiments expressed, by the promoter of opposition to the general sense of the assembly; and, latterly, something too warm seemed to pervade it, of which I feared the increase and the consequences. Under the influence of this fear, and in hope of checking the heat of debate, I reluctantly yielded to the impulse of addressing the meeting: and, as argument was unnecessary, where there was nothing like argument to answer, after what had fallen from other gentlemen, I only hung a few rags of ridicule on the step-ladder of "gradual emancipation", which were eagerly laid hold of, and, in the heat of imagination, formed into a mantle, under which Mrs "time to time" looked so silly, that her God-fathers were ashamed of, and abandoned her. In consequence, Lady "Total and Immediate" was adopted, embraced, and cheered.

From the publications in the Irish papers, and the multitudes, from all the neighbouring counties, who were present on this occasion, the decision of the day was proclaimed far and wide, and everywhere approved of. As a number of gentlemen from Dublin, warm friends of reform, and of their country, attended the meeting, it was soon known in the metropolis, by all ranks of people, and celebrated with rapture. New life, strength, and activity, were infused into the friends of union. The public papers teemed with resolutions in its favour, from every town, every village, and every volunteer association in Ulster, so as to scarcely leave room for the toasts, *wet* and *dry*, of the semi-patriotic societies, denominated "Whig Clubs", which embraced a great proportion of the nobility, and landed property of the province.

Towards the end of the year, the idea of parish and county meetings was started, and eagerly pursued, till it led to the provincial convention, at Dungannon, February 15th 1793. The object of these meetings was so clearly expressed, in the language of the county of Down, January 21st and of the Dungannon meeting February 15th 1793, that it can neither be misunderstood, nor misrepresented, while words are allowed to have any meaning, or those who use them, to possess common sense. The object was that "by free and general communication, the provincial will, regulated by the wisdom of the province, may be concentrated in a point, from which it may be directed to other provinces of the kingdom, and flow, with clearness and harmony, and strength, into the Houses of Parliament and the preserve of Majesty; in order that a complete and radical reform may be speedily effectuated".

That, with a view to this reform, I used every exertion, of which I was capable, both in public and private, to convince all, with whom I was conversant, of its necessity to restore our paralysed constitution, conciliate the public mind, and establish his Majesty's throne in the affections of the people; and of the equal necessity of *union* among Irishmen, in order to obtain, perhaps, I might say, *extort*, it from the faction of the day, I need not attempt to deny. Were I so meek as to do so, the public thanks of my congregation, which embraced the Presbyterians of half a barony, and my own publication of part of what I preached, as the politics of the bible, on days set apart, by proclamation, for praying the politics of the existing ministry, would shamefully confute me.*
Besides, as I was, by particular desire, as well as public appointment, present at

---

I have come across reports of meetings of inhabitants held in 60 Parishes in December 1792 and January 1793 to discuss reform of the Constitution and elect delegates to County meetings. The County meetings in turn elected delegates to the Provincial Convention at Dungannon and considered resolutions for it. In all of these meetings—which might be regarded as the high tide of the United Irish movement—there was overwhelming agreement in support of the aim of making the British Constitution functional in the governing of Ireland by reforming the electoral franchise and repealing the Penal Laws against Catholics. But while the aristocratic Volunteer Conventions of 1782 and 1783 are presented in all history books, the great democratic Convention of 1793 has been dropped out of history. The reason for this must be that the aristocracy gave the Volunteer Conventions an all-Ireland character, while the democratic Convention of 1793 marked Ulster off from the rest of the country. Appeals to the other provinces to follow suit in 1793 went unheeded.

and took a decided part in all the meetings of the county of Down, previous to the Dungannon convention [sic]. Meetings, unprecedented in numbers, and embracing the rank and property of the county—and, afterwards, at the Dungannon convention, as a delegate for the Barony of Ards. As I had no inconsiderable share in preparing, and modifying, the resolutions of both, and fully expressed my ideas, in the discussion of the whole—and as these resolutions were extensively published—my political creed, sentiments, and views, could not be unknown, either to the people, or government, of Ireland. I say, "government", as to Dungannon in particular, as, I believe, it is well known that it, not only, had eyes, pens, and tongues, these, to watch, record, and report, all that passed; but a friend, in the disguise of a delegate, to offer the people of Ulster a frothy collation of whip-sillabub, garnished with a few faded flowers of oratory, instead of that substantial bread of reform, so necessary to restore the Irish constitution, and which the voice of Irishmen so eagerly called for.

The liberality, wisdom, and moderation, of the Dungannon resolutions had very great, and opposite effects, on the government and people. With the people, all was hope and confidence, that parliament, *pledged as it was by promise*, would take up the question of reform, and wisely concede something conciliatory. This season, however, was of short duration. Government were alarmed, or pretended to be so; and, in their alarms, whether real or pretended, gave themselves up to madness, instead of profiting by the lessons of wisdom, and imitating the moderation and liberality of a loyal people. Hence, a series of acts of parliament, which followed each other, with hasty pace, and voice terrific, extinguished hope, revived alarm, and excited a mixed feeling of sorrow, indignation, and horror. And indignation nearly kindled into rage, on the apostacy of a majority of the delegates, who had appeared at Dungannon, as the

* At this time, every art was used, and every power exerted, by the enemies of emancipation, to seduce and intimidate my congregation, and not without a partial success. Many families withdrew from my Ministry, for a season; and an attempt was made to have a new meeting-house erected, for their accomodation. These things only enlivened my sense of duty, and roused me to increased exertion. To public addresses from the pulpit, I added local visitations of the districts into which my parish was divided, and even domiciliary calls upon the *disaffected*. Thank God, my efforts succeeded. The wanderers returned to my fold, and in the gratitude of their hearts, published the address of thanks to which I have alluded. But, strange to tell, these things reached the eye, or ear, of the noted sir R. Musgrave, who has presented them to the world, with his usual colouring of *malignity* and *falsehood*, in his *medley of misrepresentations*.—NB. A specimen of the sermons, as published in 1793, is subjoined to this Narrative. [The entire pamphlet, **Scripture Politics**, is added as a 118 page Appendix to the Narrative. BC]

The friend of Government in disguise of a delegate was probably Joseph Pollock, the most radical pamphleteer of the Volunteer period, who became a judge under the Camden Government.

zealous friends of a parliamentary reform, which would embrace all religious denominations: and enemies, equally zealous, to a war with France; a war which they had reprobated, and the British empire, has, long since, pronounced "accursed". The concurrence of the same apostates, afterward, in proclaiming the Northern counties, out of the king's peace, without cause, or provocation, except in the case of one county, and a few small districts on its borders, so completely exasperated the people, that disturbances would certainly have taken place, had it not been for the exertions of those very persons, whom the agitating parliaments afterwards devoted to ruin, *perhaps for these very exertions.* During the years 1795 and 6, when public provocations did not succeed, private emissaries were sent abroad to circulate alarms, and provoke jealousies. In my neighbourhood, it was not uncommon to see the lower Presbyterians on one day, and the Catholics on another, running from house to house, under the alarm that a massacre was to take place on the succeeding night, and that their neighbours, with whom they had lived in peace and friendship, were to be the perpetrators. These alarms and alarmists I encountered and exposed; and, happily, with success. The effect, however, as to myself, was only charges of sedition, and threats of vengeance, as opportunity of executing them did not then occur.

In October 1796, an attack was made on my congregation, in which it was confidently expected that I must fall. On the information, as was said, of one *Carr*, a poor weaver, a few of my hearers of great respectability, and with some of whom I lived in habits of the closest intimacy, were made prisoners, by Col. Savage of Portaferry, Lord Castlereagh, and some other gentlemen of the neighbourhood, and brought in custody to Portaferry-house, where they were confined for a night, and, on the day following, transmitted to Downpatrick. At the same time Carr was sent off to Dublin, lodged in Kilmainham, and, for a season comfortably supported; nor were his wife and children in the country unprovided for. His information was confidently depended on, as sufficient to convict all to whom it extended, and strong hopes were entertained that he might be induced to implicate me. This circumstance was communicated to a friend of mine, by an officer of the North York Fencibles; and, being whispered about, I was warmly solicited to take the benefit of a proclamation, which had been formerly issued, or to leave the country. Conscious that truth could not charge me, with word or action, which could expose me to prosecution, I refused to do either. On the contrary, I visited my hearers, confined in Down, every week, until the end of December, which added fresh fuel to the flame which was to consume me.

Luckily, for my friends in confinement, I was tempted to make a trip to Dublin at that time. While there, I frequently visited a number of gentlemen, from Belfast, then prisoners in Kilmainham. On one of these visits I was told of Carr, that he was in solitary confinement, precluded from all intercourse with

---

"war with France": Edmund Burke, the arch-enemy of the French Revolution, declared that the war against France launched in 1793 was merely "a society for pillage" (**Letters On A Regicide Peace**).

those in the goal [sic]—that he was frequently visited by people from the castle, and then treated with great severity, *because his information fell short of his promises*—that he was sometimes nearly distracted, from a sense of guilt, and the distress of his wife and children, whom his seducers had then abandoned—and, that he could not prosecute, to *conviction*, one of the persons against whom he had sworn.

On my asking how this could be ascertained, I was told that I might hear it all from his own lips, if I chose, and my own character also, before I left the gaol. I need not say, that I embraced the opportunity with avidity, and begged that I might be gratified. One of the prisoners immediately went out, and, returning in a few minutes, told me that the yard was clear. Having received my instructions to keep close by the wall, I, and two of the prisoners, went out into the yard. One of them took a ball, and after various attempts, succeeded in throwing it, through an open window, into an upper room. A man came to the window, returned the ball, and enquired what was wanted. Something was mentioned, respecting himself, which led him to a detail of all he had done, and all he had suffered. The detail was melancholy and infamous. It confirmed every thing told me, and discovered vastly more. On my name being mentioned, he gave me a most excellent character—better than I deserved, declared that he had never *seen me, nor even heard of my being seen*, in any society of united Irishmen, *though every body believed that I was one*—that he had been frequently questioned about me, both in the North, and in Dublin—and, that the most tempting offers were made to him, if he would give information against me. On being pressed, in respect to these offers, he declared that a *thousand pounds was to be his reward, on my conviction*.

Possessed of this information, my mind was easy in respect to my friends confined in Down; and, I own, I felt some satisfaction in the thought, that, should they be brought to trial, at the Spring assizes, I would have it in my power to expose their persecutors, through the very person, on whose information their conviction was thought certain, and my own not impossible. However, they were not brought to trial, and I was disappointed. The prisoners in Kilmainham, knowing that *Carr* was to be brought to Down, to prosecute, informed him, from the yard as before, that his evidence would be rebutted, and himself exposed to prosecution, as I had overheard all his declarations in January. However, he was brought down, under a guard; but, when he saw me in Down, he *stagged*, and, unfortunately for me, assigned his reasons. Hence, resentment against me was increased; and the prisoners were holden over until the Summer assizes.

During that Summer, the spirit of reform was ardent and general as ever, and meetings called, in many countries. At a numerous meeting of gentlemen, in the county of Down, a call of the free-holders was unanimously agreed to, and advertised; but, before the day appointed, those of the King's county were dispersed by the military, and a meeting of the county of Kildare prevented by threats. This being known, the gentlemen of Down prevented a county meeting, by another advertisement, lest disturbances should arise, were the military to interfere; but, to convince the people that they had not abandoned them, or their cause, they agreed to meet at Ballynahinch, on the day previously appointed for a county meeting, and publish such a declaration and resolutions, as should be approved of. The wisdom of this measure was justified by the event, as the military were ordered to Down, and the last of a large body from Blaris Camp, had passed through Ballinahinch, only a few hours before the gentlemen met there, of whom I had the honor, as usual, to be called as one.

The resolutions unanimously passed, at that meeting, fully satisfied the public mind, and the two last, as I am convinced they spoke truth, should have satified government, as to the great object of public desire. These declared, "that reform alone was sought for"; and "that if any such reform, as had been brought into parliament, *by Mr. George Ponsonby,* was granted, *the public mind* would be *quiet, content,* and *happy."*

At all these meetings I was present, and, as formerly, took an active part, and expressed my opinions and sentiments, fully and explicitly, so that all my ideas and views, at this time, were as well known to every gentleman in the county, as they had been in the years 1792 and 1793.

Previous to the summer assizes, it was understood that my friends, in gaol, would, not only be tried, but prosecuted with keenness; and whispers were circulated that *particular* lists of jurors were in preparation for the sheriff. Under these impressions, I went to down, the day previous to their commencement, to procure what information I could, consult with the prisoners, and, convinced as I was of their innocence, render them what assistance might be in my power. On the evening of my arrival, my success, in point of information, far exceeded, even, my hopes. I learned, from undoubted authority, that the *capital* conviction of my immediate connexions was despaired of, but that, in all probability, their trials would be again put off, on some pretext or other, in order to prolong their confinement, and aggravate the distress of themselves and families.

With this information I went to the gaol; and having communicated it to the prisoners, advised them to instruct their counsel, to demand trial, or liberation, as they had been so long confined *without any charge brought against them,* to the great injury of their health, distress of their families, and ruin of their circumstances. To this they instantly acceded, and requested me to communicate their wish to counsellors Curran and Sampson, and enjoin them to be guided by it. This I did early next morning; in consequence of which counsellor Curran immediately waited on the attorney general, and demanded the trial, or liberation, of the five prisoners from Portaferry, but received no answer. On this, I requested him to repeat his application, the day following, which he

---

John Philpot Curran of Newmarket, Co. Cork, was the leading barrister of the time on the progressive side. He was seconded in many cases by William Sampson of Derry. Sampson was also one of the main contributors to The Northern Star. He was exiled in 1798.

did, to no better purpose. On the third day, he did the same, tho' with reluctance, but, on his return, told me, that he had some hope of good, as the attorney general seemed surprised and agitated by the repetition and peremptoriness of his demand, which was then made for upwards of thirty prisoners, who had determined to follow the example of the other five. That counsellor Curran was not mistaken, respecting the effect of his last application to the attorney-general, was rendered probable, by his (the attorney general) being in conclave with the judges, for two or three hours afterwards, and the consequent dispatch of an express, supposed to be for Dublin, which returned in about forty eight hours—by the judges not coming into court, till twelve o'clock, though notice had been given, the day before, that they would enter on crown business, at nine, or ten—and, by their proclamation, on taking their seats, that persons, in the neighbourhood, summoned to attend as witnesses on trials for treasonable practices, might go home to their harvests, till Friday, as no business, of the kind, would be brought forward before that day. On that day, the express returned; soon after which the attorney general asked Mr. Curran, if his clients, on being liberated, would enter into recognizance to keep the peace, for a given time. As he could not answer this question, without consulting them, he and I left the court, for that purpose. However, all that could be effected was their consent to enter into personal recognizance for their appearance, when called in. This being reported to the attorney general, were [sic] accepted with eagerness, and the whole were turned out, on the day following. And, as their liberation was, principally, attributed to my intermeddling, the resentment of their prosecutors arose almost to madness. In justice to the gentlemen of the country, I add, that few prosecutions were conducted, with eagerness, except where outrages were committed, which justly deserved the vengeance of the law; and, among these few, that of the people from my neighbourhood was conspicuous. The quarter, from which this proceeded, was suspected, from the zeal and activity of the Rev. John Cleland, who had been private tutor to lord Castlereagh, and then was vicar of Newtown Ards, and agent to the earl of Londonderry. This zeal was obvious, both at the Spring and Summer assizes; and presumptions were so strong, of his having returned packed panels to the sheriff, that the array was twice challenged on that account. That he made returns was not denied, so far as I recollect, but the triers determined that they were not partial. That my persecution proceeded from the same quarter I was tempted to believe, for reasons to be mentioned afterwards, as well as from what I have already written; and from which the public may judge, whether or no, my belief was well founded.

Thus far, I have detailed every part, which I can possibly recollect, of my public conduct, from my first interference in the political concerns of my country. In this detail, I have neither concealed, nor attempted to palliate, either

---

The Rev. John Cleland, Anglican clergyman at Newtownards, was Lord Londonderry's Agent and jury-rigger, and he served as secretary to many Courtmartial trials in 1798.

act or motive. I have even related more than my enemies knew, or all their band of informants could communicate, that the public may be enabled to view my character, in all its bearings, and in every light; and form an impartial judgment of my merits, and demerits, as a member of the state. And I have paused here, because I can prove that, previous to this period, my arrest was frequently in contemplation, which implied that, some parts of my conduct, were politically criminal, or, at least, deemed so to be.*

That my conduct, from the Summer assizes, 1797, until the time of my arrest, may be known, as well as that period, which I have detailed, I shall now recount every circumstance of it also, so far as it would claim any public notice, or be supposed to implicate me in crime.

During the latter end of 1797, and Spring of 1798, I passed unnoticed, being

* For the reasons of my mentioning the family of Stewart so frequently, and, in some measure, embodying part of their political history with my own, see appendix, No. 3.
[This Appendix reads as follows. BC:
The name of Stewart I have frequently mentioned, for different reasons, and with feelings widely different. One of these reasons, as I have already said, was to express my high esteem of the father of the family, and my sincere gratitude for his kind attentions paid me in early life.

A second was to shew that his son, now earl of Londonderry, became representative of the rich and populous county of Down, not from a stupid respect to an overgrown fortune or long train of titled ancestors—not from mean adulation or facinating manners, nor base compromise with other great men to obtain a popular interest as a step to political power; but, from a confidence in his integrity, supported by the presumption that, with his father's fortune he would inherit his liberty and patriotism.

A third reason was to shew that such is the principle of the county of Down, that when the father's patriotism became problematical, the early and blooming virtues of the son retrieved the public confidence, called forth their affectionate support, and placed him in the seat, which his father had filled, in opposition to a combination of interests as formidable as ever candidate encountered: And, that from the same principle, when he had buried these virtues in the grave of Ireland's independence, they released him from the *slavery* of serving them, and left him at *liberty* to seek employment in the patriotic corporation of British borough-mongers. [i.e. Castlereagh was defeated in the Down election of 1805 and got an English seat. BC]

Another reason, as will appear from the preceding narrative, was, that they were the cause of my first appearance, in a political character, and in their support all my exertions were made, previous to the year 1791, and that Alexander Stewart Esq. brother to the earl of Londonderry, was present at every meeting, which I attended, until late in 1793. They, therefore, could not be strangers, either to my political principles, or general character. In fact, they were so connected with every public act of mine, until that period, that the mention of their name appeared to me unavoidable.

My last reason was, that of the early virtues, and engaging manners, of lord viscount Castlereagh might be known—virtues and maners, which, commanding the affection, esteem, and confidence of his native county, led him into the *high* way of honor and promotion, in which the end of his career is known to every body.]

mostly confined by bilious attacks, frequently accompanied by fever. Early in March, I set out for Scotland, to visit an uncle of Mrs. Dickson, who, as I was informed, was dangerously ill. His death, and the unsettled state in which he left his affairs, detained me there, till the month of April. On my return, my servant, who brought my luggage from Donaghadee, was stopped in the street of Portaferry, and carried to the guard-house. There, every thing was scrutinized with a minuteness, which excited the ridicule of the officers, who were obliged to perform the task. After every thing, in which dangerous concealments seemed likely to be contained, was tossed, shaken, and turned outside in, to no purpose, a large tobacco-box, which had formerly belonged to a sea-captain, and which I had brought from Scotland, as a curiosity, was eagerly laid hold of. As this box, supposed to be fraught with more evils than that of Pandora, was of steel, and had lain by, time immemorial, it was so rusted that the inquisitors could not force it open. In their hurry, they overlooked the cause of its obstinacy, and, attributing it to a concealed spring, were about to demolish it, till captain Marshall, hereafter to be mentioned! having pointed out their error, saved it from destruction. The cause of all this was a first surmise, and, afterwards, an assertion, that my visit to a dying friend, in Scotland, was only a pretext, while my real business was to *form and promote united societies there, and a correspondence, between them and those of this country.* This being taken for granted, it might be naturally supposed that my common documents were concealed in my luggage, and my diploma in my tobacco-box.

Tho' my bilious complaints were nearly removed, by sea-sickness, change of air, and exercise, during my excursion, yet the symptoms returned soon afterwards; and I was advised, by a medical friend, not to resume my usual sedentary life, but to take exercise on horseback daily, and drink the Ballynahinch waters. The former part of this advice I immediately adopted; and, as the sacrament of the Lord's supper was administered, in the month of May, not only in my congregation, but in others, where I assisted, the riding from place to place, and the services which I had to perform, afforded exercise in abundance; but, at the same time, prevented me going to Ballynahinch, as soon as I wished. In the third and fourth week of May, I spent several days in Newtown Ards, on sacramental duty; during which, I rode twice into Belfast, and returned, on the following morning. As, about this time, the king's troops and insurgents had frequent engagements, in the counties of Wicklow and Wexford, the public mind was very much agitated, and the public ear was occupied, by rumors, often as inconsistent and unfounded, as they were numerous and alarming. In Belfast, I had not only an opportunity of reading those contained in the public papers, but of hearing such as were communicated by private letters, or wafted by the breath of popular fame. These reports, I freely, and, as far as I could, correctly mentioned, in company, on my return to the house of Mr. Sinclair, Presbyterian minister, at Newtown Ards; and passing, without remarks, the extravagance of some, and the glaring inconsistency of others. Among these, I mentioned one, viz. "that a party of the black horse had gone over to the insurgents"; which, by the bye, was confidently asserted, and generally believed, for several days. The cause of my now recollecting this, more correctly than others, will soon appear, and, at the same time, shew, how eagerly cause of crimination against me was hunted for, and, on what slight pretences I might expect to be laid hold of.

On Tuesday morning, May 29th. I left Mr. Sinclair's with a view to spend the day at Crawford's burn, the seat of John Crawford Esq. and ride thence, to Belfast, in the evening. However meeting some gentlemen, on their way to Belfast, who told me that major Crawford was not at home, I accompanied them thither. Next day, I rode out to Ballygowan house, the seat of Robert Rollo Reid Esq. where I spent the afternoon and night, that I might be convenient to Saintfield fair, in which I intended to buy a horse, next day. On Thursday, I paraded the fair, for several hours, and in the most public manner, but did not find a horse, such as I wished for. On mentioning my disappointment, to some gentlemen present, one of them said, that he knew a horse, such as I had described and that the proprietor wished to dispose of him, but that neither he nor the horse was in the fair. On learning that captain George Sinclair, of Belfast was the owner, I expressed a wish to have the horse sent to town, as I was obliged to be there, on the following morning. On this, a gentleman, having looked around shouted, "M'Ginn". M'Ginn immediately came forward, and being requested to call at captain Sinclair's, and order his servant to take the grey horse to town, next morning, as there would be a gentleman there to buy him, promised that he would.

This being settled, the day far spent, and my appetite keen, I went to, what was called the best Inn, (I believe, Elliots) to get some refreshment. From the hurry and confusion of the place, I could not get a morsel, with any comfort. On this disappointment, I called at the house of a David Shaw, where I got some excellent cold beef, drank one tumbler of punch, and immediately left town, with an intention of returning to Belfast, without having entered a house in Saintfield, except the Inn, as above mentioned, and that of David Shaw; or spoken to an individual, except in the public fair.*

These circumstances, tho' seemingly trivial, will afterwards appear of some importance, from their relation to M'Ginn, as the message about the horse, is

---

* I have mentioned the two nights, spent with Mr. Reid, as they were the fifth and sixth before my arrest, for several reasons. 1st he had been my pupil, from his seventh to the end of his tenth year. 2dly. in consequence of this I had lived in perfect confidence with him whenever we met. 3dly. from these circumstances, I might be supposed to have unbosomed myself, to him, respecting my military command, etc. etc. especially, as fame had conferred on him the rank of Colonel. 4thly. on the latter of these evenings, he expressed great uneasiness, from the apprehension that *Mr. Cleland* would call, while I was with him. And 5thly. he was one of the reputed informers, after my arrest, and, on whose information, my conviction was deemed certain; as he had been obliged to flee the country in 1797 and permitted to return, thro' interest so *special*, that under the Influence of reviving loyalty, cherished by gratitude, his testimony was counted on, as a matter of course, and great things expected from it.

transformed, by John Hughes, into a message to him, then in Belfast, relative to my intended removal to Ballynahinch. I mention them, also, for another reason. During the whole of my stay, in Saintfield, on that day, I was so faithfully attended, at humble distance, by a few gentlemen, that, whenever I looked round, they met my eye. I say "gentlemen", because one of them was possessed of a considerable landed property, and another a dignitary of the church; and, to all such, courtesy and custom allow that appellation*.

In the evening, instead of proceeding to Belfast, I stopped at Ballygurn, where I slept that night also; and, next morning, set out for Belfast, on business, and in hope of seeing Capt. Sinclair and his horse; but, unfortunately, the Captain was not at home, and the horse was not sent to town. I suppose Mr. M'Ginn had mistaken his route, as well as the purport of his message.

On this disappointment, as the horse which I rode, was not only a slow traveller, but weak, I intended to go part of the way, that evening to Ballee, where, by appointment of Presbytery, I was to preach next day, and administer the sacrament of the Lord's Supper, on the day following. However, as I was mounting, I was accosted by Mr. John Coulter, of Collon, who, on knowing my situation, pressed me to go home with him, and he would accommodate me with a horse, which would carry me to Ballee, in due time next morning, with ease and safety. I did so, and, setting out early in the morning, reached Downpatrick, twenty miles distant, before eleven o'Clock.**

On my arrival, a new circumstance occurred, which proved, with what avidity my inculpation was sought for, and with what eagerness every word of mine was laid hold of, by the minions at Newtown-Ards, which, even by implication, could possibly lead to it. Before I could enter the inn, at which I stopped, Captain Marshall, of the York Fencibles, whom I have already mentioned, came up to me, and, accompanying me into a room, told me, with affectionate agitation, the he had been at Portaferry, in my absence, with a message from Colonel Stapleton, to enquire on what authority I had said, at Mr. Sinclair's, on Monday, "that a party of the Black Horse had gone over to the insurgents". Let it not be forgotten that Colonel Stapleton was an entire stranger to me, and, *that he was then resident in Newtown Ards ! ! ! !*

I immediately gave Captain Marshall an account as before written, of that and other reports of the day, which I had repeated there, and begged that he might

* Whatever ideas the *particular* attention of these gentlemen excited at the time, I have frequently reflected on it since, with equal pleasure, and gratitude, though not gratitude to *them*. It supplies a strong presumption, at least, that I was neither in improper company, nor improperly employed, on that occasion; whatever may have been surmised afterwards, on the authority of Mr. Hughes, who will be introduced in the sequel.

** I hope this circumstance will be recollected, when the testimony of John Hughes shall be brought forward; as he is made to swear that I was to go to Mr. Pottinger's not one mile from Belfast, on that day, and wait there till seven o'Clock in the evening, that he might have an opportunity of sending me the intelligence for which I had come to Belfast; which intelligence, he also swears that I communicated to *him* at the same time.

communicate it to Colonel Stapleton. He said, he had much rather I would write to the Colonel. I, therefore, got pen, ink, and paper, and wrote him, that I had repeated the "rumor of the Black Horse", and several others, at Mr. Sinclair's, on Monday, as the common reports of that morning in Belfast—that, if I had been there, two days afterwards, on my return from the same place, I could, and perhaps would, have repeated many more, which were in general circulation—and that I would not have thought myself blameable in so doing: but that, if any farther inquiry was deemed necessary, *"I would be found at Ballee, the two following days, and in Portaferry at night; and that, for some weeks afterwards, I would be found at Ballynahinch, from noon on Monday, until the same hour on Saturday, and, on the intermediate time, in Portaferry, on the road between the two places."* This letter I read to Captain Marshall, sealed, put into his hand, and saw him deliver it to a dragoon, then mounted at the door, and waiting for his dispatches to the Colonel.

This done, I hurried off to Ballee, four miles distant, where I arrived in time to perform the service allotted me. Agreeable to what I had written to Colonel Stapleton, I went to Portaferry, in the evening. Next morning, I returned to Ballee, performed the duties of the day, and went back to Portaferry. On Monday, I attended again, at Ballee; and, after the service of the day, baptized a child for, and dined with, a Mr. John M'Neown, a very respectable farmer of that neighbourhood. After dinner, the conversation turned on *"the floggings"*, *"shavings with red-hot iron"*, and *"half*-hangings", which for some time had been practised in the country. "Very well", said one of the company, "if they do not proceed to whole-hanging". "Well, indeed"; said I, "for my part, from what I am experiencing, and the manner in which I am hunted, I am sure they will hang me if they can find any plausible pretext": or words to that effect. This circumstance, I mention, only on account of the base use that was made of it, several years afterwards, by a reverend brother, as will appear in the sequel of this Narrative. And I beg it may be remembered that this conversation took place in presence of two clergymen, a wealthy linen-draper, and a large company of respectable country-people, with one of whom I was not personally acquainted, *except the clergymen* and *linen-draper*.

A few minutes after this conversation, *the linen draper*, a *Mr. James Brown*, and I mounted our horses, and travelled together until within a mile of Ballynahinch. Captain Magenis, of the Castlewellan yeomanry, and another gentleman were my companions, for that mile. When we parted, I drove to the inn, where I supped alone, and slept that night. Anxious to receive benefit, as soon as possible, I rode out to the well, at seven o'Clock, next morning, and drank the water; did the same at one; and a third time, at five in the evening. On my third trip, I felt happy in meeting Edward Smith, Esq.—a man of excellent character, *approved* loyalty, and an officer in his Majesty's revenue, with a sister, on their way to lodgings, which they had taken, for the season. Thither I accompanied them, and spent some time with them, devising means of getting accommodation in the same house; after which I returned direct to town.

As the hour of this return was the last of my liberty, *for three years, seven months, and seven days,* I quit it with regret. Let me therefore pause, and request my readers to review the occurrences of the last two months, as I have related them; and the relation of which I challenge any man living to controvert. I believe, it has never been alleged that any plan of the Northern Insurrection was digested, previous to the month of March. As I was out of the kingdom, during the greater part of that and the month following, I could have no part in what was then done. Indeed, none of the informers, so far as I know, have brought any charges against me, during that period. The succeeding period, of less than six weeks, I have accounted for, almost to a day, and even that day no one of them has filled up, as might have been supposed from their accounts of themselves, by mentioning a single meeting with any *brother General* to concert a plan of operations; or with the *Colonels under my command,* to give them necessary instructions. Yet, I may have been a General, for aught that appears to the contrary; and I may not have been a General, though people said I was. But be that as it was, General, or no General, it appears from the cases of the "tobacco-box" and "Black Horse" as well as other circumstances, that my doom was pre-determined, though, contrary to expectation, it did not prove *fatal.* Perhaps, however, as Mr. Pollock said afterwards "had I been left to myself two days longer, it might have been otherwise".

It was on the evening of the 5th of June, that I returned, from my interview with Mr. Smith, to Ballynahinch. I had scarcely sitten down in my room, when a servant informed me, that a gentleman, in the street, requested to speak to me. On going out, I met Captain Magenis, already mentioned, in company with a Lieutenant Lindsay, of the same corps. We walked out of town, at the request of Colonel Magenis and, after much hesitation and embarrassment, he informed me, in great agitation, that there had been a meeting of yeomanry officers, that day, in Clough; and, that he had received a letter, from Colonel Lord Annesley, ordering him to detain me, as a prisoner, till he should receive farther instructions. I begged that he would be composed, for that I was perfectly easy, as I could bid defiance to malice itself, if unsupported by villainy, in respect to

---

"Yet I may have been a general": Steel Dickson was imprisoned without charge or trial for three and half years. In 1799 the Synod of Ulster named him in a resolution as one who had been involved "in seditious or treasonable practices". His point is that the Government had used bribery and intimidation in an attempt to produce evidence against him on those lines and had failed, and that unless the Synod had evidence against him which the Government did not possess it ought not to have stated that he had engaged in treason and sedition. In 1813 the Synod agreed that the 1799 resolution had been improper.
I have argued in **Thomas Russell And Belfast** that although the United Irish of the North were forced into military conspiracy by the Camden Government after 1795, they never gave up on their original aim of reforming the British Constitution as it operated in Ireland. That divided mind did not make for effective conspiratorial activity. I cannot say whether Steel Dickson had agreed to be considered General for County Down. If so, all that existed up to his arrest on June 5th was an understanding. I do not doubt that if there was such an understanding he would have acted on it on June 7th. But he was in the custody of the state on June 7th.

every part of my conduct. On asking him for his warrant, he told me that *he had only his Lordship's letter;* and that, *as I had a horse, I might take a ride.* This I declined, and asked him and Mr. Lindsay to accompany me to my room, as I had saddle-bags and papers there, which it might be proper for them to examine. This also they positively refused to do. I then told them, that I would retire, and requested them to place sentinels on the inn, lest they should be charged with neglect of duty. This also they refused, saying, that they supposed my detention was only a *whim of his Lordship,* and that I would be discharged in the morning. However, at my earnest request, they placed a serjeant in the house, a distant relation of the family, who took his rest, during the night, without giving himself, or me, any trouble. This politeness and confidence I mention with pleasure; and am sorry that I shall have so few instances of the kind to record, as having occurred during my confinement in Ireland.*

About noon, next day, a Colonel Bainbridge arrived in Ballynahinch, from Lisburn, gave orders for my transmission thither, and, *without seeing me,* proceeded to Montello, to call on lady dowager Moira. Being informed of this, I dispatched a messenger, after him, to request, that, as I was in a delicate state of health, and the weather intensely hot, I might be permitted to ride, or travel in a chaise. The answer I received was not only blunt, but cruel: *"A chaise, and be damned! Let him walk, or take a seat on the car, which goes to town with the old guns."*

Irritated with this harshness, so different from the treatment, which I had experienced, on the preceding evening, I determined to walk, be the consequence to my health, what it might. About four o'clock, in the afternoon, I set out with a guard of 14 men, and a car loaded with old guns, over a very rough and hilly road of eight miles, under a scorching Sun, and enveloped in clouds of dust. We reached Lisburn, about eight in the evening. I need not say that I was exhausted, almost to faintness. The moment that I was refreshed by some wine and water, and a change of the flannels next my skin, I waited on General Goldie, who received me, with all the politeness of a gentleman and a soldier. On observing the exhausted state, in which I was, he expressed his sorrow that he could not accommodate me with a bed in his own lodgings, and told me that the place of confinement in Lisburn, was such that my passing a night in it might endanger my life; but, added, that I might take a carriage, in which he would send a discreet serjeant, with me, to Belfast, under an escort of two dragoons, and that he was sure General Nugent would immediately release me, *"as there was no charge, of any kind, against me";* a suspicion only existing that, as I had a general acquaintance with Scotland, spent a considerable time there, in Spring, and had been very much on horseback, since my return, I might have been promoting a connexion between the disaffected here, and people of the same description, in that country."

Gratified with the attention and openness of the General, and flattered with

---

* This confinement commenced in the fifth month of my 53d year.

the prospect of immediate liberation, I ordered a chaise, and, my escort being ready, I hurried off to Belfast, little thinking that all my fairy prospects should so soon be blasted, and my expectations disappointed. On my arrival at the General's quarters, I sent in the Serjeant to receive his commands. Instead of liberation, these were to "carry me to the *black-hole*, I was *politely* shewn in, and admitted *without much ceremony*. On admission, I there found Mr. Robert Hunter, a merchant of Down, who had been introduced a few minutes before, and was undergoing an examination, about arms found in his stores. In this all were so interested, that my entrance was little noticed, till some of the soldiers of the Monaghan Militia, who were on guard, observing my exhausted situation, civilly offered me a seat, on a large platform, which served them for chairs, table, and bed. This offer I gladly embraced, as I was extremely fatigued. Mr. Hunter's examination being finished, I was asked some questions, my answers to which *secured me possession of my seat*, of which Mr. Hunter came and took part. I then inquired, where we were to be accommodated, during the night, and was answered, in a very rough tone, "you are to stay where you are". After some time, I asked, if I might be permitted to send for some refreshment. This, as we were told by a serjeant, no commissioned officer being present, was positively forbidden. However, on sending for the Captain of the guard, he came to us, and being told *my* situation* in particular, he kindly ordered that whatever we wanted, or might want, during the night, should be procured for us. His orders were obeyed; and we, having refreshed ourselves, asked if there was any spot where we might enjoy a few hours rest; on which, one of the soldiers, civilly enough, offered us a part of their platform, on which we could stretch ourselves at length; and, as no better place could be procured, here we were obliged to lay ourselves down on hard boards, covered with filth and dust, without covering, and with my saddle-bags as our common pillow. To aggravate our feelings, we were nauseated with stench, and stunned with a continued torrent of ribaldry, oaths, and obscenity during great part of the night. Disgusting as this scene was, and painful to our feelings, to us these pains were only the beginnings of sorrows.**

In the morning we had breakfast brought us, from Mr. Hunter's, after which

* The Captain of the guard was Robert Wallace, Esq. then an Officer in the Belfast yeomanry, and now a Major of Brigade. He is son to the late Joseph Wallace, Esq. whose memory will ever be revered by all who knew him. That his son inherits his mild and amiable virtues, I have no reason to doubt. That he may ever enjoy that inheritance, is my fervent wish.

** That this charge may not lie against the Monaghan regiment, justice requires that its weight should be laid on one of their officers, by whom the scene complained of was acted, and patronized. His name, as I was informed, is Cross. Of the wretch I had no previous knowledge, nor do I recollect that I ever saw him afterwards, during my confinement. The vileness of his conduct delicacy will not allow me to mention. Let him recite it if he dare. Of the other officers, I must say, that their conduct, so far as I ever knew or heard, was equally becoming gentlemen and soldiers.

we were detained, in this loathsome abode, till about two o'Clock in the afternoon, when we were removed to the Donegal Arms, then the Provost prison. There, four others and I were thrust into a room, about sixteen feet by ten broad, without table, chair, or any other furniture, whatever; and, as our only window was unsecured, by iron bars or bolts, a chalked line was drawn across the floor, about six feet from it, and intimation given us, not to set a foot over said line, under pain of instant punishment. This left a space, of about ten feet square, in which, five people, accustomed, at least, to the comfortable conveniences of life, some of them to its luxuries, were to take their exercise, eat, and sleep. Besides, as there was but one window in the room, we were obliged to have it kept open, to prevent suffocation, as the weather was intensely hot; and, as the yard was covered with filth, and the offices a horse-barrack, we were annoyed day and night, with offensive smells, noise and uproar. Thus accommodated, we were allowed to send for beds to lie on, and clothes to cover us. We, therefore ordered two mattresses, having room for no more; but as they did not arrive till a *few minutes after four o'Clock*; which, as we were informed, was the latest hour of ingress to our prison, they were not permitted to be introduced. Hence we were obliged to lie, another night, on bare boards. They were clean, however, which rendered them preferable to those of the *black-hole*. In addition to all this, we were obliged to sit up, to be counted, on the exchange of sentinels, *which took place, every second hour.*

Hitherto, nothing like Insurrection, had taken place in Ulster...

Steel Dickson was arrested on June 5th, 1798. The insurrection in Antrim and Down began on June 7th. There had been disturbances in Dublin, Kildare and Meath since May 23rd, and insurrection in Wexford had begun on May 26.

Chapter Two

The American War

[Introductory Note

This chapter consists of extracts from two sermons included in a pamphlet which is
undated but was probably published in 1778 and which has the following title page:

Sermons
On The Following Subjects
I. The Advantages of National Repentance
II. The Ruinous Effects of Civil War
III. The Coming of the Son of Man
IV. The Hope of Meeting, Knowing, and Rejoicing with
Virtuous Friends, in a Future World
by
William Steel Dickson
Belfast
Printed by James Magee At The Bible And Crown, In Bridge-Street

These sermons were delivered on days "appointed by Government, as a General Fast". It
was not unusual in those days for the Government to order certain days to be kept as Fast
Days for some public purpose. The object was usually to concentrate the public mind in
support of some government policy. These sermons are a prime example of how
Presbyterian ministers, when they did not consider the purpose of the Government
worthy, complied with the orders of the Government in a way which tended to obstruct
rather than reinforce its policy.
The war between Britain and its American colonies began in 1775. When Britain failed to
crush the independence movement in America at the outset, the war naturally began to
take on a European dimension. Though there was no affinity of political character
between the "rights of man" movement in America and the French and Spanish
monarchies, it was only to be expected that Britain's traditional enemies on the Continent
should help the new enemies which Britain had made for itself in the New World. The
American alliance with France was no problem for the Americans but, as the greater part
of the British Army got tied down by the American resistance, the French dimension
began to loom large in the minds of America's most enthusiastic supporters in Ireland.
While opposing the policy of the British Government in America, Steel Dickson at the
same time showed a lively appreciation of the progressive and libertarian character of the
political framework of life under the British Government. He did not see the British and
French states as being two of a kind. One of his criticisms of British policy in America
was that it had the consequence of making Ireland vulnerable to France.
The second sermon deals with the war in America as a civil war. While that may now
seem an unusual view, it was not so at the time. Presbyterian Ulster had extensive
family connections with both Britain and America.
The second sermon is also a first-rate example of how the Bible served as a fund of
historical experience on which to base political reflection. Classical Rome served a
similar purpose for the ruling English aristocracy of the time—in my view the most
remarkable ruling class there has ever been. The histories of the Jews and the Romans
have in recent times both been displaced by the arid sociological abstractions of "political
science", and the effect on political reflection has not been good.]

PREFACE

The two following Sermons were written, entirely, with a View to the Congregation before which they were preached. The Author, so far from intending to submit them to the public eye, positively refused to comply with the warmest solicitations of many Friends, who urged him to publish them. However, the Circulation of some Reports concerning political Sentiments, said to be contained in them, hath obliged him to expose them, in his own Vindication. How far they may serve this Purpose Time must shew. Be that as it may, he assures the Public that he hath not presumed to retrench, add, or in any Manner, to modify, a Sentiment in them, since they were preached. He hath, even, omitted some Corrections, both in Stile and Arrangement, lest they should be supposed to be made with this View. He hopes this Circumstance will apologize for any Incorrectness, or Inelegance of expression which may occur in perusing them.

For the Sentiments he means no Apology. He trusts they are neither inconsistent with the Rights of Mankind, nor the Peace and Interests of the British Empire: And he wishes to hold them with that spirit of Moderation which Christianity, every where, recommends and inculcates.

Should these Discourses have any Influence in promoting a Return to Virtue, and a Love of Peace, the Author will think himself happy in the Accomplishment of his chief End in composing them. If they fail of this, he flatters himself, that they will descend, harmless and unoffending, to the Regions of Forgetfulness, to which so many Trifles of the Kind have gone before them, and many more must follow.

Sermon I
On The Advantages Of National Repentance,

Preached to the Protestant Dissenting Congregation of Ballhalbert, December 13th, 1776, Being a Day appointed by Government, as a *General Fast.*

II Chron. VII.14
"If my People, which are called by my Name,
will humble themselves, and pray, and seek my Face,
and turn from their wicked Ways; then will I hear from Heaven,
and will forgive their Sin, and will heal their Land."

Whatever unbecoming Sentiments Men may entertain, in prosperous Circumstances, it is evident that Afflictions, in general, tend to correct them, and powerfully minister to their chief Good. This holds, equally, with Respect to Individuals, and Bodies politic. For this Reason, God hath closely connected Sin and Suffering, under his Government, and, sometimes, sensibly interposes in the Chastisement of Iniquity. This appears, remarkably, in the History of the Israelites, whose Obstinacy, frequently, exposed them to severe Correction. Yet, no sooner did they return to a Sense of duty, than the Rod was withdrawn, and

Evil removed from them...

Fasting, as appointed to the Jews, was to be rigidly observed, in its literal Sense; and was, always, performed in the most humiliating Manner. A total Abstinence from Food was absolutely required; and the Person fasting clothed himself in Sack-cloth, and sprinkled his head with Ashes, as Expressions of his Unworthiness.

These Circumstances were perfectly adapted to the rude and unpolished Periods of Society, in which, every Thing spiritual, and abstracted, is represented, and judged of, by external Signs. Such was the State of the Jews when their law was given; and for this Reason, a vast Variety of outward Observances was enjoined, either as expressive of inward Sentiments, or in Order to excite them. However, instead of considering these Appointments, in this Light, they overlooked the End, entirely, which they ought to have served, and placed all their Religion in the outward Action. Their fasting, therefore, came to consist in Slovenliness, Filth, and melancholic Looks. The Reason of this is very obvious. It was much easier to submit to these, for an appointed Day, than to sacrifice Ambition, Covetousness, and Lust, to a sense of Duty, and the Interests of Mankind. However, this was far from answering the Purposes which fasting was intended to serve, and is therefore disapproved of by God in the plainest Manner. *Is it such a Fast*, says he, *that I have chosen? For a Man to afflict his Soul for a Day? Is it to bow down his Head as a Bulrush, and spread Sackcloth and Ashes under him? Will thou call this a Fast, and an acceptable Day to the Lord?*

These Inquiries imply, not only a strong Denial of the Acceptableness of such a Fast; but a Charge of Absurdity against the very Supposition. And, our Lord condemns such Observances, attributes them to Hypocrisy, and recommends a Conduct directly contrary. *When ye fast*, saith he, *be not, as the Hypocrites, of a sad Countenance; for they disfigure their Faces, that they may appear unto Men to fast. Verily, I say unto you, they have their Reward. But thou, when thou fastest, anoint thine Head, and wash thy Face; that thou appear not unto Men to fast, but unto thy Father who is in secret; and thy Father who seeth in secret, will reward thee openly.*

As this Affectation of Sanctity, and external Humiliation, serves no better Purpose than to impose upon Mankind, it is justly exploded; and there is another Circumstance, often connected with our religious Confessions, which deserves to be ranked little higher. This is the general Acknowledgement of the Prevalence of Sin, and a fruitless Lamentation over the Wickedness of the World, without any Regard to *ourselves*, or Endeavour to amend *it*. This, we find, was objected to the Jews by God himself... *I hearkened and heard*, said he, *but they spake not aright: No Man repented him of his Wickedness, saying, what have I done? but they turned, every one to his Course, as the Horse rusheth into the Battle*
...

I would not, however, be understood to insinuate, that we are now more wicked and profane, than ever any Nation was before. But, only, that Wickedness abounds too much; and that as the Wickedness of other Nations hath often been severely punished, in the Course of Providence, we have Reason to fear that we also shall be chastised. That we may be, only, chastised, and not entirely given over, should be the Prayer of every one of us. Nor do I mean to charge every Individual, with Profanity, Intemperance, Fraud, Oppression, Cruelty, and Violence. No! God be thanked, there are still some, among us, who *love the Lord in Sincerity*, and *hate Iniquity*, I hope, *with a perfect Hatred*. Yet, that these are few, compared with the Workers of Iniquity, I may safely appeal to Experience — Nay, I appeal to your own Knowledge of the World, and the Feelings of your Hearts, for the Truth of the Fact.

As the general Considerations, deduced from Morality and Religion, have hitherto produced no good Effect upon such — As they have not prevailed upon them, *to humble themselves before God, and seek his Face, by turning from their wicked Ways*, we may now turn our Attention, a little more particularly, to our present Situation, and consider what Motives it offers to engage us to a national Humiliation, and return to Deity.

And here, the State of our Affairs upon the Continent of America, first arrests our thoughts, and claims our Notice — A State of Affairs, gloomy, perplexed, and, truly, unpromising! There, War already rages with, even, more than its natural Horrors. Brother points the fatal Minister of Death against Brother, and Father against Son: and Children imbrue their Hands in their parents' Blood. Nor is that all. Should the Contest be prolonged, America must be ruined; and, in its Ruins, we must suffer. This is equally true, succeed who will, if the Sword must be the only Arbiter. If America supports her Independence, Commerce must be arrested in her Channel, and, under the prodigious Expence of a fruitless Attempt to conquer, we must inevitably sink. On the other Hand, should the Arms of our King prove victorious, and drive the, now, enraged Americans, from all their strong Holds, what must be the Consequence? A prodigious Armament will be always necessary to keep them in Subjection, thro' such an immense Territory, the Expence of which, I am afraid, will be greater than Britain and Ireland will be able to bear. Moreover, the Extent of the Continent, the Cover of the Woods, the numerous Fens, Morasses, Rivers, and dangerous Defiles, will enable them to keep-up a constant Skirmishing, to execute Plots, and harrass their enemies, in numberless Ways.

It is true, the British Arms may derive considerable Assistance from Co-operation of the Indian Nations. It is not to be supposed that their just Resentment, against European Plunderers, will be lulled to Sleep, on such Occasion: or that their known Sagacity will desert them, when so fair an Opportunity offers of glutting their Revenge with Blood, and recovering their long-lost Territories. But, what will be the Effect of this Assistance? We may call it *Victory* for a Time; but it will prove to be *Depopulation*. The *Scalping-knife* and the *Hatchet* will come forth, at a Call; but it is only the Terror of more powerful Arms that can force them back into Peace. This the Americans have frequently experienced; and, if their Strength be once broken, it is natural to expect, that they will flee, for Shelter, to any Clime, however inhospitable, rather than be again exposed to savage Fury. Should this be the Case, what can remain to us, as the Fruits of our Conquest, but Savage nations, to re-conquer, and a barren Wilderness to replant with Colonies?

But, (Conjectures and bare Probabilities apart) does it not appear that we are already suffering, by the Restrictions of our Commerce, the Capture of our Vessels, and the growing Weight of our Taxes; and that, if the present Contest continues, we *must* suffer, more and more, every day? Should not these Things, then engage us to inquire into the Source of our Sufferings, and endeavour to have them removed?

I do not mean, that we should begin to discuss the political Questions so much agitated, concerning the Omnipotence of Parliament, the Rights of America, etc. etc. or to determine whether the Americans were forced into the present Opposition by illegal Extensions of Prerogative, and Claims of Power—or have rushed into Rebellion against Law, without a Cause. These are Inquiries for the Solution of which, I frankly confess, I have neither Taste nor Inclination. They are, in many Circumstances, by me unfathomable; as many of the Facts, on which their Solution depends, are yet veiled in thick Darkness.

What is more; such Inquiries would be to *us*, totally unprofitable. *We* are so far removed from Power, that it cannot be supposed that our Opinions can ever enter a Council-chamber, or ascend a Throne. Or if they could, they must there be light as the Down, that floats in the Wind, or the Feather, which skims the Deep.

Further, from whatever Cause the present Distraction and bloodshed originated, the Effects are the same. Nor, are we to charge these Effects, *wholly*, either upon destructive Counsels, at home, or rebellious Dispositions abroad. Moderation will readily admit that there may be, and indeed have been, Errors on both Sides. How vain, then, for us, to indulge our Rancour, or expose our Ignorance, by forming uncharitable, indigested Opinions; or venting Torrents of Scurrility, and abusive Language, either against Administration, or its Opponents?

Again; If we consider this Matter in another, and, I am persuaded, in its true Light, we will find Cause to look farther back, than we are generally willing to do, for the Source of our national Evils, and gloomy Prospects. Tho' they may may have immediately arisen, either from wicked Counsels, and oppressive Measures; or from rebellious Dispositions — Yet the evil Counsellors, or rebellious Subjects, may be raised up, as Instruments, in the Hand of god, for our Correction as a Nation; and our national Wickedness may be the true and ultimate Cause of all. I am sure none of us can prove, satisfactorily, even to himself, that it is not. Yet every one of us ought to be assured that it is not; before we begin to look for, much more, lay the Blame upon another. Let us, therefore, carefully examine into our own Conduct, how far we have been chargeable with adding to the Guilt of the Nation, by our Transgressions — *Let us know, every one, the Plague of his* own *Heart*, and root *it* out, before we begin to arraign others. Then shall our Judgments be clear, and our Censures attended to...

The Consideration arising from this View of our present Situation is plainly this. That, as national Wickedness is the probable Cause of our divided Opinions, and distracted Counsels, and of that Confusion, War, and Blood-shed which rage thro' our King's Dominions, we, as we tender the Restoration of Peace abroad, and unanimity at Home — As we regard the Lives, Liberties, and Happiness of ourselves, and Brethren *should humble ourselves, and pray unto God, and seek his Face, and turn from our wicked Ways.*

Another Circumstance, from which this Consideration derives no little Weight, is the seemingly, undetermined Disposition of several Europeean Courts, at present. Their Professions, it is true, are full of Peace. Yet, that open Trade which is every where carried on, with the Inhabitants of America, contrary to the spurious ["spurious" crossed out and "specious" written in on British Museum copy. BC.] Prohibitions; and the powerful Armaments fitted out, in all the principal Ports of *France* and *Spain*, seem to announce approaching War. However, tho' we should not be the immediate Objects of these Preparations; yet, if the present Dispute between *Spain* and *Portugal* comes to an open Rupture; we must, of Necessity, be engaged in it, and share its Consequences. And, how fatal these might be to us, in our present distracted and defenceless Situation, is hard to say.

Should either *France* or *Spain* be in a Capacity to invade us, they must, at present, meet with feeble Opposition. Not, that our Armies are less numerous, or less brave, than our Enemies have often found them; but, merely, because they are dispersed far and wide, and their Force divided. The British Arms may be justly compared to a mighty torrent, which, confined to a narrow Channel, burst along with foaming Rage, and, with irresistible Impetuosity, beats down all Opposition; but diffused over a far extended Plain, loses all its Force, and, with a languid Motion, faintly creeps along. Nor, is this All. Our Power is not only weakened, by Division, but labours to destroy itself.

In this Situation, let us for a Moment, suppose, (and Heaven forbid it should ever be more than Supposition)—let us suppose, I say, that *France* and *Spain* should invade our Land, and that their Arms should be crowned with Success. What must be the Consequence to us? With all our Murmurs and Complaints, do we imagine, our Liberties would be extended, our Taxes diminished, or our Properties better secured? Neither is the Case with the Subjects of either Power. And do we presume, that their Attention to us would be more tender than they have ever shewn to others? Or that our Interests would be dearer to them than those of their natural-born Subjects? Vain Thoughts!

The truth is; we are never satisfied with our Condition; nor do we know the value of our Blessings but by their Loss. Do you not now enjoy the most extensive Liberty of Thought, Word and Action? We may publish every Sentiment of our Minds, in Speech, or Writing; and upon every Subject too, without Restraint. It is true, we are accountable for the Abuse of this Liberty. But, then, we are not accountable to Men; but to Law, the Principles of which are founded in Equity, and the Expressions unequivocal. Is this, then, the Case in *France*, or in *Spain*? Or would it be the Case with us, if subject to their Authority? No, certainly! Every Sentiment, which appears to imply Disrespect to any established Form, whether in Religion or Politics, must be accounted for to interested Men, and atoned for, by the Privation of Property, or Life.

With Respect to Taxes, nothing need be said. In that Particular we are certainly more easily dealt with than any other Nation. And as to Property, the poorest Peasant, in these Realms, has the Advantage of the greatest Subject under arbitrary Governments. The meanest Cottage is, as, an impregnable Strong-hold to the Possessor, in which he defies the Iron-hand of Oppression; and into which, even, Law itself dares not, violently, enter. How enviable is such a Situation, compared with the most exalted Rank, where the most princely Fortune may be destroyed, in a Moment, by the almighty Word of an arbitary Monarch! And the poor Man's little *all* reduced to Nothing, by the Covetousness of an artful Financier, or the Rapacity of a Farmer-general! And, yet, such a Change of Situation must we feel, should an Invasion take place, and be attended with Success.

There is another Circumstance, in which we must suffer intolerably, if we retain the least Dignity of Sensibility, or Regard to our Dignity as rational Beings. We must deny ourselves the Use of our noblest Powers, and implicitly resign our most valuable Privileges — We must renounce Reason, and make over Conscience to a designing Priest, resign the Bible to be sealed up, for ever, and devoutly kneeling, at the Shrine of Infallibility, receive with Thankfullness, our spiritual Chains — We must, at once, forego all those Privileges which our Fore-fathers purchased with their Blood, and in the peaceable Enjoyment of which we have long been happy. In a Word, we must embrace Popery, with all its absurdities; or encounter Death with all the Terrors which Malice can devise.

Let us, then, seriously ask ourselves, whether we would willingly submit to these Things. Tho' we would often act contrary to Reason, and labor to silence the Voice of Conscience, would we feel no Reluctance in disclaiming the Guidance of Reason and Conscience, altogether? — 'Tho we treat Religion with Indifference, neglect its Appointments, and violate its sacred Precepts for every fleeting Gratification, or trifling Gain, could we freely renounce the Name and Profession of it, all at once? 'Tho we seldom open the Book of God for religious Instruction, and more seldom still, to form our Tempers, and regulate our Actions by its heveanly Influence, could we voluntarily resign it into the Hands of another, or suffer it to be wrested from us, for ever? Until we can submit to these Things, without Reluctance, we should endeavour, by every Mean, to prevent our being exposed to them: And, surely, the most effectual Mean, for this Purpose is to improve our present Privileges, and act a Part truly becoming them—to be good Men, good Subjects, good Neighbours, and good Christians.

From our present Prospects, then, as a Nation professing Religion, the Consideration is plainly this— That, as we value Liberty of Conscience and private Judgment—as we value the Bible, its sacred Contents, and the Privilege of reading, judging of, and worshipping God according to it; In a Word, as we regard the Interests of Protestantism, and desire to continue in the Possession of it, we should *humble ourselves before God, and seek his Face, and turn from our Wicked Ways*, in Hope that he will *hear from Heaven, and forgive our Sins and heal our Land*.

But, perhaps, it may be asked; *will these Things, really, avail us? If our Enemies be disposed to invade, or enslave us, will our Humiliation, Prayers, and Repentance prevent them from putting their Designs in Execution?* I freely answer; They probably may; and, if not, they will certainly tend to defeat their Intentions.

A brief Observation, or two, will plainly illustrate these Assertions.

1st. Wherever a Sense of Religion and private Virtue prevails, in a Nation, public Virtue, and a Desire of promoting the general Good are in Exact Proportion; and these must ever render a Nation formidable. Accordingly, we find from Experience, that, in every Age, a few virtuous and brave Men, equally Strangers to Luxury and Corruption, have led in Chains the most numerous Armies composed of the Luxurious, Effeminate, and Debauched: And the Vices of such have done more, towards their being conquered, than the Power of their Enemies. If our Return, then, to Duty, will recover our public Spirit, and replant the Principles of true Patriotism within us, is it not probable that upon such a Foundation our Councils will be unanimous, and our Arms Objects of secret dread, rather than of Contempt — That our Enemies will view us with Jealousy, or Fear, rather than with the Vain Presumption of triumphing over us?

2dly. Vice, in its own nature, tends to enervate the Mind, unhinge its Resolution, and inspire a servile Fear of, *we know not what*; Whilst Virtue invigorates every Principle, inspires Fortitude, and fills the Soul with cheering Hopes, and Confidence, more than earthly…

3dly. As God is the Ruler of all Things, and disposeth of every Event as seemeth good unto him… is it not probable, that, upon our Repentance and Return to Duty, he will *bring to Nought the Counsel of our Enemies, and render vain the Device of the Crafty?*

These Observations plainly shew the Probability that our Repentance *will* avail us and that *if we turn from our wicked Ways, God will hear our Prayers, forgive ours Sins, and heal our Land.*

The Sum of all which hath been offered upon this Subject, amounts to this; That in Order to the Deliverance of a Nation from present Distresses, or its Escape from those with which it may be threatened, God certainly requires a national Repentance, and return from Wickedness; and that it is such a Fast, as is attended with this Change of Temper and Conduct, of which he will approve…

Sermon II
On The Ruinous Effects Of Civil War
Preached before the Protestant Dissenting Congregation of Ballyhalbert,
February 27, 1778, being a day appointed, by Government, as a General Fast.

II Samuel, 11.26
"Then Abner called to Joab and said, Shalt the Sword devour for ever?
Knowest thou not that it will be Bitterness in the latter End?
How long shall it be, then 'ere thou bid the People
return from following their Brethren?"

[This sermon begins with a long review of events in the Jewish civil war following the
death of Saul. Abner, Saul's army commander, established Saul's son, Ishbosheth, as the
king of all Israel, excepting Judea. David was king of Judea. Abner, attempting to unify
Israel under Ishbosheth, was defeated at the battle of Gibeon. But he held his army
together and made peace overture to Joab (David's military commander) which is the text
for this sermon. Joab rejected the overture. His brother Asahel pursued Abner's retreating
army. Abner tried to persuade Asahel that peace should be made. Asahel insists on battle
and is slain.
Some time later Abner married Respha, who had been Saul's concubine. Ishbosheth took
this to be a sign that Abner himself aspired to the throne and their trust was broken.
Abner then tried to to unite Israel under David. He went to David and made an agreement
with him, but before he left the palace he was killed by Joab in revenge for his brother
Asahel.
These events, and a resurgence of the Philistines made possible by divisions in Israel,
provide Steel Dickson with a rich ground of reference for his consideration of the war in
America. BC.]

...

However dreadful the Ravages of War may be, its Barbarities are never so
shocking, as when it riots in kindred Blood: And, in the Case before us, the
Connection was peculiarly tender. The Parties contending were but a few
Generations removed from the common Parent which gave them Birth: and their
Relation was cemented by a Variety of Circumstances. Frequent Inter-marriages,
a Community of Goods for many Years, a Participation of various Distresses,
fighting together in the Battles of the Lord, the Peculiarities of their Religion,
and a common Interest in the divine Promises, all tended to bind them together
by the Cords of Love. And the four hundred Men whose Debts, Distresses, or
Disaffection to the Family of Saul, had driven them to join David in his Exile,
and who then advanced to fight in his Cause, were, no doubt, severally related to
the different Tribes. How bitter, then, must the Conflict have been where Father
stood opposed to Son, and Brother to Brother! ...

The Circumstances of Israel thus divided against itself, as well as the
Occasion of this Day, naturally suggest the Thoughts of our own Situation, and
the War, so shocking to Humanity, and ruinous to our Interests, which now
rages thro' the American Continent.

Tho' it be painful, in general, to trace Similarities of this Kind, yet the Likeness is so striking, in the Case before us, that it is impossible to review the Contest in Israel, and, at the same Time, exclude the Thoughts of our own. The same tender Connection subsists between the contending Parties; and the same Circumstances of Horror attend the Ravages of the devouring Sword. A few Generations lead us back to the Origin of American Colonization, when the Inhabitants of the British Isles first explored its pathless Desarts, in Quest of that Liberty and Peace which their County denied them: And every succeeding Year has transported Multitudes from every Corner of these Lands, so that there is scarcely a Protestant Family, of the middle and lower Classes among us, who does not reckon Kindred with the Inhabitants of that extensive Continent. How many Parents, in the narrow Circle of our own Acquaintance, are agitated with the most painful Anxiety for the uncertain Fate of favorite Children whose Habitations have become the Seat of War; and against whom the Profession of a Soldier hath obliged an Acquaintance, Friend, or Brother to go forth! And these Apprehensions derive additional Terrors from the improved Artillery of Death. In ancient Times, while the Sword or Spear decided the Contest, the Features of a Friend might be distinguished in the Combat, and the fatal Blow turned aside. But now the Manner and Place of Attack, the uncertain Aim, Intervention of Smoke, and many other Circumstances render this impossible. Friend and Foe are equally exposed, fall promiscuous, and often lie undistinguished.

Nor are the Violations of private Friendship and social Obligation left obvious, or terrible, in the present Conflict. In the late War, many of the Forces who now fight (to use a favorite Expression) *to lay America at the Feet of the Ministry*, fought, on the same Ground, for nobler Purposes—to repress the Insolence of French Policy, and repel the Incursions of savage Fury—to banish Slavery from the Colonies, and extend the Interest and Glory of Britain. And, as the Operations of War have, in great Part, proceeded in the same Line, many, who formerly rejoiced in Offices of mutual Friendship, or fought together in the common Cause, must now meet in hostile Array, and feel the Effects of mutual Enmity. What must be the Feelings of the Colonist when he beholds the Briton who repelled the Tomahawk and Scalping-knife from his Borders, and restored him to his Family, Habitation, Liberty, and Peace, rushing foremost to drive off his Flocks or his Herds, plunder his Granaries, or lay his Dwelling in Flames! And, what the Feelings of the Briton, while he recollects, in the smoking Ruins, the now desolated Mansion under whose hospitable Roof he had sheltered his weary Limbs; while he perceives that his Hand hath reduced to Beggary, the Youth, who had watched over his stolen Slumbers; or the Virgin, who, with tender Hand, had applied Balsam to the Wounds under which he languished!

Yet, even these scarcely deserve the Name of Sorrows when compared with those which arise from a Review of the slaughtered Hosts, with which a Day of Battle strews the Ground. Would we form an Idea of these let us consider how many Natives of America, who were Hewers of Wood and Drawers of Water to the British Troops—How many, who bravely shared the Dangers and Fatigues of

War with Britons, and fought by their Sides—And how many Britons, who, at the Conclusion of Peace, married Daughters of the Land, and sat down to enjoy the Fruits of the Fields which they had enriched with their Blood, now fight in the Cause of America, and support her Claims. In the Multitudes who have been slain many of these may certainly be numbered; and, in the different Engagements, many Britons must have fallen by their Hands. What, then, must be the Distresses of the Briton, when he beholds the Man who had assisted his Arms, levelled the Forests before him, or, by some secret path, directed his wandering Steps, thro' Morasses, Desarts, and dangerous Defiles, to Security, or Conquest, slaughtered by his Hand! Or, of the American when he beholds the mangled Remains of the Avenger of his Wrongs, the Protector of his Infant Offspring, or the Instructor of his Youth, who *first taught his fingers to fight*, and finally to conquer, and whom Necessity hath obliged him to sacrifice to his Country! Will he not be ready to exclaim with Lamech; *I have slain a Man to my Wounding, and a young Man to my Hurt?* Or, to take up the pathetic Lamentation of David over Saul and his beloved Jonathan: *The Beauty of Israel is slain: How are the mighty fallen in the Midst of the Battle! I am distressed for thee, my Brother! How are the mighty fallen, and the Weapons of War perished!*

...

Should we, then, persevere, in our present Measures, till our Armies be destroyed, and America lost, will not the Recollection of these Things whet their Revenge, animate their Councils, and invigorate their Arms! And, should Providence permit them to prevail over us, with what Haughtiness of Spirit would they proclaim their Triumphs, and insult our Wretchedness! "These are the Heroes of the Age, before whom the Nations bowed; who claimed the Sovereignty of the Ocean; and boasted that their Victories and their Empire extended from Pole to Pole! But, now, their Strength is become Weakness; their Laurels have faded; and their far-extended Empire is shaken from it's Foundations!"

Such Reflections as these are sufficiently mortifying, from whatever Causes the Calamities spring which give them birth; yet, they might still be supported, could we resolve them into any acquired Strength, new Connection, or formidable Alliance among our Enemies. But, when a Moment's Reflection will remind us that they originated from our Folly or Wickedness—that it cost us a painful Struggle of several Years, a Profusion of Treasures, and the Blood of Thousands, to lay their Foundations——Nay, that we were obliged to ransack Europe for a Troop of Mercenaries to press us down to Ruin; the Feelings of Remorse become envenomed as the Stings of Scorpions. Then, the Recollection of the Liberties we possessed, the Plenty in which we rejoiced, the Pinacle of Glory, on which we stood, the Victories which followed our Standards, and the Terror of our Arms, which held in Awe the vanquished Nations, will serve, only, to imbitter our Reflections, and mingle new Ingredients with our Cup of Wretchedness.

I know, it is alleged by some, that these Apprehensions are groundless, and the evils imaginary to which they point. To support this Allegation it is said, not only, that the Declarations of France and Spain are full of Peace; but, that, if their Intentions were unfriendly, they are not in a Capacity of putting them into Execution. This last Assertion, however, requires more Evidence than hath yet been produced to give it Credit. The general Levy of Troops through both Kingdoms, the Strength of their Fleets at home, and Reinforcement of those abroad, neither indicate Weakness nor Dispositions to Peace. They rather give Reason to conclude, that they are in a Capacity of annoying us; and, that, their not doing so, is the Effect of Policy, not Weakness.

But, when all, that is here alleged, is taken for granted——When we suppose that our Enemies are really incapable of destroying us immediately, our Apprehensions are not, on that Account, altogether groundless. If we may reason from what is past, America may continue her Resistance a few Campaigns longer; and, if it does so, France may continue to talk of Peace, while she prepares for War. Each of these few Campaigns will weaken our Hands, while her's become strong: And, the very Trade which we have forced into her Ports will accelerate her Progress, and supply her largely with the Sinews of War. Nor, is it improbable that the Experience of this will induce her, when Necessity requires, to unsheathe her Sword for the Support of America, and Protection of her Commerce. These Allegations, therefore, imply no more, than that our Enemies cannot, probably, effect to day, what a few Years may render easy, or even accomplish to their Hands. But, is our Situation, therefore, free from Danger? Must the Sword on that Account, *devour for ever?* Or, if it does so, is it less obvious that it will be *Bitterness in the latter End?*

However, as Precedents are often hunted after, in such Cases, and rested in as decisive, let us have Recourse to Precedent, and try what Instructions it will afford us: Nor will it be difficult to find one to our Purpose. The Case of Israel and Judah, with which we set out, is directly in Point.

The Kingly Form of Government was introduced in Israel at the joint Solicitation of the twelve Tribes, and Saul clothed with Authority by the Direction of Heaven. These Circumstances gave him every possible Claim to Obedience; and while his discharged his Duty, every Attempt to divide or overthrow his Kingdom was altogether inexcusable. Yet, we find that in the Reign of his Son, the Tribe of Judah, which may be considered as a Colony descended from the Loins of Israel, revolted, erected themselves into an independent State, and anointed David to be their King.

This Erection was condemned as rebellious, at the Court of Ishbosheth, and Abner marched out with the Armies of Israel in Order to suppress it. For this Purpose, he was clothed with full Power to make Peace, or carry on War, as Circumstances might require. In this important Character he marched to Gibeon, flushed with the Hopes of an easy Conquest, and a complete Subjection of the revolted Tribe. As the Kingdom of David was not fully established, he imagined that the Appearance of an Army in the Territories of Judah, would awe him into Submission, and reduce his Adherents to their wonted Obedience. However, he soon discovered his Error. He found them prepared to meet him in the Field, and determined to oppose them with Firmness. And, in the first Engagement, his Army was routed, put to Flight, and narrowly escaped total Destruction.

When the Discontents appeared in America, the same mistaken Politicks prevailed in our Councils. Measures of Force were immediately adopted, and Troops dispatched from Britain under the same Presumption which led Israel astray. It was confidently asserted that a few Regiments would, not only, awe the disaffected into Submission, but march, without Interruption, from one End of the Continent to the other. As the Error was in common with Israel the Event was so too. After many Difficulties, Fatigues, and Encounters in which thousands were slain, the shattered Remains of a powerful Army were obliged to abandon the Province which they were sent to reduce, and flee for Shelter to a distant Region.

Thus far the Parallel holds exactly between Israel and Britain. The End to be accomplished, the Means adopted for that Purpose and the Success which attended them are perfectly similar. But, from this forward, the Measures which we have followed are totally different from those of Abner. When he felt the Force of the Arms of Judah, and perceived the Expence of Blood at which they were to be reduced, he renounced his Measures of Coercion, and held forth the Branch of Peace. Tho' he fought in Support of a Family, in whose Favor the divine Right of Kings might have been pleaded with greater Propriety than any other which ever swayed a Sceptre—Tho' he came to reduce a revolted Tribe to Subjection, and re-establish an Authority which had long been acknowledged; yet, when he perceived the Inexpediency of the Means proposed for effecting these Purposes, he immediately rejected them. He neither pleaded the Supremacy of his Prince, nor the Omnipotence of the general Council of the Nation in Support of his favorite Measures.—He did not consider the Honor of Israel as injured by receding from his original Demands; nor was he afraid of strengthening the Hands of Rebellion in Judah, by offering Terms of Peace. As he perceived that the public Interest would be more effectually served by a friendly Accommodation than the Ravages of the desolating Sword, he chose to acquiesce in the Determination of the revolted Tribe, and suffer them to enjoy their new-born Independence, rather than push his Claims of unlimited Submission, and thereby protract a War, the End of which, he foresaw, must have been Bitterness.

Had the first Repulses of our Troops been thus attended to, and the Consequences, to which they pointed, duly weighed, Counsels of Peace would have prevailed with us also; and, even now, we would have been rejoicing in their Influence. However, different Measures were preferred and the Effects are notorious to all...

Chapter Three

Volunteering

[Introductory Note
In 1760 a small French squadron landed on the Northern shore of Belfast Lough. It was blocked by a Volunteer force assembled locally. That event was not forgotten. In the spring of 1778, a more formidable French invasion was anticipated. The British Army was locked up in America, and only half a regiment of dismounted horse was available to repel an invasion through Belfast Lough. A large body of Volunteers was quickly assembled to meet the contingency. During the following months, with the approval of the Government, bodies of Volunteers were organised in all parts of the country.
Steel Dickson's sermon to the Echlinvill Volunteers was published with the following title page:

A
SERMON
On The
Propriety *and* Advantages
OF ACQUIRING THE
KNOWLEDGE AND USE OF ARMS,
In Times of public Danger;
PREACHED BEFORE
ECHLINVILLE VOLUNTEERS
On SUNDAY the 28th of MARCH, 1779;
AND PUBLISHED AT THEIR REQUEST;
BY THE
REVEREND W. S. DICKSON.

B e l f a s t
Printed by James Magee, at the Bible and Crown, in Bridge-Street. M.DCC.LXXIX.

To CHARLES ECHLIN Esquire, and the Volunteer Company under his COMMAND, this SERMON is most respectfully inscribed, by HIS and THEIR, sincere FRIEND, and Humble Servant, The Author, Moab, April 4th, 1779.

I have broken up some very long paragraphs in this section, indicating where I have done so with the symbol ^.**]**

Nehemiah IV. 14.

And I looked, and rose up, and said unto the Nobles, and to the Rulers,
and to the rest of the People: Be not ye afraid of them;
remember the Lord which is great and terrible, and fight for your Brethren,
your Sons and your Daughters, your Wifes and your Houses.

The Occasion and Propriety of this Address are obvious from the slightest
Attention to the Circumstances of the People to whom it was made. Their
Situation, for an hundred and fifty Years, had been uncommonly painful.
Seventy Years they had languished in Captivity; and, from the Decree of Cyrys,
impowering them to return to their own Country, and rebuild Jerusalem, they
had been tormented by the Jealousies of their Neighbours, the Samaritans.
These were Circumstances sufficient to depress the Spirits of any People, and
give Terror to the Name of an Enemy: and their Effects are but too notorious
from the Reports of Hanani, which induced Nehemiah to leave the Court of
Artaxerxes, and join his Countrymen at Jerusalem. *The Remnant who are left of
the Captivity,* saith he, *are in great Affliction and Reproach; the Wall of
Jerusalem also is broken down, and the Gates thereof are burnt with Fire.* Upon
this Intelligence Nehemiah immediately determined to put an End to the
Affliction of the People, and remove their Reproach, by repairing the City. But,
his Purpose was no sooner known to the Governor of Samaria than he used
every Mean to defeat it, which had been used, eighty Years before, to obstruct
the Execution of the Decree of Cyrus.^

When the Force of Ridicule, and Keenness of Satire had been exhausted in
vain, the Cry of Rebellion was raised, Threatnings denounced, and Forces
mustered against them, on every Side. That these Things should inspire a
people with Terror, who had been long estranged from the Use of Arms, and
whose Spirits had been broken by a galling Servitude, is not at all surprizing.
How terrible for them to look forward, and encounter, even in Imagination, the
Wrath of a Monarch, the Scars of whose Chains they had scarcely worn out, and
at whose Frown they had been taught to tremble! And, however bitter their
Reproach, and contemptible the Situation to which they were reduced, Fear
might dispose them to acquiesce, rather than provoke new Calamities, or
encounter Evils, with which they had been, as yet, unaquainted. There is
something in Man which inclines him, rather *to endure, with Patience, the Ills
he suffers, than flee to others which he knows not of.* To these Fears the
Prophet opposed a Sense of Religion, and the tender and endearing Relations in
Defence of which he summoned them to Arms. *Remember the Lord,* saith he,
*who is great and terrible, and fight for your Brethren, your Sons and your
Daughters, your Wives and your Houses.*

The first Part of this Address may be considered, either, as a Threatning
against the Jews, should they desert the Work, in which they were engaged, from
the Fear of an Enemy: or, an Encouragement to proceed, from the Consideration
that, while they were dutiful and obedient, the Power of God would protect them,

and his terrible Judgments be executed against those who accused them falsely, or oppressed them without a Cause. And, the Reflection on the Experience of their Fathers, and the Victories with which they had been often crowned by the Favor of Heaven, would tend to rouse their drooping Spirits, invigorate their Resolutions, and confirm their Hopes of Success.

Yet, however powerfully a Sense of God may act upon the Mind of Man, it must derive it's principal Influence from conscious Virtue and Integrity of Heart; And, tho' the Name of Religion hath been often prostituted to give false Colourings to Schemes of Rapine, Persecution, or Deceit, it can never support a Mind intent upon Violence, labouring in the Cause of Oppression, or thirsting after Blood. Our Designs must correspond with the great Purposes of Providence, else we can never look up to God with Hopes of Success, contemplate his Greatness with true Satisfaction, or with religious Confidence, implore his Aid. In this Point of View the Designs of the Prophet will bear the strictest Inquiry. He did not summon his Countrymen to Arms to serve the Cause of Ambition, by extending their Territories, enslaving their Neighbours, or binding the Iron-yoke of Oppression on the Neck of the Unfortunate. His great Purposes were to induce them to protect themselves and their Property, and to defend *their Brethren, their Sons and their Daughters, their Wives and their Houses,* against the Outrages of a jealous and insulting Enemy.—Purposes, of which Heaven must ever approve; to which Religion gives Sanction; and every generous Feeling, and tender Affection must rouse the Spirit of Man...

As the Principles by which the Jews were actuated, on this trying Occasion, are highly important, and honorable, so are they deeply rooted in the Nature of Man. They are originally implanted by the Hand of the Creator, and display themselves in every Circumstance of human Life. The Savage and the Sage, however they may differ in their particular Opinions of God, jointly acknowledge his Being, and reverence his Greatness. The Love of Country is an universal Principle. It attaches the Laplander to his barren Rocks and howling Tempests, and the Lybian to his burning Sands, as firmly as the Native of more temperate Climes to his milder Sun, flowing Vintage, and plenteous Harvests. Nor is there a Nation upon Earth where the Love of Offspring doth not surmount every Difficulty. The Instances are innumerable, in which Parents drag on a painful Life, devoted to Care, Weariness, and Danger, merely to set a beloved Issue above the Reach of Evils, which they daily encounter. Nor are Examples infrequent, where the Thought of entailing Poverty or Disgrace on an innocent Offspring hath roused an abandoned Parent to a Sense of Honor, after every other Consideration had pleaded in vain. Nay, sometimes the Coward himself becomes bold in their Cause, and encounters Dangers, which even courage might wish to decline. When these Principles, then, join their Influence—when Religion gives it's heavenly Sanction to the Glow of Patriotism; and the Infirmities, or Dangers of a Parent or Brother ——a beloved Wife, or darling Child call for Protection or Defence, who can resist their Claims, or restrain his Hand from the Weapons of War!

These Pleas of Religion, Patriotism, and Humanity derive powerful Support from the Principles of sound Policy. The Safety of a Nation must ever depend on the Spirit of the People, unless it's Povery is so great as to place it below the Notice of Ambition. Riches invite the Hand of War, as they are the Support of lawless Power, and Handmaids of Luxury. And, wherever they abound, the People must either be Slaves, or cherish a warlike Spirit for their own Defence. The Misfortune is, that the very Circumstances, which render a warlike Spirit necessary, tend most effectually to destroy it.^

In barbarous Nations, where Men are at continual War with Beasts of Prey; Where all their Labor is necessary for the Acquisition of Food; and Hunger often prompts to mutual Destruction, a savage Fierceness is acquired which Opposition cannot terrify, and Death alone can subdue. And, even, in Countries somewhat civilized, the Love of War prevails over every other Principle, and every Man commences Soldier, as soon as he is capable of bearing Arms, or using them against an Enemy. However, when Tillage becomes general, it supplies the Means of Subsistence in Abundance, soothes that Ferocity of which Want is the Parent, and quiets those Jealousies which the Fear of it creates. It affords Time, also, for the Cultivation of Genius, which gives Birth to Arts and Sciences; And they, by multiplying Objects of Desire, or varying their Forms, and giving them the Semblance of Novelty introduce Luxury, the Bane of every manly Principle.^

When Men are accustomed to Idleness, and the Enjoyment of Plenty, they become indolent, weak, and fearful. The Horrors of War appear insupportable; And even where some Spark of native Dignity remains, which kindles at the Name of Slavery, it is unable to give Vigor to enfeebled Bodies, which sink under the Fatigues of War, and yield an easy Conquest. But, in a State, where Luxury prevails, even this last expiring Gleam of public Spirit is seldom to be seen. The Approach of Danger, instead of rousing to manly Exertions, sinks the Effeminate to abject Despondency, which invites the Tyrant's Lash, and hurries on the Ruin which it dreads.^

The first Symptoms of this Degeneracy, in a Nation, should be carefully observed, and the Evils guarded against which they forebode. The Necessity of this all seem to be aware of, yet, unfortunately, instead of striking at their Root, all rest satisfied with substituting one Evil in Place of another, or hanging up a flimsy Screen which hides the dreaded Evil from their Sight, yet gathers Strength from Time, and grows at last more dangerous than that which it was meant to cure.^

Thus it hath fared, hitherto, with the greatest Empires where standing Armies have been established. Tho' formed for Protection, they have, in the End, usurped the Reins of Government, and enslaved the People whom they were paid to defend. Yet, from Men's Unwillingness to forego their Ease and Pleasure, the dangerous Scheme hath become general; and some Nations have carried it so far as to trust their Protection entirely to foreign Mercenaries, while they stupidly pursue the Path to Gain, or sensual Enjoyment. However fair an

Aspect such Appointments may wear, it is not to be doubted but they are, at Bottom, as deceitful as ever. Indeed, it is absurd, in the highest Degree, to trust the Safety of a State to Persons who have no other Tie to it's Interests than the scanty Pittance which they are paid for their Services.^

Nor can much better be said of standing Armies, in general. The principal Circumstances in which they are serviceable are, where an Ally stands in Need of Assistance, or War is carried on in distant Regions. To these Purposes the Body of a People can never be carried without a total Neglect of Arts and Manufactures, on which the whole depend. But, where internal Defence rests entirely on a standing Army, the Situation of a County is extremely precarious. The Confidence reposed in it, in Time of Peace, lulls the People into a drousy Security; and, in War, leads to the dangerous Conclusion that, while it is superior to that of an Enemy, all is safe; but, if inferior, the State is undone.^

Examples of this are very common; but a more striking cannot be produced than these Nations afford. tho' our Troops do not bear a greater Proportion to those capable of bearing Arms than one in an hundred; and, Tho' a small Proportion of them can be brought into Action, at the same Time and Place, it is not uncommon to hear the Politicians of the Times graveiy asserting that the Loss of this or the other Post will endanger the Nation, and a single Defeat ruin Us for ever; while the credulous Throng, who revere them, as Oracles, rise or fall in their Expectations of Safety, as the Circumstances of an Army may seem to fluctuate, tho' thousands of Miles distant. From these Things a Man, unacquainted with our Resources would readily conclude that our whole Strength was exhausted, and the Flower of our Youth cut off by the Sword; and that nothing remained but the Aged and the Infirm, the lame and the blind, with the Women and Children. He could never suppose that, of those able to bear Arms, and *fight for their Sons and their Daughters, their Wives and their Brethren*, ninety nine in an hundred were sauntering in Idleness, pursuing the Arts of Life, or hunting it's unhallowed Pleasures. Or, if he was informed that this is our real Situation, with what Contempt would he treat the Alarms which every Rupture with a neighbouring Power raises amongst Us; and the Terrors which the Name of Invasion spreads far and wide! Would he not be astonished to perceive that we are so quick-sighted to Danger, and sensible to the Fears of Violence before it comes near; and yet are incapable of discovering that God hath given Us Strength to oppose, and Hands to defend Ourselves against them!^

May we not, then, ask, with Propriety, Whence do this State of Mind, and these Terrors arise? The Answer is obvious. The former proceeds from Luxury's accursed Influence; the latter from a total Decay of that generous Spirit, which diffused itself thro' the Inhabitants of the British Isles, covered our Ancestors with Glory, laid the Foundations of our Liberties in Blood, and rendered the Name of Britain illustrious. If the Decay of this Spirit, then, be the Cause of our Fears, surely a Revival of it will be sufficient to dispel them. Nor, is it less evident that a general Knowledge of the Use of Arms would render Us superior to any Force which the most formidable Enemy can send against Us. Every Hill would, then, be a Stronghold; and every Village would pour forth an Host to defend it. And, however strange it may appear, we may venture to affirm that, were our standing Army destroyed, we would be better fitted for internal Defence, by the Prevalence of such a Spirit, than we are, at this Day, or ever have been. The Rumor of Invasion, instead of sinking the Nation into abject Despondency, would serve only to rouse it to noble Exertions, call forth it's Strength, and prepare it for Victory.

I would not, from any Thing here offered, be supposed to consider standing Armies as useless: Far from it! In every extensive Empire they are highly useful, and serve many valuable Purposes. Besides assisting Allies, and carrying on War at a Distance, as already mentioned, they serve to protect Colonies, keep Fortifications in Repair, and instruct others in the Use of Arms; while a brave People co-operate with them, in protecting themselves, and the Fruits of their Industry at home. Nor would Industry suffer by such a Regulation. The Avocations, in Time of Peace, would be very trifling; And, in a Country which is the Seat of War, every Kind of Industry is as much at a Stand, as if the whole People were, actually, under Arms.

Further; If the Inhabitants of a Country were generally instructed in the military Art, the chief Commands, and the Care of public Concerns, would fall principally on Men of landed Property, whose greatest Bane is want of Employment. This would naturally lead them to useful Inquiry; and the Desire of excelling would lead many to join the Study of Politicks to that of Arms, and unite the Soldier and Statesman in one illustrious Character. The Cabinet would be no longer disgraced by visionary Projectors; nor the Camp with Commanders incapable of understanding the Nature of the Service, in which they are ordered. Tho' Justice obliges Us to own that, in the Camp, we must look for some of the most respectable Characters of which we can boast. But, in the Parliament of the Nation, these Advantages would be remarkably evident. The Benches of the House would no longer groan under a cumbrous Load of Mutes, and nominal Representatives; nor would a Man be revered, as an Oracle, because he could publickly express a few Sentences without degenerating into Nonsense, or Absurdity.^

Gentlemen would rise to a true Sense of their Importance, and Dignity of Character. Ignorance would be every where contemptible; and a Want of military Skill, in particular, would be an indelible Reproach. How many young Men would thus be raised from Obscurity, or allured from the Vanities and Vices of Life, to the Service of their Country and Pursuits of Honour! How many, in the Circle of our Acquaintance, of whom little better can be said, at present, than that they possess so many Hundreds, perhaps Thousands, a Year, would be revered as the Patrons of public Spirit and Guardians of their Country's Rights! And, if this Spirit prevailed in the higher Orders, in Society, it would immediately diffuse itself thro' every Rank. Gentlemen of Property would never Want a spirited Tenantry to support them, in Defence of their Liberties; and, in Case of an Alarm, the whole People would be instantly embodied. Nor is it to be doubted that the public Interests would be more secure, under their Protection, than in the Hands of an Army, who have Nothing to lose, but every Thing to grasp at. They would evidently serve the double Purpose of strengthening such an Army's Hands against a foreign Enemy; and checking the rapid Strides of military Ambition towards unlimited, and arbitrary Sway.

If these Observations be not altogether groundless, every real Friend to this poor ill-fated Island must rejoice in the Spirit which begins to rouse it's Protestant Inhabitants: And his Joy must be enlivened by the flattering Prospect which will open before him, when he considers that it is not owing to the Policy or Influence of Statesmen, but rises spontaneous in the Breasts of a generous, tho' neglected People.

IN whatever Light we view our Situation this Spirit appears equally important, honourable, and praiseworthy; As Men, we have Rights and Privileges, Wives and Children; As Members of Society we have a Country and Brethren; and, as Christians, a God, who is great and terrible, whom we ought to remember, and a Religion, which we owe to his Goodness, by which we hope to be saved. These are the only valuable Concerns in human Life. They comprize all that is worth struggling for, in this World; and the only Means of rising to the Glories of that which is to come...

...

I beg Leave, in the Strength of this Conviction, to suggest a few Observations...

1st. As ye have voluntarily taken up Arms in Behalf of your Country, and the endearing Relations which bind you to it's Interests; And, as ye have, thus far, proceeded with a Degree of Spriit which doth Honour to your Names, and will render your Characters respectable; Ye ought to persevere, in Opposition to every Difficulty and Inconvenience, until ye have fully attained the Knowledge of Arms, and be thereby qualified for rendering that Service to your Country, which ye profess to have in View...

2dly. As ye appear in a Character highly important and interesting, there ought to be Dignity, in the Whole of your Conduct, becoming the Station which ye fill...

3dly. Your Views of doing Good ought to be generous, and extensive; unconfined by the narrow Limits of party, or external Denomination, whether in Politicks, or Religion. The Names of Party often excite Jealousies; and these, again, are apt to resolve the most generous Actions into the worst Designs. This is, particularly, the Case with us, in Time of War. As our Enemies are generally of the Popish Persuasion, those of that Denomination, among us, are apt to construe Measures of public Security into private Design, and attribute every Armament to Enmity against them. To remove such injurious Suspicions is an Object well deserving your serious Attention; and your Conduct ought to shew that ye have not taken up Arms for this, or the other Denomination; but for your Country——That it is not your Purpose to spread Alarm, Terror, or Desolation; but to check them in their wild Career——That it is, only, against the Enemies of your Lives, Liberties and Peace that your Arms are pointed——And, that whoever is the Friend of these is your Friend, and the Object of your Protection.

4thly. Ye ought to cherish the most cordial Affection towards every Man, and every Company, who appear in the same distinguishing Character which ye support...

5thly. If the Invasion of our Country should endanger our Property, or the happy Constitution under which we possess it, it is evident that a spirited Preparation to meet the Enemy in the Field, and oppose Force to Force, is the only Mean of Safety. Servile Fear encourageth the Insolence of Pride, and Phrenzy of Ambition; and tame Submission serves only to sink the injured lower in Contempt, and invite new Injuries...

Lastly. With the Love of your Country and every other virtuous Attachment, ye ought to cherish a lively Sense of God, and Regard to Religion. These constitute the only Foundation on which Virtue itself can stand secure...

Ballyhalbert:
March 28th, 1779.

Chapter Four

Scripture Politics

[Introductory Note

Three
Sermons
On The Subject Of
Scripture Politics
By The Rev. W.S. Dickson D.D.
Belfast
Printed In The Year 1793

Scripture Politics was the basic orientating pamphlet of the popular movement in Belfast, Antrim and Down in the 1790s. It expressed the amalgamation of politics, philosophy and theology which was the world outlook of Presbyterian Ulster, and by expressing it developed it. Among its sources were John Locke's **Treatises On Civil Government**, which shaped the political philosophy of the ruling class that took power in England in 1688; the historical conception of social evolution expounded in John Millar's **The Origin Of Ranks And Distinctions**; and William Leechman's liberal development of Calvinist theology. (See notes to page 13.)

Though Tom Paine's **Rights Of Man** was very popular in Belfast in the 1790s, it was by no means the guiding light of the progressive movement there. Paine was read into the Ulster Scots world outlook as it had developed in Ulster during the preceding generation, and I can imagine that certain aspects of his writing were discounted by such reading.

Paine's Rights Of Man is entirely secular in conception, but it lets Christianity be. However, in **The Age Of Reason** (1794), Paine dismissed Christianity as a concoction of fables which obstructed clear thinking. If, as is often said, The Rights Of Man had been the Bible of Belfast in the early 1790s, publication of The Age Of Reason would have sent the town into trauma. But in fact the Bible of Belfast was the Bible, therefore Belfast experienced no difficulty in rejecting The Age Of Reason while continuing to appreciate The Rights Of Man. Paine had never been its prophet, so it could agree with him on one point and disagree with him on another. The Northern Star urged its readers to read the pamphlets in defence of Christianity published in reply to The Age Of Reason, but it did not denounce Paine for publishing The Age Of Reason. It felt absolutely secure in the mental world of **Scripture Politics**, and was confident that free public debate could only strengthen that world.

There was a small, elite group in Belfast which was discarding Christianity as a form of earnest belief. Foremost among them was Dr. Alexander Haliday, secretary of the Northern Whig Club, correspondent of Lord Charlemont, and frequent visitor to "the family" at Mountstewart as it rocketed up through the ranks of aristocracy. Dr. Haliday did seize on The Rights Of Man as a substitute for the Bible in which he no longer believed in any serious way. Dr. Haliday expressed his enthusiasm in letters to Lord Charlemont, the leader of the Volunteers. If this had been a purely personal matter Charlemont would have agreed with Haliday—but *pas devant les domestiques*. And with Paine it was very much a case of *devant les domestiques*. Whatever Paine said was not said amongst gentlemen in private after a good dinner. It was blurted out in cheap popular editions. And, as Charlemont, the wordly wise aristocrat, explained to his enthusiastic friend, Dr. Haliday, that would not do. And Dr. Haliday came to see that it would not do, and confined his free-thinking to after-dinner conversation in the Temple Of The Winds at Mountstewart.

That was two hundred years ago. Dr. Haliday has ever since had social heirs and successors—people with a groundless sense of superiority because of a philosophical scepticism which renders them politically impotent. In my twenty years in Belfast I met some of them, while others have been far too important for me to meet them.

Here then is the finest expression of the world outlook within which Protestant Ulster acted in one of its finest hours, and which is still far from exhausted.

It was published in February 1793, immediately after the Ulster Convention held at Dungannon. Steel Dickson had played a crucial part in the deliberations of the Convention by curbing the republican enthusiasm of a minority of radicals and persuading them to support the existing Monarchical Constitution on the condition of Catholic emancipation and a reform of the system by which the House of Commons was elected. The meeting ended as follows:

"Mr. *Sinclair* begged the attention of Gentlemen to a piece of important information which he had to communicate, and in which he thought the question of reform was materially involved—Doctor Dickson (of whom he need say nothing after the sample which the meeting had experienced of his abilities this day) had now in the Press three Sermons, in which the necessity of reform and emancipation was enforced, on the basis of christianity—he recommended it to the Delegates to be active in circulating these Sermons in their respective districts for the purpose of enlightening the people.

"Mr. *Knox* thanked Mr. Sinclare for the communication and said he was sure whatever fell from the Doctor's pen would not only tend to enlighten the People at large, but he was confident, there was not a delegate in the Convention, but would find himself instructed by the Sermons alluded to—the whole Convention seemed to concur in this sentiment." (Northern Star, 20 February, 1793.)

Publication was advertised in both Belfast papers in late February:

"Scripture Politics

"**Dr. Dickson**, encouraged by the flattering attention of the **Ulster Convention**, assembled at Dungannon, on Friday last, takes the liberty of informing the Public, that his three Sermons now in the Press, will be published in a few weeks, Price 1s-1d—The Gentlemen who had not an opportunity of subscribing at Dungannon, are requested to specify the number of Copies with which they wish to be furnished, to Mr. Henry Joy, or Mr. Samuel Neilson, Belfast. Such Societies, Congregations, or other collective Bodies as chuse to encourage the Publication, may send their orders as above, that the impression may be extended, so as to answer the demand. To prevent disappointment, the Types will be kept standing till the 20th of March.

Portaferry, Feb. 20, 1793."

Henry Joy was editor of the News Letter and Samuel Neilson editor of the Northern Star.]

PREFACE

In the following sheets, the reader is not to expect any of the characters of a laboured production. The circumstances which forced them on the public eye, must render such expectation vain. This was the unqualified assertion that, their contents were *"Sedition, Treason, Popery"*.

How far the assertion is founded in truth, the public are now to judge; and they may rest assured that they are laid before them, exactly as preached, without alteration, and without correction. The second and third were, each, the production of three days, before their respective dates, and never underwent the polish of a second copying.

The first was written, at an early period of the Author's life, and preached before the general Synod of Ulster, in June 1781. Since that time it has not undergone the alteration of a single word. The circumstance, is mentioned to show that the liberal sentiments of the Presbyterians, towards their Catholic brethren, are not the hot-bed plants of the moment, as has been invidiously represented. They have been the sentiments of the Author these twenty years. And from the favourable reception which this Sermon met in 1781, he thinks himself justified in saying, they were then the sentiments of his Rev. Fathers and brethren. It was preached in the congregation of Portaferry, word for word, as it is printed, (the concluding address accepted [sic]) on the Sunday before Christmas last. But as this address was part of what was delivered before the Synod it is now printed with it.

This is the second time which the Author has been obliged to expose his abortive offspring to the world, by the ignorance or malice of wicked men. To the former attempt to calumniate and destroy him, he owes the origin of what little reputation the partiality of the public has allowed him. What may be the issue of the present, rests with the same tribunal. He adds, that whatever construction may be put on his words, there is not a heart in his Majesty's dominions more warmly attached to his real interests, or the principles of the British constitution, than the heart which dictated the following sentiments; and that the warmth with which he has occasionally mentioned Catholic emancipation, and reform, arose, not merely from the principles of justice and humanity, but from the full conviction, that as the happiness of our King must be inseparable from that of his people, so their union among themselves, and attachment to his person and government, founded on equality of right, privilege, and protection, according to the original principles of the constitution, form the only solid base on which that happiness and his throne can rest secure.

He is aware that many apologies ought to be made for troubling the public with the concerns of an individual, or the calumnies to which he may be exposed. These, however, he shall leave to the good nature of his countrymen, whose indulgence hitherto, has far exceeded his deservings. And if the following sheets shall be the means of conveying, or confirming one just idea, or liberal sentiment; or in any manner promoting the dignity, peace, and prosperity of his countrymen, he will rejoice in the calumnies which have been uttered against him, while he prays for the reformation and forgiveness of their Authors.

Portaferry, February 1793

[Sermon 1]

John, chap.18, verse 26
"My Kingdom is not of this World"

The extraordinary power displayed in the miracles of Jesus, and the benevolence with which it was exercised, seem to have produced a general disposition to receive him, as the great deliverer, which prophecy had foretold to the people of Israel. And when they saw him raising the dead, and feeding multitudes in the Wilderness with a few loaves [sic] and small fishes, they concluded that, as he could thus easily support armies, and rescue the slain from the hand of death, he would realize the hopes of temporal dominion, with which they had long been intoxicated, and urged him to assume the title of King.

As this overture was founded on mistaken apprehensions of his kingdom, instead of compliance, he endeavoured to correct the prejudices from which it proceeded, and the passions connected with them. But they were so firmly attached to the hopes, which ambition and revenge had long cherished, that they were offended; turned that resentment against him, of which they had attempted to make him the instrument; joined issue with his enemies in a scandalous prosecution, and obliged the Governor of Judea to consent to his death.

The most remarkable circumstance in this transaction, is that on which they founded their accusations. They charged him with the seditious designs, in which they had laboured in vain to engage him; and, as they pretended, they brought their charge *merely* because his claims were unfriendly to Caesar— That Caesar whose claims they wished to shake off, in overthrowing whose empire they would have gloried, and in opposition to whom, they had endeavoured, by compulsion, to make him a King.

...

To Pilate's inquiries on this subject, Jesus admitted, in answer, that he was a King; but informed him that his claims, as such, did not interfere with those of the Emperor, from whom Pilate derived his authority, and to whom he owed allegiance; and added a circumstance from which he might be assured that this information was true.

"My Kingdom is not of this World; if my kingdom were of this world, then would my servants fight, that I might not be delivered to the Jews; but now, is my Kingdom not from hence."

Whatever ideas Pilate entertained of the kingdom of Jesus, from this declaration it is evident that he did not imagine there was any interference between it and the interests of Caesar; ...for he immediately went out and declared publicly, that he found "in him no fault at all". (John 18.3.)

However favourable this may appear to the character and pretensions of Jesus, no satisfying argument can be deduced from it in favour of christianity. Pilate had no fixed principles, nor any clear views of it, to enable him to pronounce upon its merits. The only obvious conclusion was that which he formed, by connecting the idea of "Kingdom" with that of "bearing witness to the truth", that a man who professed only to teach and support truth, and acted agreeably to his profession, could not be an enemy to good government, or the interests of society.

Yet many inquiries remain concerning truth in general, and particularly concerning christianity as teaching the truth, or exhibiting just views of the various important subjects of which it treats. But as it would be impossible to comprise them all in the bounds of a Sermon, we shall confine our attention at present to one which arises directly from the declaration before us.

Previous to the discussion of this inquiry, it may not be improper to ascertain the meaning of the declaration itself.

"This World", from its inordinate influence on the passions and conduct of men, is often contrasted with "the Father", who is the source of all good; and from the distresses in which the immoderate love of it involves them to "Heaven", which is the seat of perfect happiness. Hence, those who devote themselves principally to the indulgence of appetite, are said to be "of the World"; whilst those who cherish more exalted sentiments, and pursue the more valuable attainments of wisdom, truth, and virtue, are denominated "of the Father". Thus Christ addressed the Jews; prejudices and worldly attainments rendered them blind to the purposes of Heaven: "Ye are from beneath, I am from above: Ye are of the world, I am not of this world" (John 8,23). In the same sense he used the phrases frequently in his discourses to, and concerning his disciples: "Because ye are not of the world, but I have chosen you out of the world, therefore the world hateth you" (15,19)...

These passages shew that, "to be of the world", is to adopt the designs, indulge the passions, or engage in the pursuits which center on it. And to be "not of the world", is to be free from their destructive influence.

In this sense the phrase applies as strictly to collective bodies as to individuals. They also take their characters from the ends which they have in view, and the means by which they propose to accomplish them. The character, therefore, which is here given of Christianity, may be comprehended under the following particulars:

I. It did not originate from worldly policy.

II. It doth not affect pomp, magnificence, and perishable wealth, which flatter the vanity, and gratify the ambition and avarice of men.

III. It disclaims every idea of being extended by violence, or supported by oppression. And,

IV. It exercises no dominion over men but what truth and righteousness fully justify, and the reason of its subjects must ever approve and rejoice....

But though christianity is a system purely moral and religious—though it is not marked with the characters of human policy, nor dependent on it; we are not to conclude that it bears no relation to civil government, or is unconcerned in the laws by which it is regulated. This would be a conclusion, rash, unwarranted, and dangerous. It would at once remove the strongest barrier which ever hath been, or ever can be opposed to the passions of men.

We shall, therefore, inquire how far and in what manner the kingdom of Christ is, or ought to be connected with the kingdom of the world; or in other words, how far, and in what manner, religion and politics are related.

In this inquiry, the kingdom of Jesus is to be considered as a system of pure and universal morality, enforced from religious considerations. That this system hath man as its object, and in all parts tends to his improvement and happiness, will not be denied in this place. We may add too, that it respects him in every relation in which he may be placed, as this is necessarily implied in the idea of universal morality.

This morality, which is the great object of religion, and ought to be the basis of all government, is in itself unchangeable; and under whatever form it hath been exhibited, or motives enforced in the different stages of civilization, is intrinsically the same.

Should this remark be thought to require any illustration, Revelation amply supplies it. We can hardly conceive of any systems more widely different, in many particulars, than the two which form its principal contents. The one is calculated for a particular people, proposes to keep them distinct from all the nations of the earth, is loaded with rites and ceremonies, and confines its prospects to the present life. The other presents itself to all mankind, proposes to abolish distinctions in respect to religious privileges, and unite the whole in one great family; is divested of the artificial aid of ritual observance, and brings forward all the treasures of immortality to enrich its votaries, and its horrors to appal the spirit of iniquity. Yet with all this difference of circumstance and motive, the morality of both is exactly the same, "Thou shalt love the Lord thy God, with all thy, heart, with all thy soul, with all thy strength, and with all thy mind, and thy neighbour as thy self".

As these general precepts comprehend the sum of human duty, they express the principles by which it should be regulated, and are the great objects of both systems.

In the latter of these precepts, it is taken for granted, that men are uniformly induced with the principle of self-love, in a degree sufficient to impel them to the pursuit of happiness. And as this principle is the standard by which the love of others is to be regulated, the least which can be inferred is, that those who acknowledge the authority of the precepts, should so far cherish the benevolent affections, as is necessary to engage them in promoting and securing the happiness of others. With this inference the descriptions of love enjoined in the gospel, and the effects which it ought to produce, are perfectly conformable. It restrains from injury, disdains the narrow limits of religious or political associations, and rises superior to enmity and insult. "Love worketh no ill to his neighbour; suffereth long and is kind; envieth not; rejoiceth not in iniquity, but rejoiceth in the truth" (Rom. 13, 10, 1 Cor. 13,4,6).

Nor are the claims of christianity satisfied by that indolent complacency which expresseth itself, only in unavailing wishes of prosperity, or for possessions of good-will. The love which it enjoins must press forward into action; set opposition and dangers at defiance; and if the public good requires, bravely encounter death itself. "Let us not love in word, nor in tongue, saith the Apostle, but in deed and in truth" (1 John, 3,10). "To do good, and to communicate, forget not; for with such sacrifices God is well pleased" (Heb. 13,16). And saith Jesus, "This is my commandment, that ye love one another, even as I have loved you". "Love your enemies, bless them who curse you, do good to them who hate you, and pray for them who despitefully use you".

From these expressions we perceive that as christianity inculcates the generous affections, the happiness of man is the great end which it proposes, to which it directs his activity, and to the promotion of which it lends its solemn sanctions. And the more any relation in life affects this happiness, the more important it becomes, and the more immediate object of religious inspection and religious influence.

Among these relations, various and interesting as they are, that which binds an individual to the state of which he is a member is the most important. In it the influence of one may occupy a wide extended circuit, and materially affect the security and happiness of many. Nay! the instances are not infrequent of kingdoms rescued from the very brink of destruction, by the wisdom or prowess of an individual; while on the other hand, we have seen empires hurled from the summit of prosperity into the gulph of confusion, and all their proud trophies buried in ruins, at the feet of one ambitious mortal. On it the duties of subordinate relations depend for protection, and from their tendency to raise men to the exalted character of citizens, much of their importance is derived. This too must every vary with the extent of a state, as duties and ranks multiply in proportion to its increase.

However, all this variety of rank is comprehended in the general division of men into magistrate and subject, the former of whom is entrusted with the execution of laws, which the latter have sanctioned with their approbation, and to which they are amenable. The laws which respect this arrangement, and mark the reciprocal duties, of which it lays the foundation, have received the name of politics, and constitute a most interesting branch of morality, considered as a science.

In the first stages of society, and in small states, subordinate distinctions are few. Hence their internal politics are simple, and comprised in small bounds. A moderate share of prudence and sagacity, connected with personal courage, a sense of justice, and patience of hardship, are sufficient for all the purposes of counsel or war. In ordinary circumstances, old age, which is the repository of knowledge, and in which experience hath rescued the understanding from the influence of the more turbulent passions, holds the seat of executive justice; and when external dangers threaten, or counsels of war prevail, he whose bravery and patience have been formerly proved is called forth to command, and the most implicit respect is paid to his authority. But as soon as the cause for which he is promoted ceases to operate, his authority expires, and he sinks, as before, to a level with his brethren. However, if his exertions are crowned with success, his tribe is emboldened, new enterprizes are undertaken, and his appointment is renewed; the fame of his prowess spreads around, his alliance is courted, and fear induces a submission to his arms. Yet, still his authority expires with the enterprize for which it was given him.

But though his authority is shortlived, the effects of it are often permanent. The nations whom his arms have subdued, or virtues conciliated, unite in one common interest, and become objects of jealousy or fear to all their neighbours. Hence combinations are formed to check their growing power, and balance their influence.

Thus states proceed from small to great; and in this process, the face of things takes on a new aspect and complexion. As population increases, the necessaries of life come into greater demand. And, as the resources of nature fail, after many struggles, art is called to her assistance. Hence originates private property; and the variety of success which attends the efforts of individuals, in time, lays the foundation of a permanent distinction in ranks. He who is indolent or unsuccessful, must submit to him whose labours have produced more than his wants require: And dependence for bread gives an influence, which is often lasting, and generally increases, as superiority in wealth prevails.

This inequality supplies new matter to excite and employ the dissocial passions. Pride demands humiliating expressions of the dependence which wealth hath created; ambition aspires to an increase of power; whilst poverty, *galled by insult* and *oppression*, complains, that power is overstretched; becomes clamorous and turbulent, and labours to throw off the painful yoke. Hence endless discord is introduced, and in its effects, plainly demonstrates, that something more stable and just, than the capricious will of an interested individual, is necessary to ascertain the rights, regulate the interests, and secure the happiness of men united in society.

The conviction of this gives a new turn to human affairs. Laws are established as standards of right; and one, or a few, are deputed to give them activity, and regulate their execution. Hence as government stands on fixed principles, it takes a regular form; and this form is originally modelled by the prevailing taste or circumstances of the state.

It appears, in general, that states delegated but a small part of their power at first. A jealousy of their rights induced them to reserve matters of national concern for national debate. Accordingly, in new-born states, war and peace were never determined but in the public assembly of the people. But as population increased, and territories were enlarged, such assemblies became inconvenient, and sometimes impossible, even on the most important occasions. Hence, more extensive delegations were adopted; and the most valuable interests, and solemn deliberations, were instructed to a few.

These delegations, however well adapted to the purposes for which they were made, seem to have been early perverted. Power is always intoxicating; and whatever the sources or means of power may be, ambition will endeavour to perpetuate and increase it. In these struggles for pre-eminence the more knowing or powerful prevail; success secures friends; and authority is erected on the basis of corruption. Sometimes, indeed, the very fear of tyranny creates tyrants; and the apprehension of slavery gives birth to despotism. In the hardy struggles which men make for liberty, some favourite patron is called in, by whose generous efforts the dreaded evils are averted for a season. On such occasions the overflowings of gratitude despise all bounds. An infatuated people throw themselves into the arms of a deliverer, as if he rose superior to human infirmities. But alas! experience soon proves the contrary. He, in turn, is intoxicated with power; he considers unlimited submission as scarcely adequate to his past services; and popular confidence lulls suspicion asleep, 'till he rivets the chains of slavery too fast to be broken without violence and rebellion.

But in whatever manner these changes are introduced, and power centred in individuals, the event is the same. All governments tend to despotism; and by degrees, more or less rapid, terminate in it.

From all these circumstances, taken together, we see, that the desire of security and peace gave birth to civil societies; and that all the revolutions, in the mode of governing them, have arisen from it. We see too, that all civil authority is originally derived from the people; that no individual hath any right to govern but what they bestow; and, of consequence, that their protection, safety, and happiness are, or *ought to be*, the great ends of government; and the supreme law to which all others should be subordinate.

This doctrine, however ungrateful to ambition, will ever be supported by reason and humanity. The spirit of despotism may counteract, but cannot invalidate, or disapprove it. Indeed it carries its evidence in its own bosom; and in its certainty, brings us to an important point in the present inquiry. It shews us that the end of christianity and good government is the same; and consequently, that in this important particular, religion and politics are inseparably connected.

If this end is the happiness of mankind, as we have endeavoured to shew, we are led from it to a conclusion of great importance. We are obliged to acknowledge, either that this happiness may be attained and secured by means essentially different; or that, in them also, the connexion between religion and politics must be preserved inviolate.

The alternative can never subject us to any difficulty. Experience shews, that virtue alone leads to true happiness—and religion inculcates virtue, as the only means to promote and secure *it*, and the favour of God, with whom the treasures of it remain. In this view it marks distinctly the duties of every relation, and claims an authority to enforce them. It represents every individual as under the cognizance, and subject to the controul of Heaven: And from the influence which men in authority may have, and ought to use, in the cause of virtue, it speaks of Magistrates, in particular, as the Ministers of God: *i.e.* as servants acting under him in promoting that happiness which is the great end of his administration. When they depart from this character, Revelation charges them with guilt, commands repentance, and points out the measures by which the destructive tendencies of injustice and oppression may be corrected, "Thus, saith the Lord God; remove violence and spoil; execute judgment and justice; take away your exactions from my people" (Ezek. 5,9). "Loose the bands of wickedness; undo the heavy burdens; let the oppressed go free; and break every yoke" (Isa. 5,6). "Keep mercy and do judgment" (Hos. 12.6). "For mercy and truth uphold the King; his throne is established by righteousness: (Pro. 20.28. Isa. 16.4). It marks also, the popular effects of such conduct, and contrasts it with the issue of licentiousness and oppression. "When the righteous is in authority, the people rejoice; but when the wicked beareth rule, the people mourn" (Prov. 29.2).

From the certainty of these observations, and the many temptations to which magistracy is exposed, Revelation asserts, that a sense of religion is the only principle on which their influence can be counteracted; and prescribes it as an indispensable quality in men who are to be intrusted with civil power. "Provide, out of all the people, able men, such as fear God, men of truth, hating covetousness" (Exod. 18.21): "Wise men, and understanding, known among your tribes, and place such to be rulers over you" (Deut. 1.13). "For he that ruleth over men must be just, ruling in the fear of God" (2 Sam. 23.3.)

There is a circumstance in these words, which is too important to be overlooked. While they strongly mark the characters of men, who may be safely intrusted with civil authority, they give a solemn sanction to an observation already made. They resolve all authority into an appointment of the people; and place the rights of choice and investiture entirely in them.

But though this be the case, we are not to suppose that Revelation places the people above the reach of government and law. Every individual owes subjection to the state: and though the magistracy derives its power from the people, it possesseth also the sanction of divine approbation... "Submit yourself to every ordinance of man, for the Lord's sake..." (1. Pet. 2.13)...

The Jewish law consigned those who disobeyed magistrates, in the exercise of their duty, to "imprisonment, confiscation of goods, banishment, or death" (Ezra. 7.26), according to the nature of their crimes: and christianity carries its vengeance still farther, and declares "that the Lord knoweth how to reserve the unjust to the day of judgment; but *chiefly*, those who despise government, and speak evil of dignities" (2 Pet. 9,10). Still, however, religion admits, that disobedience is criminal, *only* when the power of the magistrate is exercised *"for the punishment of evil doers, and the praise of them who do well."* When this order is inverted, magistracy violates the principle upon which it was established; every claim to respect and obedience is cancelled; and resistance becomes, not only lawful, but necessary and honourable. On this principle the midwives of Egypt have immortalized their names; the army of Saul will be mentioned for ever, in terms peculiarly honorable; and the name of Daniel will be remembered with reverence, as long as sun and moon endure.

Upon the whole, the kingdom of Christ claims a strict connexion with the kingdoms of the world. It challengeth authority over them, marks distinctly, the duties of every station: and enjoins the performance of them by its solemn sanctions.

Should it be asked, "How far doth this connexion extend?", what hath been offered on this subject, will help us to a ready answer. It extends to every measure which can affect the persons, reputations, properties, or enjoyments of men. Whatever, therefore, is unfriendly to human happiness or improvement, tends at once to defeat the end of the Gospel, and of good government...

The only circumstance, relative to government, over which religion does not claim controul, is the form under which it may be administered. It leaves this as a matter of perfect indifference, and, provided the end of government is accomplished, it allows the taste and circumstances of states to determine, whether their executive powers shall continue in the body at large, be intrusted to a few, or resigned intirely into the hands of an individual.

Having proceeded thus far, it remains to inquire, in what manner religion and politics are connected. However obvious the answer to this inquiry may appear, from what hath been already offered, it seems to have been almost universally mistaken. Though men have seldom denied the reality of this connexion, yet they have arranged the parties connected in an order which reason and the nature of things disclaim, and religion must ever abhor. Though politics is only a part of morality; and though religion comprehends the whole, and gives it energy by her solemn sanctions, yet the part assigned to religion is subordinate to policy, and the dependence to which she hath been reduced, truly humiliating. She hath been shackled by forms of human device, as if the parent of happiness was in danger of destroying her favourite issue; bedizened with ceremonies, as if such taudry ornaments could add to her native beauty; fortified by penal statutes, and guarded by gibbets, racks, and flames, as if the solid arguments, on which she rests her claims, and the power of God.—the only power which she acknowledges—was not sufficient to protect and support her.

The effects of this arrangement have fully proved that it is not more impious, than it is absurd. *Impious* it is, because God alone is the light of the understanding, and Lord of conscience: And it *must be absurd*, as opinion is independent, even of him, who holds it. It owns no influence but that of evidence; and as this may vary, it will continually change. It is *even worse* than absurd. It hath sacrificed religion to appearances—realities to a shadow—by diverting the attention of mankind from the important matters of the law, with which their interests, improvement, and happiness, are inseparably connected; and instead of that mild and gentle spirit, which proclaims glad tidings, and diffuses peace and joy among men, it hath substituted a daemon which sounds the trump of war, spreads havoc and desolation through the world, and deluges the earth with human blood.

The same presumption which hath degraded religion to a slave, and armed her with the terrors of death, hath attempted to subject the Deity to human policy, and render his power subservient to the passions of men. Examples of this are scarcely noticed in the history of the heathen world. From the extraction and character of their gods they seem perfectly natural. When we reflect that Mercury was a thief, and Venus a prostitute, we cannot be surprised that the one should be invoked in the schemes of theft and rapine, and the other of debauchery. Here religion is the natural parent of corruption; and the grossest enormities take shelter under the example of the gods.

Though the character of the true God is widely different from those of the heathen world, yet we find the same attempts, which we have mentioned, made to interest him in the cause of inequity. When states have adopted schemes of conquest, whether from avarice, ambition or revenge, religion is strained hard to justify their execution; its Ministers are made the echoes of political mandates; and Heaven's lofty arch resounds with loud invocations to God, that he would divest himself of his excellence, accommodate his will to the passions of men, and bless their attempts to undo his creation, and defeat the designs of his gracious providence.

Whoever thinks seriously, for one moment, will perceive that, as this is an office abhorrent from the nature of God, it is also founded upon a station to which he rises far superior. As He leans not on the feeble authority, He will not stoop to become the pliant tool of human policy, or abject slave to passions which He implanted at first, for wise and good purposes, and hath absolute right to controul and regulated.

From these things we may conclude, that religion is not connected with politics, as an equal, much less as a dependent. Every argument which proves that God hath a right to govern the world: and that the Revelation comes from God; proves also, that the principle of Revelation should regulate the counsels and designs of men; and that human laws can never justify measures, which those of God condemn.

This principle is urged with remarkable strictness under the Jewish dispensation. On all important occasions recourse was had to the law, before any important decision in public affairs was made; and, least magistrates should err in their duty, they are injoined to have a copy of the law for their private perusal, and to devote a part of every day to the study of it. "When thou art come unto the land, which the Lord thy God giveth thee, and shall possess it, and shalt dwell therein, and shalt say, I will set a king over me, like as all the nations which are about me: Thou shalt, in any wise, set him king over thee, whom the Lord thy God shall chuse. And it shall be, when he sitteth upon the throne of his kingdom, that he shall write him a copy of this law in a book, out of that which is before the Priests the Levites: And it shall be with him, and he shall read therein all the days of his life; that he may learn to fear the Lord his

God, to keep all the words of this, law and these statutes to do them." (Deut. 17,14,15, 18,19.)

The same principle is laid down for the direction of subordinate rulers, with this additional circumstance, "that in matters of difficulty, they should have recourse to the Priests, whose office it was to expound the law, and that the sentence pronounced by them should be final." (Deut. 17,8,13.)

...

If the politics of the Jews were thus subjected to the morality of their religion; does it not evidently follow that the same morality, under the gospel of dispensation, should regulate, with commanding influence, the politics of states professing christianity? This conclusion is so just and obvious, that it cannot be denied; and I am convinced it will be adopted in this assembly, with that candor and cordiality, which its importance justly claims.

In the strength of this conviction, permit me to subjoin a few plain inferences from what hath been discoursed on this subject. And 1st. As the kingdom of Christ is not of this world—As it did not originate from worldly policy; doth not join issue with the passion and prejudices of men; disclaims the aid of violence and oppression; and arrogates to itself no authority but what truth and righteousness should possess over the minds and conduct of men; we may infer that every attempt to influence belief, or regulate modes of worship among men, by human policy or power, is inconsistent with its spirit. It is a kingdom purely moral and religious; morality and religion are personal; and the religious belief of every individual must depend upon the light in which religious subjects are presented to his understanding.

2dly. As christianity proposes the happiness of mankind as its end, prohibits the violation of his person, character, and property, and denounces its judgements against those who counter-act it; we may infer that every act of perfidy, oppression, cruelty, and injustice is highly offensive to that merciful and righteous god, from whom it derives its solemn sanction. If this inference be just, in respect to individuals who fill private walks of life; it cannot be less so, in regard to those, who, from more elevated stations extend their influence through a wider circle; or states, the effects of whose rapacity and ambition, are still more dreadfully destructive. As Jesus came to subdue the passions of men, direct them into proper channels, and regulate their influence; all offensive wars, for wealth, empire, fame, or even religion itself, are evidently inconsistent with his character and dominion. We can never suppose that he would forbid the poor man to purloin a morsel of bread, or lift his hand against his neighbour, under pain of damnation, and yet, suffer the great to plunder and destroy with impunity; or states to deluge the earth with blood. The thought is too big with absurdity to find reception, for a moment, into an enlightened mind.

To us, my Revd. Fathers and brethren, who hold the character of Ministers, under the Messiah's kingdom, what hath been offered upon this subject, applies with more than common force. We have undertaken the dispensation of a trust, the most important which can be committed to mortals—A trust, on the discharge of which, it is universally acknowledged, the improvement and virtue of the multitude depend. Nor do the duties of our office affect men as individuals only. From the connexion of religion with politics, and the authority which she claims over the kingdoms of the world, we derive a political character highly important, and become the dispensers of that knowledge which unfolds and ought to regulate their political interests; and patrons of that virtue which alone can secure them. While, therefore, we point the way to Heaven in our religious character, let us not forget the duties of the other; or the additional weight which love of country may give to the distant prospects of futurity. Let us consider that while true patriotism stands on virtue as its base, it rears its head above the regions of mortality, and claims an interest in that eternal world where truth and righteousness shall reign for ever, without controul: And let us endeavour to infuse into the minds of our people a full persuasion that strict honor, incorruptible integrity, and inviolable attachment to truth and righteousness, are absolutely necessary to national prosperity; and that without them patriotism is a bubble, and religion only an empty name.

The present situation of our native country, affords us but too many melancholy opportunities of introducing and inculcating this interesting truth. While every village murmurs complaints against the corruption of superiors, and charges the representatives of the people, and the nobility of the nation, with corruption, venality, and evil design, are we not called upon to remind them that their own meanness, venality, and corruption are the sources of all? Do not the representatives derive their powers from the voice of the people? And doth not the people—that very people which complains so loudly—prostitute its voice for a smile—a promise—nay, a night's debauch?...

Further, we ought particularly to cherish and diffuse that liberal spirit in religion, which views the Redeemer as sole Lord in his own kingdom; and all christians as *his* subjects, and accountable *to him alone in religious matters.* We should endeavour to banish that blind and tyrannic daemon which can see no worth, but in the name of party, and under the name of liberty, is busied only in the forgery of chains. We have much reason to rejoice and be thankful, that the influence of this daemon hath long been declining in our country. That it may soon be annihilated for ever is an event devoutly to be wished! We have lately seen toleration extend her soothing arms, and offer an embrace unknown before. Let us rejoice in the prospect which this opens before us; and let us join our helping hand to extend them wider still. Since policy hath so far foregone her claims over religion, let us endeavour to raise the kingdom of Christ to its proper dignity, and reduce its connexion with the kingdoms of the world, to those principles by which we ought to be regulated for ever.

[Preached before the General Synod of Ulster in June, 1781.]

[Sermon II]

Luke 2.14.

"Glory to God in the highest, and on earth Peace—Good-will towards Men."

...

God is the common father of the universe: the nations of men are his family on earth; and consequently, connected by the relation of brethren. To him, therefore, they can never unite in the devotion of children, while their hearts are alienated from each other by envy, enmity and strife. Nay, while they are strangers to that mutual good-will, which is the parent of peace among men, they must be incapable of that love of God, which is essential to his worship. This seems to be the meaning of the Apostle John: If any man say, I love God, and hate his brother, he is a liar; for he who loveth not his brother, whom he hath seen, how can he love God, whom he hath not seen...

These, and a thousand other passages, clearly shew, that the spirit of christianity is the spirit of peace...

Nor are we left to suppose, that the blessings of peace, and obligations to pursue it, are confined to men as individuals. Nations are represented in the glowing language of prophecy, as objects of Messiah's peace, and actuated by its spirit. Thus saith Isaiah: "He shall judge among the nations, and rebuke many people: and they shall beat their swords into plough-shares, and their spears into pruning-hooks. Nation shall not lift up sword against nation; neither shall they learn war any more"...

...

"It is true, for upwards of three hundred years after the publication of the gospel, the mutual affection of christians, and the peaceableness of their demeanour, were subjects of wonder, even to their enemies. But no sooner was their religion connected with the politics of kingdoms, and the intrigues of statesmen; and their priests seated among *nobles*, and ranked with the princes of the earth; than the bond of union was broken, the mild spirit of religion swallowed up by ambition, and the light of the gospel converted into a firebrand of discord. That the passions of individuals had introduced personal disputes, before this period, the Apostles inform us, but that these ever affected the public harmony, we have no reason to believe. However, from the days of Constantine, in which the honors and emoluments of the state were connected with party or office in the religion of Jesus, down to the present, peace has been interrupted in the christian world; and the lust of power, riches and pleasure has been stronger, not only than the obligations of religion, but the ties of nature. Of this, the history of fourteen hundred years is a continued testimony; and the present moment an unhappy demonstration. In all the religious contests which have distracted nations, and terminated so often in scenes of blood, *the religion of the state*, and not the religion of Jesus, has been the subject, and the love of power, pre-eminence, or riches, the leading principle. And whatever party prevailed, sufficient care was taken to humble the vanquished, sink them into insignificance, and brand them with infamy. Nor can we attribute this spirit, *exclusively*, to any church, sect or party. It has uniformly diffused itself *through* all, and operated *in* all. Of this, the lands of our nativity have afforded melancholy but undeniable examples. During the reigns of the Stuart family, all parties were favoured in turn; and as power changed sides, Catholic burned Protestant, Protestant persecuted Catholic, and the Presbyterians in their momentary triumph, denied toleration to both. In later periods, we see the same scenes acted in all their parts. We see Scottish Presbyterians proscribe episcopacy; English episcopalians exclude Presbyterians from the honors and offices of the state; and a scion of the same stock, transplanted to Ireland, shedding its baneful influence over the Presbyterians, who first gave that stability to its root, which has clothed its branches with fruits of gold. And, over all, we see the devoted Catholics bound down with the twisted chains of mental darkness, and corporal incapacity, by a body of laws, which humanity views with horror, justice reprobates, and religion pronounces *accursed*.

...

The same causes, which have rendered the *peace of the gospel* an empty name, and banished it from among christians, have hitherto prevented the *extension of the gospel* to the other nations of the world. The covetousness, rapacity, cruelty, and violence of the professors of christianity, have universally caused the name of God to be blasphemed among the heathen, and the religion of the Messiah to be rejected. Of this we have many instances in the conquest of America by the Spaniards: and it is not improbable, that succeeding generations will be informed of the like barbarities, practised by our own countrymen, in the east; though few of them have been yet published among us. These enormities, while they strike us with horror, and cover humanity with a blush, enable us to assign a reason, why the knowledge of the Lord hath not yet overflowed the earth, as the waters cover the sea: and at the same time convince us that the peace of the gospel can never prevail among men, till the passions, the political interests, and the domineering spirit of religious party, be swallowed up in the ocean of universal goodwill.

If prospects may be trusted, that blissful period is at hand, even at the door. One great and enlightened nation has burst the chains of prejudice and slavery, disclaimed the idea of conquest for dominion, opened the temple of liberty for all religious denominations at home, and sent forth her arms, *not to destroy*, but *restore* the liberty of the world, and extend her blessings to all who dare, and by daring, deserve to be free. Tyrants already tremble at her name; while oppressed nations exult in her success, receive her sons with gratitude and joy, and unite in her cause. Happy! thrice happy the people, whose rulers may become wise, by the lesson which she has been obliged to write in letters of blood—Where the ear of the prince may be open to the voice of humanity reciting her grievances, and supplicating redress; and the necessity and horrors of revolution precluded by *seasonable* and *radical* reform! That this may be our case is the prayer of my heart.

...

...If we value the peace, which we have been considering, as we ought; and from a sense of its importance, wish to preserve it—If, for this purpose, we are willing to acknowledge the offences we have committed, and repair the injuries we have done; and in order to secure it, keep a watch upon our hands, our hearts, and our tongues, in all time to come; should we not likewise, shut our ears against the poison of the slanderer, the malicious whisperer's artful tale, and the base insinuations of the cringing sycophant, and the false representations of the officious partizan? Reason says "it is right"—Prudence says, "it is our interest"—Religion says, "it is our duty"—and experience proclaims, with ten thousands tongues, that "if we do not, jealousies, discord, and strife will reign for ever—that Heaven-born peace will be eternally banished from the society, and soothing comfort from the hearts of man".

Let us then, be determined to obey their united voice. Let us no longer listen to the tale of malice, or of art, which tends to deceive, to irritate and inflame; and by representing men as enemies to each other, to convert them into such. And if this be our duty, where misrepresentation extends, only to an individual, or a family; it is, if possible, *more than duty*, where it goes to calumniate and vilify, not only a neighbourhood, but a nation; by calumny and falsehood, to revive and inflame mutual prejudice, jealousy, and contention; and under their influence, to perpetuate oppression, slavery, and wretchedness.

Such are the slanders, now and lately inculcated among you, against which your ears should be shut, and your hearts double-fortified. The subject of these are the Roman Catholics of Ireland—*three fourths of its inhabitants*. Ye are told by malicious and designing men, that they are not only *"ignorant*, but *incapable of liberty"*.

The latter part of this assertion, is a *libel* on *human nature*, and *blasphemy against God* ! The wretch must be equally lost to religion and shame, who dares assert that God is so weak, or so wicked, as to form a nation of men, insensible to the first right of humanity, and incapable of enjoying it. Nor is the former part of the assertion less false, than the latter is impious. That there should be ignorant Catholics is not wonderful, when we consider how they have been so long shut out from the means of knowledge, by the laws of their country...
...Yet under all these discouragements, the Catholics have refuted the charge of ignorance, and proved its falsehood...

However, my friends, this charge of *Catholic ignorance* and *incapacity* is only for *your* ears. The same lips convey to *them* a different tale. They are told, with great affection and regret, "that their abilities and their merits are well known; and that they ought to share the benefits of the constitution in common with their brethren; but that such is the ignorance, bigotry, and illiberality of a great majority of the Protestants, that nothing can be done for the Catholics, without offending *them*".

Now, who constitute this great majority of Protestants, not only in Ulster, but in Ireland? *Presbyterians!* Are ye Presbyterians then, such *ignorant, bigotted*, and *illiberal wretches*, as those double tongued tattlers, first attempt to *make*, and afterwards *represent* you? With you it lies, either to justify or refute the charge. And be assured, such charge lies against you. I speak not on the authority of idle rumour. It has been made in my own hearing, again and again.

...Ye are told, that "the Catholics are combining against you, meditating the overthrow of our happy constitution and preparing to embrace the nation in war".

This is as false as the former. Notwithstanding the sage prognostications of our wise masters, all their proceedings are legal, orderly, and peaceful. And at this moment, they are supplicating—humbly and dutifully supplicating—his Majesty, for a redress of their grievances, and a share in the blessings of the constitution, which would bind them to their country, by interest as well as affection...

There is yet another suggestion, founded on, and addressed to, your jealousies and interests. That is, "that the restoration of *their* rights and liberty would abridge and destroy *yours*".

This is absurdity too gross for any thing above idiotism, or childhood to swallow. Are your fields less fruitful, or your harvests less abundant, because those of your Catholic brethren share the benefits of the enlivening sun, refreshing showers, and dews of Heaven, in common with them? No! Nor would your liberties be injured, if slavery were banished from the earth; and not only your Catholic brethren, but the whole human race, as free as ye are—or, *in justice ought to be*. Liberty, like the light of Heaven, though extended to infinity, is not diminished in its influence. No individual is deprived of its blessings, though ten thousand times ten thousand share them with him...

These are only a few of the political forgeries of the busy-body and slanderer, at this eventful moment. But they are such glaring instances of the baseness of his heart, and the venom of his tongue, that they could not be overlooked: especially in a case so nearly connected with your honour and your interest...

...

But believe me, my brethren, the public peace, and the *public purse*, are more in danger from those who originate such alarms, than from *all the Catholics in the kingdom put together*. Who are they? — I will tell you in a few words who they are. — They are the official heirs and successors of the very men, who *less than ninety years ago*, represented to Queen Anne, that your forefathers were enemies to her government, and a dead weight on *their interests*; that allowing them the rights of men, and the benefits of the constitution, would destroy both church and state; and who procured, by their outrageous clamour, the continuance of the infamous test-act, which excluded the Presbyterians from every trust, honor, and office of state, above that of that of a petty constable. At that period every calumny was levelled against them which is now pointed at the Catholics, and every alarm sounded, which now disturbs the public mind. And all this was done by a faction, which now arrogates the *lofty* title of *ascendancy*.

...

Preached to the Presbyterian congregation of Portaferry, December 25, 1792.

[Sermon III]

Tim. II 3.16,17.

"All Scripture is given by inspiration of God, and is profitable for doctrine, for reproof, for correction, for instruction in righteousness; that the man of God may be perfect, thoroughly furnished unto all good works."

That all scripture was given by inspiration of God, we firmly believe. That it became necessary, from the degeneracy of man into ignorance, error, and sin; that its design was to teach, reprove, correct, and instruct him in righteousness; and that it contains a perfect system of precepts, the observance of which would secure his happiness here, and lead him to happiness hereafter, we cannot deny.

In these particulars the christian world is nearly agreed: and protestants have universally pleaded for, and supported, the principle, "that the Bible is the only infallible rule, both of faith and practice".

This principle necessarily implies, that the doctrines and precepts of the Bible extend to, and comprehend, every part of human duty, and every relation from which it arises; and consequently, that its principles, reproofs, and instructions, should be applied for the correction of every error and every sin, which may lead *man* astray, or impair that happiness, to which wisdom is the guide, and of which virtue is the parent, and religion the guardian.

...

In these principles and consequences, considered as abstract propositions, we are all agreed. Yet such is the perverseness of man—such the partial prejudices, passions, and pursuits, that he thinks they should be excepted from an universal law, and the denunciations of religion levelled against those sins only, from which he is free.

...

Hence, it is the duty of Ministers of religion, as watchmen of souls, stewards of the manifold grace of God, and guardians of truth, to observe errors and iniquities as they rise; to expose them in their destructive tendencies; to display their enormity and guilt; and to reprove and correct them with freedom and boldness...

That this preaching, exhortation, and reproof should extend to every sin, and every transgression of the law of God, cannot be denied. And that no rank, order, or office of men, is exempted from, or placed above, them, I shall afterwards prove... by... the decisive testimony of the word of God...

To an attentive mind it must appear surprizing, that such proof should be necessary; as the very supposition, that any man is above the reproof and correction of religion, or any action beyond their reach, implies, that such man is above the authority of God, and such action beyond the controul of his law. Yet, that such proof is necessary, we cannot doubt, while the interference of religion and its ministers is boldly condemned, in the most important concerns, not only of life, but of truth and justice. These are, where the duties of men, united in society, and placed in the relations of *governors* and *governed*, magistrates *and* people, come under consideration. Though all allow that the personal duties of temperance, sobriety, and chastity—that mutual love, fidelity, and order in families and even justice, truth, moderation, friendship, charity, and peace, in a town or neighbourhood, should be recommended and enforced, under the sanctions of religion; and every violation of them exposed, reproved, and execrated, with all the terrors of damnation, though their effects are confined to individuals, or extend only to a few families; yet, when power is abused by governors, and those who act under them, to the purposes of partiality, oppression, rapine, corruption; and violence, till whole nations are distracted, plundered, and enslaved; and every right of man presumptuously trampled under foot; the abettors of slavery and corruption maintain, that religion should stand by, as an idle spectator; and that all her exhortations, reproofs, and instructions in righteousness, should be buried in slavish silence. In other words, that religion and her ministers have no concern, either with the duties or interests of men, as members of a state; nor any right to interfere with the conduct of rulers, and the affairs of nations.

Groundless and absurd as this position is, when applied to that religion, of which God is the author, and the Bible the statute-book; it must be admitted, as resting on something *like* solidity, in respect to political religious establishment, created, protected, and supported by states. Of these, kings are the head, policy the only principle, and political influence the end. For such, therefore, to claim authority over rulers; or their ministers to expose, reprove or correct, the corruptions, usurpations, or profligacy, of governments, would be unpardonable presumption, and political blasphemy. Shall the creature say to the Creator, "I have power over thee; thy ways are evil, and thy doings unjust?" No, surely! or shall the Priests and the Levites, who minister in the tabernacle of the state, and *wax* fat on the sacrifices of the people's substance around its altars, lift up their voice against the oppressions, which raise them to seats among the princes of the land? This never *has* been the case—nor can it ever be supposed possible, till *principle become stronger than policy, and religion be rescued from the mean drudgery of a political engine.* Till this period shall arrive, the voice of the priesthood will be the echo of the Prince—his will their religion—his power the object of their slavish veneration—and the measures of government will be the standard of devotion. The father of mercies will be solicited, *in prescribed forms,* to become partner with the oppressor, the plunderer, and the assassin, of nations...

All this is natural and consistent. As admirers of consistency in others, let us, therefore, examine the religion, *not of the state, but of the Bible,* that we may see what *it* teaches, and what consistency requires of *us* who *profess* to believe it.

That *it* considers all men, *and of every rank,* as subject to its controul—that it directs its precepts *to all*; and that it censures the violation of these *in all,* whether *princes, priests,* or *people.* I now *assert,* and shall endeavour to prove, not by doubtful disputation, but... by the *decisive testimony of the word of God, and the facts which it recites.*

The first fact to be adduced is so extensive that it could not be composed into the bounds of a sermon. That is, the great body of the Bible is almost entirely *political*. Of this, the prophetic writings, from beginning to end, are one continued testimony. They scarcely contain a single exhortation, precept, promise, or threat, addressed to men as individuals, or members of a family, but as *states*, or *nations*. And, whenever they descend to particulars, it is to denounce the tyranny of kings, the corruption of governments, and the *unprincipled* connivance and rapacity of Priests and Prophets. This is so plain, that any man who has read them, *if not more than half asleep*, could not avoid seeing it. To them, therefore, *who can read*, I seriously recommend them...

The next fact is, "that the Bible interferes with the affairs of government, by the precepts which it gives for directing the conduct both of magistrates and people, governors and governed, in the discharge of their political duties.

In proving this fact, I shall present you only with the language of the Bible...

[Twelve pages of quotation from the Bible follow at this point.
Chapter and verse are not given, presumably because United Irish readers

"The prince, who wanteth understanding, is also a great oppressor... Scornful men bring the state into a snare; but wise men turn away wrath. If a ruler hearken to lies all his servants will be wicked... Hear the word of the

The political activities of the prophets who reproved corrupt priests and rulers are listed. The prophets named are Ezekiel, Shemaiah, Hanani, Jehu,

From the passages brought together on this subject, the following particulars appear plain and undeniable:

I. The controul of religion over governors, governments and nations.

II. Not only the right, but the duty of teachers, to expose, reprove, and censure, the partiality, oppression, and tyranny of rulers, the destructive influence of evil counsellors, and the corruption of governments.

III. That this duty extends, not only to the concerns of magistrates and people—governors and governed, but to leagues, treaties, and combinations of Kings with Kings, and nations with nations, for the purpose of injustice, oppression, and bloodshed. And,

IV. It has come to light, as by accident, from several of the passages I have quoted, that the necessity of sending extraordinary Prophets, to reprove and correct political fraud, oppression, and violence; and thereby, prevent national ruin, arose from the ignorance, indolence, covetousness, and profligacy of a worthless priesthood; and the meanness, obstinacy, and folly of a silly people, who preferred flattery and delusion to the law of the Lord, and the words of truth, soberness, and a sound mind.

...I shall now shew that religion carries her authority farther still; and that the Bible teaches us other doctrines equally important.

I.   It teaches us, that as it is the duty of the teachers of religion to rebuke the partiality, injustice, and oppression of governors, and expose the abuses of government; so it is the duty of the people to call for and enforce reform.

II.   That where any particular body, or description of men labours under partial grievances, hardships, or oppressions in a state, it is not only the duty of the existing government to redress and remove them; but where they neglect such redress, or refuse it to·the dutiful petition and remonstrance of the aggrieved, it is the duty of their brethren and fellow-subjects to espouse their cause, and support their claims, by every fair and justifiable mean.

In support of these lessons, I shall only recall your attention to two or three sentences of what I have already quoted.

"Wo unto them who decree unrighteous decrees, and write grievousness, which they have prescribed; that is, who enact partial, unjust and oppressive laws; to turn aside the needy from judgment, and to take away the right from the poor of my people."

"Hear the word of the Lord, O King of Judah, thou, and thy servants, and thy people, deliver the spoiled out of the hand of the oppressor, loose the bands of wickedness, undo the heavy burdens, and break every yoke: give ear unto the law of the Lord ye people; learn to do well, seek judgment, relieve the oppressed. Take away the wicked from before the king; and his throne shall be established in righteousness."

Here we see, that the commands, "seek judgment, relieve the oppressed, and take away the wicked from before the king" were directed, not only to the prince and his servants, but to the people...

These lessons... are for the direction of every nation, and the instruction of all people, who believe the bible. It cannot be wrong, therefore, for us to learn, know, and practice them. Would to God, we had no occasion to apply them!

This, however, is not the case! Wisely as our government was originally constructed, and solidly founded in the principles of justice, and the rights of men; yet in the lapse of ages, it has been removed from its original foundation, perverted in its principles, deranged in its structure, and converted into a mis-shapen and monstrous pile of venality, corruption, and partiality!

...

In these circumstances, the nation could see no prospect of relief, or safety, but in a radical reform, which would remove all these evils, or a total revolution. From a just view of the convulsions and horrors which attend revolutions, and a conviction that nothing but incorrigible despotism, and dire necessity, can justify the experiment, they have wisely determined, in obedience to the call of duty, to look for and demand reform. And though "oppression sometimes makes wise men mad"; they have proceeded with temper, moderation and order...

...

That the method proposed for obtaining reform, is the way of peace, as well as of prudence, every attentive mind must see. If pursued with unanimity and discretion, it must terminate in happiness. If not, "confusion and every evil work" may be reasonably expected from the present agitation of the public mind, and the provocations which have occasioned it. And should division among the people tempt government to reject requisitions, founded in right, and sanctioned by religion, to loose the bands of wickedness, and break the yoke of oppression", something more expressive than requisition may be justly dreaded...

...

Preached to the Presbyterian congregation of Portaferry, January 13, 1793.

Chapter Five

Confinement And Exile

[Introductory Note

In this chapter Dickson's own story, as told in his **Narrative Of Confinement And Exile**, is picked up at the point where it left off in Chapter 1. But, from this point onwards, the main line of the story is abstracted from the wealth of circumstantial detail in which it was told. The entire text of the Narrative is being prepared for publication at a later date.

The Narrative is for the most part self-explanatory. But one matter needs some explanation.

Lord Cornwallis, the new Viceroy who replaced Lord Camden in June, 1798, was quickly disgusted by the attitude of the Irish ruling class, the Ascendancy. He was appalled by the irresponsibility of the Ascendancy gentlemen who clustered around him and urged a policy of ever greater terror. His official correspondence oozes contempt for them. And their correspondence (for example, the letters to Lord Downshire from his informants in Dublin) shows that they got his message and began to regard him as a United Irishman in power.

Cornwallis aimed to suppress the insurrection with as little bloodshed as possible, to minimise resentment on the popular side, and to subvert the Ascendancy through a Union of the Irish and British Parliaments. To that end, he negotiated a 'Treaty' with United Irish leaders in prison in Dublin, granting them amnesty in exile in America, in return for which they agreed to answer questions in general terms about the United Irish movement—that is, they were not expected to give information about individuals other than themselves. (The questioning was recorded and was subsequently published, first in a version by the Government and then in a version by the United Irish leaders themselves. The latter was reprinted by Athol Books under the title, **The Origin & Progress Of The Irish Union.**) In the event, the American Ambassador in London refused them permission to enter the United States, and they spent a couple of years along with Dickson in confinement in Scotland.

Steel Dickson, while in prison in Belfast, was approached about a similar sort of deal. He rejected it out of hand.

Because Belfast was beyond the immediate reach of the new Viceroy's influence, and because Dickson was within Londonderry's sphere of influence, the approach was much more brusque and intimidatory in Belfast than in Dublin. Londonderry, and his agent, the Rev. John Cleland, were small-minded and vindictive individuals who bore a special malice towards old friends who had not turned their coats when they did. If Dickson had been held in Dublin, he would have been under much greater pressure to sign the Treaty, because it would have been more conciliating pressure. But I doubt that it would have made any difference to the outcome. The important difference between Dublin and Belfast was not circumstance, but social character.

The final leaders of the United Irish movement in the South were very unlike Dickson. They were gentry of the Ascendancy to whom it seemed that the main body of their own caste had gone mad. In 1796 they saw the country being driven distracted by the administration, and they placed themselves at the head of the conspiracy in the hope of being able to control and civilise the eruption, which they considered inevitable. But, when the eruption came, in Wexford, they were swept aside by it. Others were swept along in front as captive leaders.

Society in the greater part of the island was a patchwork of local fragments. There was nothing like a national will operative in it—unless the will of the Ascendancy be regarded as such. The popular reform movement of the early 1790s had not spread beyond the province of Ulster. There was considerable local disorder, but it was not connected with any national purpose. And law was only a sort of capricious local despotism, administered by an imposed gentry.

It is therefore not surprising that the state-prisoners in Dublin did not stand on ceremony when offered an agreement which tacitly admitted that they had tried to act for the best in an impossible situation.

Eastern Ulster, by contrast, was a more orderly and coherent society than England itself, and Steel Dickson was one of its social leaders of long-standing. And, while the Government might, until 1795, have claimed to be a force restraining disorder in the rest of the country, there was no doubt that since 1793 it had been trying to disrupt the orderliness of Ulster in order to ease the pressure for reform being exerted by Ulster. Dickson, therefore, did not find it reasonable, as the state-prisoners in Dublin did, to connive with the Government in setting aside the law and making a pragmatic settlement outside the law. He was not going to say that his life had been a mistake and that, when all was said and done, he was no better than the Government.

The Government had spouted about "law and order" while disregarding law and provoking disorder. It was holding him in prison without charge. It claimed that he was the United Irish General for County Down. He would deal with that claim, if it was formulated into a charge, and presented either in a court of law or at a courtmartial. But he would make no personal deals with the Government, even though it had him at its mercy.

Dickson was held in confinement for three years and a half. He was released, still uncharged, during the Peace of Amiens. On his release, he took issue with what the Synod of Ulster had said about him while he was in prison, but charged with no crime.]

Hitherto nothing like Insurrection, had taken place in Ulster. When we were treated, as above, previous to Insurrection, nothing, but increased severity, was to be expected, after its commencement... The number of our sentinels was increased, their passions were irritated against us, and their language became so insolent and outrageous, that we considered our lives in imminent danger. After the affray at Antrim, we were particularly alarmed and harassed by the dragoons of the 22d regiment, enraged, as they were, by the loss which they had sustained. As their barrack was in our rere, they had to pass our open window, in all their outgoings and incomings. Hence, our ears were dinned with their imprecations, oaths, and declarations to our sentinels, that "were they so placed, they would not leave one of us alive". On more occasions than one, some of them got into the Prevost, made their way to the door of our apartment, and threw in dead fingers, thumbs, etc. etc. with loose gestures and words, awfully expressive...

Though we now thought that the situation, in which we were placed, could scarcely be rendered worse, we soon found ourselves miserably mistaken. After the Insurrection took place in the county of Down, the number of prisoners was greatly increased, and they were generally huddled together, without regard to either age or station. Of these, many were destitute of the means of procuring a morsel of bred, or a wad of straw to spread over the boards on which they were obliged to lie; and, in the prevailing alarm and ferment, no attention was paid, for some weeks, either to their wants or their distresses, by the servants of government. In fact, they must have died of hunger, had they not been supported by their fellow-prisoners, and a number of families in Belfast, who generously supplied them with food, and other necessaries...

...After the several battles, in the county of Down, though the Insurrection was quelled, alarm seemed to gain strength. In consequence, on each change of our guards, the soldiers were made to load with ball-cartridge, in our presence; and, ordered, if any new disturbance should arise, to put us every man to death...

Under the uneasiness, which these orders occasioned within, we were not free from anxiety about things without. We knew that trials had commenced, and that executions, spiking of heads, etc. etc. were taking place...

Before the commencement of these trials, resolutions of extending them seem to have been formed, and measures taken to procure information against individuals, who had been arrested before the Insurrection, of whom I was one. To attain this, it was deemed *expedient* to apprehend some of their least suspected dealers in information: denounce them, *as ringleaders in sedition, whose conviction was certain*; and under this denunciation, place them among the victims devoted to death. This measure seems to have been adopted, in the hope, that compassion would be excited, among their fellow-prisoners, by the supposed certainty of their fate; and that, in the warmth of that compassion, confidential conversation might be brought about, in which something would be elicited, to confirm their information, and ensure the ruin of their devoted neighbours.

The first of those, of whom I had any knowledge, or by whom I was beset, was the *notorious* John Hughes—a man, some years before, of considerable respectability, but with whom I never had any particular connexion...

Besides Hughes, other informers were placed among us, about the same time. One of which was the Mr. Magin mentioned by him, in his deposition... Something, in his manner, on this occasion, impressed me, with suspicion...

This suspicion was fully justified, soon after, in an interview, which I had with a Mr. Pollock; not the once celebrated *Owen Roe O'Neill* Pollock—but a Mr. Pollock, whom I had known, many years before, as an attorney, not higher than second class. This gentleman, as appeared, was sent to Belfast to forward and conduct such trials, before courts martial, as he might think expedient to bring on. Anxious to see some of the objects of his mission, and as he gave me reason to suppose, *me* in particular, he visited us, on the very night of his arrival, and in a style which surprised us. At a late hour, just as we, *poor prisoners*, had laid ourselves to rest, but not to sleep, our ears were arrested by a voice, not very articulate or musical, bellowing execrations against "the D——d infernal Traitor"; and frothing out, "where is the scoundrel Dickson?"... His language to me... I shall not repeat. That I leave to Mr. Pollock, if he can, or chooses to, recollect it...

On that next day, or the day following, I was summoned, by a guard, to wait on Mr. Pollock. I instantly obeyed, and was conducted to his apartments, in the house of Mr. M'Cluncy, surgeon, nearly opposite to our prison... The

---

Owen Roe O'Neill Pollock —Joseph Pollock, the extreme radical of the early Volunteer period, who in 1779 published a pamphlet entitled, **Letters Of Owen Roe O'Niall,** but later became a judge in the service of Lord Downshire.

Rev. John Cleland was sitting with him, when I entered, and staid in the room for some time. After a few questions and remarks, respecting *Traitors, Treason,* etc., put and made in Mr. Pollock's *peculiar* manner, he asked me, if I knew *"Mr. Grattan",* as he afterwards asserted, but, as I then thought, and still think, *"Mr. Curran".* In consequence I answered that I did; which led to the following conversation: "You have often met him, I suppose?" "Not often, but always with great pleasure." "I suppose your correspond?" "Sometimes we have correspondence". "And, pray Sir, what have been the subjects of your correspondence? Irish politics, no doubt?" "We have corresponded on more subjects than one, but seldom on politics. I will shew you a specimen of our correspondence, if you desire it." This desire he expressed with eagerness; on which I handed him a letter, from Mr. Curran, which I happened to have in my pocket. This he hurried over, with devouring eyes, till he came to the subscription, when he exclaimed, in rage; "Z——ds. This is not from Grattan". "Grattan!" cried I, "No, surely! It was Mr. Curran you asked about." "No, By H——ns; I need not ask about him. I know you and he were never asunder at the assizes of last year—You were d——d busy there packing juries, and tampering with the sheriff to save Traitors from the gallows—It was Grattan I mentioned." "Be assured then", said I, "I never saw Mr. Grattan in my life; nor ever had any correspondence with him, of any kind; and, as to packing juries, I hope you do not mean to wound this gentleman, (looking towards Mr. Cleland) through my sides"—Mr. Cleland got up, and walked off, without even making his bow; and Mr. Pollock, as if recollecting himself, became calm, and seemed uneasy; I suppose, from having made a greater blunder here, than between the names *"Grattan"* and *"Curran";* as the array had been twice challenged, at the Down assizes in 1797, on the alleged ground that Mr. Cleland had given a partial pannel to the sheriff. Be this as it may, to this blunder I probably owed my dismissal, for a season, and return to my prison... Be it noted, however, that I was not dismissed, without the friendly assurance that, "if I did not do *what government expected,* I would certainly be hanged!—By the E——l G—d, I would."

This last sentence conveyed the ideas, that Mr. Pollock either had what he deemed sufficient evidence for my conviction, or was sure of procuring it; and that I might expect another interview with him, for some purpose or other. The former gave me little uneasiness; the latter was painful, principally, from the disgust excited by the indolence and vulgarity which I had experienced from the *little-great* man.

While I was, in my own mind, anticipating this interview, on the same evening, I was interrupted by the entrance of a decent-looking countryman. As he was an entire stranger, I asked his business. He said, it was only to speak a few words with me in private. On my retiring with him, to a corner of the

---

Rev. John Cleland —Church of Ireland clergyman at Newtownards; Lord Londonderry's political agent and jury-rigger; secretary to the Courtmartial which sentenced Rev. James Porter of Greyabbey to death.

room, he told me, that he lived in Saintfield—that he had called on his neighbour, Nicholas Magin— and that Magin had told him of the information he had given against several people, and me, in particular—That, in the detail of information against me, he mentioned my being at the fairs of Killinchy and Saintfield, in the month of May—that, on this, he asked Magin what information he could give about Killinchy fair, as he was at home, *all that day*, getting his barley sown... He told me many other particulars...

On the truth of this intelligence, in part, I had satisfactory proof, in my second interview with Mr. Pollock, a very few days after... "You know, Sir", said he, with a ferocious air, "what government expects from you; and, if you do not comply, by G—d I will hang you, before 12 o'Clock to-morrow." This, I alleged, was yet impossible, as he would not venture on such a step without some sort of trial; which, I was sure, his *then* master would not dare to grant me; though it was what I most ardently wished and intreated, and what I challenged him to institute. Whether provoked by the suggestion that he had a master, or from what other cause, I know not; but, for a moment, he seemed half-choaked by a paroxysm of rage; and, on recovering breath sufficient, exclaimed: "You are d——d confident.—By —— I have information against you sufficient to hang *twenty* men." Then, setting his arms a kimbo, and affecting to look uncommonly big, he said, in the most insulting manner: "Pray, do you know a Nicholas Magin, Sir?" To this I answered, with all the composure of countenance, which I could command, that, "I did know a Magin, but not that his name was Nicholas, till I saw him in prison; and that I never had been in his company, to my knowledge, at any meeting seditious, or not seditious, previous to his confinement." On this, he threw open a large book, which lay before him, in which the corners of many leaves were turned down; after inspecting which, he mentioned several places, and days, and demanded to know, whether I had not, there and then, attended seditious meetings. To this I answered, that, in some of these places, I had not been for several years, and that I had never attended *any* meeting of *any* kind, at *any* time, in *any* one of them—But that I had certainly been in Killinchy and Saintfield on the days specified by him; and that Magin was sent, from the latter place, with a message about a horse... The sound of the word **"HORSE"** seemed, for a moment, very much to affect him. But, recovering, he exclaimed: "a horse! a horse! What the Devil sort of a horse". "A horse" answered I, "able to carry my weight safely, either on the road, or across the country". "Ay! Ay!" replied he, "a charger for *a General*, I suppose! Now, pray, Sir, will you presume to say that you did not receive your commission, as a Rebel General, at Killinchy, in presence of Magin?" To this I answered, that "whether I did, or did not, receive such commission, it could not be in presence of Magin, as he was not in Killinchy on that day, or within several miles of it. He was at home sowing barley, and several of his neighbours were assisting him, from morning till night." After strutting, once or twice, across the room, he once more inspected his book, then swore, in great agitation, (half aside) "that cannot be". Seeing him thus agitated, I told him coolly, "that it was so", and begged him to send for Magin; and, "if he did not acknowledge the fact, on allowing me twenty-four hours, I would prove it to his face"... This he passionately refused, swearing "that he saw through my flimsy pretexts—that he knew *us all*, too well, to be taken in by such subterfuges—that we, *Presbyterian Ministers*, were a set of d——d ungrateful scoundrels—that, though supported by government, we were, to a man, Rebels, and fomentors of Rebellion, while we thought ourselves safe; but that, on the approach of danger, we abandoned the people, whom we had seduced, and skulked like cowards." Having proceeded thus far, he paused, seemingly out of breath, and then added, but not with an approving smile, "By —— you were not of the number—you were taken at your post, but rather too soon—Had you been left to yourself a few days longer, by the —— —— ——, government would have been sure of you."

However I might have relished this rough compliment to my own consistency and courage, I retorted the attack on my Rev. Fathers and Brethren, with pointed personality, and in such manner, as provoked his fury beyond all bounds...

...Magin was soon after sent for, told what I had asserted, and asked "whether he could personally prove his information against me". He said *"he could not*, but he had it from different people, whose authority he could not doubt". "Can you produce them, you scoundrel?" was the next question. "No, Sir, they were all concerned in the Rebellion, and have made their escape." On this, Mr. Pollock's rage was turned on Magin, and his denunciations against him terrified the wretch, almost to death.

This I was told by the same man, to whom I was indebted for my former information concerning Magin...

...

From these apprehensions, the nuisances which gave them birth, and several other disagreeable circumstances, I, with eleven others was partly relieved, early in July, by a removal to the artillery barrack. On our arrival there, we were put into two apartments, six and six; both of which were clean and comfortable, compared with those we had left... Here I add, with pleasure, that Mr. Fox, town-major, under whose roof and whose eye, we now were, never interrupted our comforts, or restrained our indulgences by any impertinent intrusion...

I shall mention a circumstance, or two, which took place, during my residence in the artillery barracks.

First, so far as I recollect, it was immediately before, or soon after, our removal thither, that the attention of government... was first directed to the wants and distresses of the prisoners in Belfast; and **Twelve Pence Irish**, per day, allowed for their subsistence. From the liberal sums allowed the state-prisoners in Dublin, to whom we proudly presumed that government thought us, *every way*, equal: and the recollection that one of us, at least, had enjoyed that allowance, in the preceding year, the beggarliness of this pittance wounded our pride, and nearly produced its rejection. This, however, was prevented by the suggestion that, if we rejected it, a Mr. Salmon and the Prevost-serjeant, by whom it was to be distributed, would put it into their own pockets; that, for this reason, we ought to accept it; and, if we did not choose to apply it to our own use, we might dispose it for the relief of those, whose confinement was embittered by poverty and disease. On this suggestion, we unanimously agreed to receive—and *did* receive it.

How inadequate this was to the subsistence of those, who were, not only poor, but far removed from every friend and relative, must be very obvious. And that, to those, who had been ·accustomed, at least, to the conveniences and comforts of life, it was a direct insult, must be equally plain. Yet, this same **Twelve Pence Irish**, per day, was the only allowance, in *money*, granted to the state-prisoners in Ulster, so far as I know, or have ever heard, during the years 1798 and 1799.

Secondly. In the latter end of July, or very early in August, we were officially informed of a compact between government and the state-prisoners in Dublin, by which it was stipulated "that said prisoners, on giving certain information therein specified, should be allowed to emigrate to such country as should be agreed upon between them and government, giving security not to return to this country without the permission of government, and not to pass into an enemy's country, if on their doing so they should be freed from prosecution; and that the benefit of said compact would be extended to such persons in custody, or not in custody, as might choose to accept it."

Such confidence in government then continued, that this intelligence was received, with gladness, by most of the prisoners in Belfast; and a paper, acceding to the terms proposed, was numerously signed, and sent to Mr. Pollock. This paper he rejected, as he said, on account of informality or incorrectness; and sent one, written by himself, for the acceptance of which, by government, he pledged his **Honor** to all who would sign it. On this pledge, the paper was signed by a great majority of the prisoners, in the Prevost-prison; but on being presented in the artillery barrack, by Colonel Barber, some hesitated, and I peremptorily refused to sign it, declaring that *"I had no compromise to make with government; and that I would not sign any paper, either implying that I was guilty of crimes which I had not committed, or admitting any thing, as a crime, which I had done as a duty"*. To prevent misrepresentation, I delivered this declaration, *in writing*, to Colonel Barber, to be given by him to Mr. Pollock.

On the receipt of this declaration, Mr. Pollock was said, to become so enraged, that he committed the paper with its signatures to the flames. However, he called on us, personally, a few days afterwards, accompanied by the Colonel and some other Officers, presented another paper to us, not in a body, but *one* by *one*, and demanded our determination. His interview with me was very short; and in our conversation embraced only the question; "will you now sign the compact with government?" and my answer; which was merely a repetition of my former declaration through Col. Barber. After this, I was waited on by William Sinclair, Esq. his brother-in-law, a man whom I sincerely esteemed, and whose memory I revere. He expressed deep sorrow, for my having so greatly *offended Mr. Pollock*, and used many arguments to induce me to sign the paper, not only for my own sake, but that of my fellow-prisoners, *as my perseverance in refusal might be made a pretext for withholding from them the offered boon.* This last suggestion impressed me with the idea that all this pressing was not well-intended; as, if government meant to grant the proposed indulgence, the want of my signature, could be no reason for denying it to others; and, under this impression, I persisted in my refusal.

That this obstinacy, as it was called, was a disappointment to Mr. Pollock, and, perhaps, to others, I had very great reason to believe; nor did the belief give me any uneasiness. But the offence taken by some of my respected fellow-prisoners, on the supposition that my stubbornness was the cause, not only of preventing their emigration, but of their detention in prison, I painfully felt, and bitterly regretted, as my feelings and convictions were invincibly opposed to their wishes. However, the event proved, about four years afterwards, that their suppositions and conclusions had not even the substantiality of a shadow to support them. The probability is that, had the signatures in Belfast been accepted and retained, the persons who signed would, after pining under a long confinement, have been transported to the Continent of Europe, in common with the fourteen who had signed in Dublin, to work, or beg, their way, through foreign lands, till the grave, or some hospitable country, should yield them rest and shelter.

Be this as it may, we twelve, comparatively comfortable *bondsmen*, were soon after destined to another change of situation. Whether this change originated from the desire of varying and multiplying our miseries, or our comforts, I shall not pretend to determine; but destined we were, and removed accordingly, to enjoy the summer-breeze on the surface of the water.

Of such removal this was not the first instance. Soon after the Insurrection, one prison ship had been stationed in the Pool of Garmoyle, three miles from Belfast, and completely stowed, as the prisons in town could not contain the multitudes dragged in, from the counties of Down, Antrim, Armagh, Derry, and Tyrone. This being found insufficient, a second, and of much larger burthen, was chartered, stationed in the same Pool, and nearly filled, both between decks, and in the lower hold, early in August. To occupy the vacant space on board, *if such could be said to exist*, was our destination. Accordingly, on the forenoon of the 12th of August, *the fair-day in Belfast*, we received notice to prepare for being carried "down the water". We had barely time to pack up our little luggage, before the guards appeared at the barrack gate; and there was neither car, nor other conveyance of any kind, even for our mattresses; so that we must have lain on *bare boards*, once more; had it not been for the exertions of our friends, who crowded round us, in alarm and agitation.

When marched to the street, we were astonished at the parade of horse and foot, ready to take charge of us, and the affectation of alarm, *lest we should escape, or be rescued;* though to a suspicious mind, this day of crowd and confusion might seem to have been chosen with a view to encourage such an attempt. The countenances and conduct of the military, and of the multitude, with which not only the street, but every door and window, was crowded, presented a curious contrast. The former, by every look and gesture, excited alarm and terror; the latter called forth feelings widely different, by starting tears, indignant frowns, and solemn silence. On reaching the quay, we found boats in waiting, embarked safely, and soon reached our floating Bastile. There, a guard was drawn up, on deck, to receive us; and, on approaching the hatch-way, we found it surrounded with a barricado of plank, from three to four feet high, from the top of which, on the inside, was hung a piece of old shrouds, to supply the place of a ladder, but not even fastened to the deck below, to keep it steady. this rendered ascent and descent, both difficult and dangerous. Indeed, for a considerable time some of us—I in particular—could neither go up, nor down without assistance.

When we first came close to the hatch-way, we were met by a *hot fœtid steam*, from the multitude below, almost intolerable. Through it, however, we were obliged to descend; and, on reaching the deck, found it literally crowded, so that there was some difficulty in clearing a corner for *us*. This done, we had time to contemplate our situation, which was truly unpromising. The length and breadth of our apartment I cannot exactly state; but it was only four feet eight inches high, so that we could neither walk, nor stand, upright: and, such was the number of its inhabitants that, when we laid ourselves down to rest, those on the deck were, not only in contact with each other,* but nearly so with a range of hammocks stretched over them, many of which were likewise occupied: whilst all the *good* air, admitted or admissible, was through four ballast-ports, two on each side of the ship. Our mattresses, which luckily arrived soon after us, we were obliged to use, both as beds by night, and seats by day, during our stay on board. In this respect, however, we were comfortable, compared with the multitude, many of whom had not even a wad of straw between them and the hard planks, when either sitting or lying. From the poverty of such, and seclusion from their friends, cleanliness was impossible, as they were under necessity of wearing their linen, such as it was, without washing, *even for weeks*. This alarmed us with apprehension,** both of disease and vermin, as the weather continued extremely hot. To this apprehension some other circumstances greatly contributed. Most of the prisoners were allowed on

---

* On the lower deck, we were not only in contact, when stretched out; but many were obliged to lie, in opposite directs, with their limbs intermingled, the feet of the one range reaching to the knees of the other.

** Our cause of apprehension was great indeed. While walking on the quarter-deck, we saw the poor wretches who got on deck, only once a day, busily employing the short time allowed them, in picking the vermin from their inside clothes, or shaking them from their rags over the ship's sides.

deck, only once a day, and for a short time—and the hatch-way was covered with a frame, and secured at eight o'Clock every evening; previous to which a large vessel was let down, which, before morning, was grossly offensive, being nearly filled with excrement of every kind.

To counteract these circumstances, necessity compelled us to use every mean, and make every exertion, which our situation would admit. Such of us, as had beds, *of any kind*, procured leave to carry them up frequently, and have them exposed to the Sun and air, on spars, or the nettings of the ship. We were allowed also to go on deck in small parties, to take up water in buckets, and hand it to our companions below, who washed, and swabbed the deck and sides, three or four times a week. These labors, though very severe, as some of us were advanced in years, some infi rm, and others totally unaccustomed to such drudgery, we all performed in turn; and I am fully convinced that they greatly conduced to the preservation of what health and strength we still enjoyed.

It is but justice to add here, that a Captain Steel, who had charge of the prisoners, did us great service, by suspending canvass tubes, from the rigging of the ship, which descended, not only between decks, into the lower hold, and carried off a part of the pestilential air. To Mr. Richard M'Clelland, Surgeon and Druggist in Belfast, the prisoners were under very great obligations. Through his interest, he procured an order for supplying them with medicines, in consequence of a representation by me; which he did, in a manner, equally honorable to himself, and beneficial to them. This I can assert, as the care of the sick, and administration of their medicine, fell mostly to my lot, the Surgeon appointed having it in his power to visit us very—very seldom. Such were the effects of these precautions, labors, and aids, under the auspices of providence, that, though many among us were occasionally sick, not one died on board.

To this account of our accommodation as to bed, &c. &c. that of our *board* I shall now subjoin, as our BLACK shilling per day, was withdrawn and our provisions supplied by government. In the distribution of these, there was no *partiality* or *respect to persons*. We were allowed to form ourselves into separate messes; and the œconomy of our *ship-hold* was, as follows. About eight o'Clock in the morning, each mess was presented with stirabout, made of oaten-meal and water, and a jug or can of small-beer. This *stirabout* was prepared in a large boiler, by a wretch as dirty-looking as ever met the eye of mortal, and served to us in *coarse wooden tubs hooped with iron*. I need hardly add that, from the heat of the weather, and other causes, the small-beer was, generally, sour or vapid. These tubs, washed or unwashed, as the prisoners chose to send them back, were returned about one o'Clock, with boiled fresh beef, or salt pork, the very coarsest ship bread, and small-beer as at breakfast; but without vegetables of any kind, or *even a potatoe*. This was our *only provision*, and the *invariable fare of every day*. This fare, however, was supplied in abundance. At least, I never heard any complaint of the contrary. But the quality of the pork was frequently and loudly complained of. One some occasions, the prisoners threw it out of the port-holes, saying, it stunk so abominably that they could not bear it. This last circumstance I mention on the authority of others, and of my own sense of smell, as the mess, to which I belonged, used very little of the government provisions, except beef, and small beer when drinkable. It is true, we took our allowance of bread, &c; but, it is equally true, that we handed it over to the poorer prisoners, who contrived to get it exchanged for butter, and such other little comforts as their friends could occasionally get sent on board. Besides, as we laid in our own provisions, beef excepted, and our own drinkables of every kind—and, as our friends supplied us, superabundantly, with garden-stuffs, sallading, fruit, fresh butter &c. we had it in our power, not only to supply invalids with many articles of useful regimen; but to enable others, with the addition of their ship-bread, to procure comfortable broths occasionally.*

Notwithstanding all these attentions, the state of many among us continued truly pitiable, and our own situation was painful and dangerous. We were, at once, suffering severely in our minds, our persons, and our purses. It is true, our minds were occasionally relieved by the visits of some friends and relatives, who procured admission to us: But this was greatly diminished by the inconvenience and hardships to which these visits exposed them; and still more by the continued mission of wretches among us, *under pretext of punishment*, to betray the ignorant and unwary, irritated as they then were, into unguarded expressions, and afterwards distort them into treason, for their destruction. This practice, though regularly persevered in, totally failed of success. Numerous as the prisoners were, not a sentence was elicited, or even forged, on which charge could be founded, or trial instituted. On the contrary, the only wretch, who made such attempt, by a forgery against two of our number (a Dr. Nixon, and the Rev. John Smith, Presbyterian minister of Kilrea) bungled the business so completely, that he narrowly escaped a flogging, and was disgracefully dismissed, *as unfit for service.*

Towards the end of September, our situation became less distressing. The heats had abated. We had gotten the port-hole in our quarter glazed, to keep out the spray, when it blew hard; and procured a small table, with a few folding stools. Several of the poorer prisoners, from whom information against the superiors had been vainly expected; others, equally poor who had been committed on unsupported charges, and some invalids, had been sent on shore. Hence, we had more room, less disturbance, and a better air. We had also gotten a canvas curtain put up, to draw round us occasionally, and afford us a kind of privacy. This last circumstance gave us occasion to observe how quicksighted the people are to every affectation of seclusion from, or elevation above, them. From the time this curtain was erected, we were denominated "the court", and our

---

* Let it be here observed, that the prisoners were not supplied, by government, with bowl, dish, plate, mug, noggin, knife, fork, or spoon. Their only food utensils were the tubs and cans already mentioned, except what they could purchase for themselves. Hence many had to tear their food asunder like wild beasts, or wait till their neighbours were satisfied, before they could appease their hunger.

corner "the castle". Thus *good-humouredly* distinguished, and apprehending that we were in no danger of a sudden dispossession by the superior forces of a greater castle, as our lives which alone they had hitherto aimed at, had proved *uncomeatable*, we began to amuse ourselves with farther plans of fortification against the attacks of the approaching Winter—the most formidable enemy, as we vainly imagined, which we had then to fear.

Here, however, we were mistaken, as usual, and all our plans proved visionary. On the arrival of Sir John Borlase Warren, in Carrickfergus road, with his squadron, and the French ships, taken off the N.W. coast of Ireland, my messmates and I were hurried into a boat, *without a moment's previous notice*, carried back to Belfast, and reinstated in the prevost prison, the place of our first confinement. From various causes, we found it less crowded than before, but still well peopled. In each apartment, we had room for our mattresses, a table, and some chairs. Sentinels were placed, only on the outside of our doors. The parade of loading with ball cartridge, and the terrific orders attending it, were dispensed with; and our rest was undisturbed by nocturnal visits. Our friends, too, were admitted with less difficulty; and our intercourse with each other was less restricted. What is more, hopes of information having expired, *overseers* were no longer placed among us, *to watch for our souls;* and pen, ink, paper, and books were allowed us, so that we could amuse ourselves with writing, reading, or conversation, as circumstances might admit. Still, however, we had difficulties and distresses sufficient to exercise our patience. The resources of some of us were nearly exhausted and we were replaced on our former allowance of TWELVE PENCE IRISH, per day. The windows of our apartments had many broken panes. Some of the rooms had neither lock, nor latch; and dirt and stench continued to prevail over all. As Winter came on with its severities, our inconveniences and expenses were greatly encreased. Fuel became necessary, not only from the inclemency of the season, but the ravages of the soldiery. The sentinels, having none for themselves, began, early in November, to tear off bases and surbases; mouldings of doors, windows, and fireplaces; and, latterly, doors, door-frames, and window shutters: all which they burned in the rooms of the poorer prisoners for their own comfort. And, as no notice was taken of this, they proceeded to such partitions, as were constructed with wooden uprights and laths. Hence, before the middle of December, the house was pervious to every blast. And, as these depredations were made by night, our rest was so much disturbed, that our situation was truly uncomfortable, and some of us suffered, severely, in our health. In a word, we continued prisoners; and these circumstances, added to the loathsomeness of our prison, as before mentioned, did not permit us to forget that we were such, or to enjoy the few indulgences with which we were favoured.

Thus situated, our only comfort arose from the expectation that, if any change should hereafter be made, in our situation, it could not be for the *worse*, as that, in the aspect and state of the country, was so much for the *better*, In fact, the country had become perfectly tranquil, and the public mind composed.

f this there could be no clearer evidence than Belfast exhibited. A patriotic and, *many of whom had been united Irishmen, and some of them active in promoting the union,* who had taken up arms to keep the rabble of their townsmen in order, laid down their muskets, unrigged their black cockades, and returned to their amusements, their country-houses, and their *pulpits;* and the *gallant* yeomen of the place were removed from permanent duty. I have inserted pulpits", because, in refutation of Mr. Pollock's vile calumny against the Presbyterian ministers of Ulster, two of the number, resident in Belfast, had regularly done duty, as private soldiers, in the brave and loyal band of BLACK COCKADES.

Notwithstanding all this, to the fresh surprise of us and our friends, we were hurried out, *on Christmas-day,* and carried back to our former apartment, on ship-board, to *enjoy* the remainder of the Winter. Our old inmates received us with great civility, and permitted us to take peaceable possession of the *castle.* Here, we were put on our former allowance of provisions, instead of our TWELVE PENCE IRISH, per day, and permitted to walk the quarter-deck* as before; but this indulgence the inclemency of the season now rendered unimportant. Indeed, when the sea ran high, the ship pitched so much, that walking the deck was extremely dangerous, as we had not gotten *sea-feet.* Hence, necessity alone compelled us to attempt it, as severe falls were generally the consequence; and one of us (Mr. Tennent) had his leg dangerously fractured, and nearly lost his life, in attempting, by a little smart exercise, to restore heat to his half-torpid limbs. Whether he had reason to regret this accident may be doubted, as it procured a removal to his own house, by which he was exempted from the miseries of our wretched situation, during the most severe part of the Winter.

After his misfortune, we seldom ventured to go on deck; and, as we could neither walk, nor stand upright, below, we were obliged, for several weeks, to sit muffled in great-coats, with our bed clothes wrapped round our lower extremities, and beating our feet on the boards from day to day, to prevent the loss of our limbs. When it blew hard, which was frequently the case, our situation was truly melancholy. Three of the ballast-ports were without stoppers, and consequently admitted both winds and waves. Hence, through all the storms of a most inclement Winter, we were reduced to the disagreeable alternative of being pinched with cold and drenched in water, by allowing them to continue open; or sitting in darkness, almost total, by stuffing them with rubbish; the only admissible light, in that case, being what passed through the two panes of glass in the port of our castle. In this situation, we endeavoured, as much as possible, to amuse ourselves with reading; but in this we labored under painful restrictions, the use of candles being prohibited, after eight o'Clock at night. This prohibition was so severely enforced, that we were frequently insulted for a few minutes excess; and, on one or two occasions, a ruffian soldier, having unbolted the cover of the hatch-way, came down and kicked our candles from before us.

Under these circumstances, without variation, except what depended on the weather, did we languish, during the three dreary turbulent months, from the 25th of December till March 25th. And, in addition to the sufferings to which they exposed us, sickness and pain prevailed to a considerable extent. In the course of the Winter, several were obliged to be sent on shore for the preservation of their lives; yet many others, real objects of compassionate attention were left behind.

With me, these months passed very uncomfortably. I had two or three attacks of Gout, though no regular fit; and a bilious complaint to which I had been long subject, was frequently troublesome. Latterly, from want of exercise cold, &c. I became very much crippled. Indeed, I could scarcely be otherwise for, dreadfully inclement as the season was, I did not enjoy the comfort of fire heat, or even the sight of a fire, for ten minutes, during the period I have mentioned, viz. from December 25th until the 25th of March. It is true, the gloom of the castle was somewhat dissipated by the kindness of a few friends who continued their visits occasionally when the weather would admit. Yet after the removal of Messrs. Tennent, Simms, and some others of my mess, my hours would have passed very heavily, had it not been for the lively, rational and entertaining conversation of a Mr. David B. Warden. Now, that I have mentioned this young man, I hope I shall be excused for adding, that he was only a *poor Probationer;* under the care of the Presbytery of which I was an *unworthy Member*—that his father was tenant to the Earl of Londonderry, father of Lord V. Castlereagh, Minister of the day—that, after the Insurrection in the County of Down, he obtained, with great difficulty, permission to emigrate to America—that, for several years, he has been, and now is, Secretary to the American Legation at Paris—and that, besides filling that department with honour to himself, and satisfaction to the state, he has been rising as *regularly,* and almost as *rapidly,* in the *literary* world, as the son of his father's landlord has been sinking, in the *political.*

Thus far, I have written, partly from memory, and partly from detached memoranda, having kept no regular journal, till after my arrival in Scotland. However, I have not related a single circumstance, but on the most perfect recollection, which I could command, aided by these memoranda...

On the 25th of March, while sitting at dinner, a voice called my name, adding that "a gentleman there requested to see me". I immediately rose, and got on deck, with considerable pain, as one of my feet was greatly inflamed. On seeing a guard there, I was very much surprised, though I supposed it to be one for my safe conduct to Belfast; but much more so, when I was informed that was to escort me to a ship, with prisoners from Dublin, which lay at anchor two miles below us; and even this surprise was encreased, when, on looking over the ship's side, I perceived my old messmates, Messrs. Tennent, Simms and Hunter, on board a boat, waiting till I should join them. Seeing this, I immediately called down to my fellow-prisoners, to tie up my mattress and bed clothes, and heave them, with my other trifles, on deck. This they did, with

---

D.B.Warden —see note on page 108

little trouble or delay. My luggage was thrown into the boat, and I followed. On this, as on former occasions, neither warrant, nor written order, for my removal, was produced, though demanded.

Whether this step was taken, from premeditated cruelty, official wantonness, or idiotic resentment; or from whatever cause; the manner, in which it was taken, with respect to me at least, was mean, vile and vengeful. On former occasions, want of previous notice was a trifling matter, as our removals were only to a short distance, and our friends had it in their power to send our luggage after us. Here, the case was widely different. We were now to be transported to another land, and immured in a military prison...

Thus scantily equipped and provided, was I, with my old messmates, shoved off from the Postlethwaite, my relatives, and my country, to enter upon a short, but stormy, voyage, and pass into a long exile; or, as my reverend fathers and brethren of the Synod of Ulster interpreted the matter; thus did I, in contempt of a law of their body, set out on my *removal to a foreign country*, and thereby forfeit all right and claim of my wife and children, on my demise, to the benefits of a fund, for the support of the widows and Orphans of Presbyterian ministers, to which I had contributed, as a subscriber, for TWENTY EIGHT YEARS.

About half an hour wafted us from the side of the "Postlethwaite" to that of the "Aston Smith", which was accompanied by an armed Tender, *for our protection*. Being ushered on Board, we were shewn down to the hold, where we found Thomas Addis Emmet, John Sweetman, John Chambers, Roger and Arthur O'Connor, John Swiney, Edward Hudson, Joseph Cormick, William James M'Nevin, Matthew Dowling, Thomas Russel, Hugh Wilson, William Dowdall, George Cuming, Samuel Neilson, and Joseph Cuthbert. On looking round, we perceived, to our great satisfaction, twenty births, tolerably decent and clean, four of which were reserved for us. We learned also, that, in addition to the provisions put on board by order of government, the Dublin prisoners had been allowed to lay in a considerable stock, at their own expense. This was a fortunate circumstance for us Northerns, as our detention on board was protracted by the severity of the weather, and we had been allowed neither time, nor opportunity, to lay in morsel for ourselves.

...

As some may read this Narrative, to whom we, or most of us, twenty are totally unknown, and who may wish to know who, and whence we were, and of what description; this place may be as proper, as any other for the gratification of their curiosity, With a view to this, as I have already inserted our names, I have only to add, that we were selected from the three provinces of Ulster, Leinster, and Munster, but, principally, from the city of Dublin, and town of Belfast; that we comprehended, in our body, three magistrates, three barristers, two physicians, one attorney, one apothecary, one printer and bookseller, one printer and proprietor of a News paper, one dentist, one military captain, one runner to a bank, one merchant Taylor, and one Presbyterian Minister, with an eminent Porter brewer; two wholesale merchants, one broker, and two young gentlemen, without profession, trade, or calling.

In this statement there *may* be one error, besides some incorrectness. The error may be, in respect to the Messrs. O'Connor, whose being Magistrates I have mentioned on report; but that they were both Counsellors is matter of certainty. The incorrectness is in saying that such a such gentlemen "then were", Magistrates &c. &c.; whereas I should have said, "they had been", viz. before their arrest. There is a defect also. To the professional part I should have added "A Clergyman of the established Church", as Arthur O'Connor was ordained as such, previous to his being called to the Bar; and, as episcopal ordination impresses an *indelible character,* he not only, then was, and now is, but ever must be, a *Clergyman.* Of our circumstances, I shall only say, that we *had* all been *independent*—most of us *respectable* in our professions—some possessed of large capitals in trade—and others of considerable landed property. Perhaps it may not be amiss to mention here, that, as we were selected from the three principal provinces of Ireland, we were respectively members of the three principal churches in the Kingdom, and which alone government has yet acknowledged *as Churches.* Nor is it unworthy of notice, that the numbers of Catholics, Protestants, and Presbyterians, in our little colony, was in an *inverse ratio* of the number of each denomination, in Ireland at large. Perhaps, the proportion may be stated as follows, though not correctly.

Catholics, two thirds of the people,	prisoners	4
Presbyterians, more than one fifth of do.	do.	6
Protestants, less than one seventh of do.	do.	10 ! ! !

From this statement, a fact truly anomalous, two presumptions arise: 1st. As a majority of the prisoners were deemed principal authors and promoters of the Irish insurrection; and, as only one fifth of said prisoners were Catholics; the representation of that insurrection as "a Popish rebellion" cannot be confided in as *the very truth.* 2dly. That, the Protestant ascendency in Ireland, however pre-eminent in splendid titles, lucrative offices, and overwhelming power, has as little pre-eminence to boast of in loyalty, as in numbers, *where loyalty is left to provide for itself.*

Having endeavoured to do justice to our convoy, and mentioned such circumstances, concerning us, as strangers might wish to be informed of, I shall now proceed with my Narrative, which will present, to my readers, persons and things, so characteristically different from those exhibited in the preceding pages, that, did it rest merely on my own credit, I could scarcely expect to be believed. And I am sorry to say that the contrast between our treatment in Ireland, and that which we experienced from our first setting foot on British ground, must ever cast a dark shade over the Irish Minister, his minions, and his measures, of the Summer of 1798, and the three succeeding years. However, truth ought to be told; and justice requires that I should represent, fairly and honestly, the conduct of the British government, and its servants with whom I was particularly connected, during *two years and nine months* of exile and imprisonment. And, in doing this, I shall confine myself to extracts from my journal, and copies of official documents, at this moment in my possession.

I have said that we were landed, at Goorock, on the 30th. of March. On the beach, the military were drawn up in two lines, between which we were conducted, with polite attention, by colonel Hay and the king's messengers, to four coaches, into which we were handed, five and five. This ceremony over, our military escort took their stations—the infantry in our front and rere, and captain Bird with forty four of the Rutland Horse, twenty-two on each side. Thus arranged, and accompanied by a multitude, which, not only crowded the road but covered the adjacent fields, we proceeded to Greenock (two miles and an half) in solemn silence, and with funeral pace. Here, our reception and entertainment excited an equal pleasure and surprise. Instead of being thrust into a *black-hole, a military guard-house,* stinking prevost, or *gloomy prison,* fortified with *bolts* and *bars,* and parcelled out in *dark, damp, cold,* and *bed-less* cells, we were ushered into *a large assembly room,* with a blazing coal-fire; and, instead of a *junk of beef* in an *iron-bound tub,* with coarsest ship-bread, and a jug of *vapid small beer;* in about twenty minutes, we were shewn across a lobby, into another handsome room of equal size, where we found a *very good dinner,* neatly laid out, and *servants* to attend us. At table, we had *good porter* and *ale,* in *abundance;* and, after dinner, a pint of port each.

In the evening, Colonel Hay, and the king's Messengers, Messrs. Smyth, Sylvester, and Scott, called on us, and told us, that they were ordered to get, from us, the money in our possession, which they would return, on our arrival at Fort-George. This demand was immediately complied with, by some wholly; by others, I believe, only in part. On receipt of this money they retired, and did not appear again for several hours, except to introduce some respectable merchants, who wished to see two of our number, Messrs. Tennent and Simms, with whom they had been in the habit of commercial intercourse.

Their introduction led to the knowledge that, on the representations in government papers, the Irish insurrection was firmly believed, in Scotland, to be a *real Popish rebellion.* One of the gentlemen, who knew that Messrs. Tennent and Simms were Presbyterians, and having learned that I was a minister of that persuasion, in a low voice expressed his surprise that *we* would connect ourselves with *Papists,* and much more that we would be concerned in a *Popish rebellion.* Overhearing this, I interfered, and asked the gentleman, in a voice equally low, why he called the insurrection, in Ireland, *"a Popish rebellion?"* He answered pertly that "he did so, on the authority of government, and that it was *known to be a fact."* I replied, that "such an assertion was one of the many falsehoods, by which the people of Britain were deceived and misled, in respect to Ireland." As this seemed to offend him, I then asked him, what opinion he supposed the Irish government to entertain of us twenty, then present. To this he answered, rather peevishly, but without reserve, that "they must consider us, *as the most guilty,* or the *most dangerous,* or they would not have *distinguished* us, as they had done." On this, with a view to remove an idea, equally unfounded and pernicious, I withdrew, to a side table, and wrote our names, classed by our religious profession, as underneath.

John Sweetman, John Swiney, Dr. M'Nevin, Joseph Cormick.	} Catholics.	T.A. Emmet, R. O'Connor, A. O'Connor, John Chambers, Mat. Dowling, Thomas Russell, Edward Hudson, Hugh Wilson, Wm. Dowdall, Robert Hunter.	} Protestants of the Established Church of Ireland.
Wm. Tennent, Robert Simms, Samuel Neilson George Cuming, Joseph Cuthbert, Dr. Dickson.	} Presbyterians.		

This done, I returned, and put my little scroll into his hand, whispering; "please, Sir, to look at that; and then tell me what becomes of your Popish Rebellion, on your own supposition that government consider *us*, as the most *guilty*, or most *dangerous* of its enemies?"

While his eyes were intent on the paper, he seemed surprised, and perplexed; and, on returning it, hinted a suspicion that I was *jesting* with him. On this I passed it round my fellow-prisoners, asking them, as it circulated, whether I had truly stated their religious profession? This question, which all answered in the affirmative, attracted the attention of other gentlemen present. The paper was, therefore, handed to each of them, and on perusing it, and being informed of the purpose for which it was written, their *faith* in the representations, which had been pressed upon them as *faithful*, seemed to be shaken. At any rate, during the remainder of their stay with us, *Popish Rebellion* was not even hinted at. Considering this development as an act of justice to the Scottish mind, I repeated it, *more than once*, during our journey.

In the course of the evening, we had tea served, which, with its accompaniments were all good. A little before ten o'Clock, our *guardian Angels* appeared, and informed us, that we were all to sleep in the room where we then were; and that, as we were to set out early, they had taken the liberty to order beds. Soon after, servants appeared, cleared off tables, chairs, &c.; and, equally to our surprise and satisfaction, brought in *twenty* good feather-beds, with blankets, sheets, bolsters, pillows, &c. perfectly clean, which they arranged neatly on the floor. This over, we were accommodated with Porter, Ale, or a draught of Brandy and water, at our own choice, previous to our going to bed; and then told, "that we need not get up in the morning, till called. " No sentinels were placed in our room, but guards were stationed in the lobby, hall, and around the house, during the night, in great abundance.

Sunday, March 31st. we were roused early, and proceeded in our coaches, under our escort of cavalry, to Bishopton-Inn, (eleven miles) where we found the family and servants all in waiting, and in full-dress; and the breakfast-table set out in a style, on which even the eye of a *Doctor Johnson* might have dwelt with pleasure. After breakfast, we were driven through Renfrew, Govan, and the Gorbals of Glasgow. During this part of our journey, not only the roads, but adjoining fields, were perfectly crowded with people, who kept pace with us for many miles. On our approach to Glasgow, the multitude became so great, that our escort seemed to have some apprehension of a rescue, though the conduct of the multitude was perfectly peaceable, and their countenances expressive, only of seriousness and anxious curiosity. About five, in the afternoon, we reached Hamilton, after a journey of thirty-three miles, where we found a pretty good dinner in readiness, with Porter, Ale, and Wine, as on the preceding day. In the evening, we were served with tea, and afterwards accommodated with a draught of Porter, Ale, or Spirits, and water, and twenty good beds, as at Greenock. Here also, the principal gentlemen of the place waited on us, and paid us the most polite attention.

The progress and entertainment of these two days I have copied, verbatim, from notes then taken; and, as there was little variety, in these two respects, during the remainder of our journey, I shall only add, that we did not, in any one instance, fare worse, and, in more than one, not only much better, but *sumptuously*. In Aberdeen, our dinner was equal to any thing of the kind I have ever seen or tasted, in variety and elegance. We sat down to *twenty-seven* dishes, including all the rarities of the country, cooked in style, and elegantly laid out. Our side-board made a good appearance; five servants attended us; our wine, both red and white, was good; and the quantity left to our own discretion. In the evening, we had several visitants, among whom were some of the magistrates, military gentlemen, and other genteel inhabitants of the place; as also captain Bird, commander of our military escort, who politely came to take leave of us, after an accompaniment of 181 miles. To him and the dragoons under his command, I feel that my feeble praise is justly due. During this long, and to them cold, and fatiguing journey, his and their behaviour to us was attentive and respectful; and, though in our approach to some of the larger towns, and passage along their streets, the crowd was so compact that progressive motion was scarcely possible, not an individual received a blow, an insult, or even an impassioned curse, except in one instance so far as I know. Justice calls for the same tribute, *without exception*, to the Windsor Foresters, an equal number of which accompanied us, during the remainder of our tour; 107 miles. Were I to hazard a supposition, I would add that we owed to the splendor of our coaches and respectful behaviour of our guards, some share of that respect, which was paid us by the multitude, in many places, through which we passed. On our route, from Barry to Fort-George, it was more than once observed, "that we must be *very great men*, or we would not have been escorted by such a retinue." This idea was not unnatural, as a troop of horse had not been seen, in that quarter, from 1746 until our arrival.

Of the military, who not only guarded the doors, but encompassed the walls, of the Inns where we breakfasted, took our meridian refreshment, or dined and slept, my feelings oblige me to express my unqualified approbation. They were, generally, the volunteers (yeomen) of the towns and villages, where we stopped. The conduct of the privates was uniformly correct, inoffensive, and discreet; and to the officers we owed some of the comforts, and much of the local information, which our journey supplied. To the gentlemen of Perth, in particular, I am indebted for personal attentions, the recollection of which I shall ever cherish with gratitude and pleasure.

Of the magistrates, and other gentlemen, who were admitted to visit us, during nine successive evenings, I must say, that their conduct was to us truly pleasing. We had not one instance of impertinent intrusion, or even an attempt, so far as I know, to procure admission to our room, without our previous consent: nor do I recollect a word, or look, which could lead to the suspicion that their object was merely to stare at, much less to insult, *"wild Irishmen"*, or *Irish rebels"*, or "both *united"*. That their curiosity was strong, not only to see, but converse with, us, cannot be doubted, from the rumors that must have preceded us; especially, as the person and manners of an Irishman were as unknown to the great mass of the Highland people, soldiers and a few sailors excepted, as those of a Hottentot, Esquimaux, or Laplander. Yet, generally, an interest in our situation seemed stronger than the desire of knowing who we were, or what we were like; and several, when leaving us, expressed, not only their wish, but *hope*, that we would be speedily released, and restored to our liberty, country, and friends.

From our outset, on this journey, till our arrival at Fort-George, the attention and services of our civil guardians, his majesty's messengers, were great and uninterrupted...

...

On Tuesday, April 9th. we arrived at Fort-George. Our entrance might be called solemn. The very aspect of the place made it so to me, who had never, before, seen a regular fortification. A numerous guard was drawn out, and the multitude assembled, which included the great part of the rank, and fashion of the country, was so numerous that persons, unacquainted with the improved state of the northern counties of Scotland, and, consequently encreased numbers of its inhabitants might have supposed that one half of their population was collected, on the occasion. Through them and the guards, our coaches drove to a stair, up which we were conducted to the rampart: and thence along a wooden bridge, thrown across the street on our account, to the third floor of the garrison; and shown into a spacious room, where we found an uncommonly large grate filled with a blazing coal-fire.

We had not enjoyed this many minutes, when lieutenant colonel Stewart, (the lieutenant governor) the fort-major, and some other officers, made their appearance. Panting as we were with anxiety to know our fates, their minds did not seem to be much more at ease than ours. After a few polite inquiries concerning our journey, health, accommodations, &c. &c. the lieutenant governor, taking a paper, from his pocket, said: "gentlemen, it is necessary that I should read to you the orders, which I have received from government; though I assure you, to me a very painful task." That he felt it such, was evident, from the tremulous voice and interrupted breath, with which he performed it. On perceiving the indignation, which these orders excited, expressed by every countenance, and hearing it from one tongue; "gentlemen", said he, As a *servant of government,* I cannot hear *reflections on government.* I own, I cannot reconcile your appearance and these orders; yet, I must obey them. However, it shall be your own fault, if ever they are executed with severity." On this, he, and the other gentlemen, retired, seemingly, and, as I believe, really, affected with our situation.*

Soon after, our table was handsomely laid out, and a good dinner, *of five dishes,* served up. We had two servants to attend us. Our allowance of drink was, one dozen of Porter, one of Ale, and ten bottles of Port. And we were informed, that we might have Tea in the Evening, or a cold supper, with a bottle of Porter, or Ale, for each, as we should choose.

After dinner, twenty rooms, each between sixteen and eighteen feet square were allotted us by ballot, sixteen of which were laid with brick over the boarden floor. On taking possession, we found them clean, dry, airy, well plaistered and ceiled, with windows sufficiently large, well glazed, and secured, on the outside, with iron bars. In each room was a neat four-poster bed with good curtains, Paillasse, Mattress, Sheets, one under and three upper Blankets, a cotton coverlet, Bolster, Pillow and Pot; a rush bottomed Chair, and small oaken Table, a bottle and Bason, a commode, fire-irons, coal-box, candlestick, snuffers and extinguisher; all entirely new, and good in their kind. To these was afterwards added a bell, on the outside of each door, with two pulls on the inside, one at the fire-place, and one at the bed, that in case of sickness, fire, or alarm, our keepers might be roused, and assistance procured. Four invalids were exempted from duty, for our service, and allowed double pay; two, to make our beds, keep our rooms clean, and do other chamber and personal services; and the other two, to keep our knives, forks, spoons&c. as they ought to be, bring our provisions from the Inn, and attend us at table. Each of us had Captains allowance of coal and candle; nor did we burn a dipped candle, except for one Fortnight, during my residence in the Fort. For our health, equal provision was made. The Surgeon of the Fort had instructions to attend us, and supply us with Medicine, when necessary, which he regularly did. In one instance of dangerous illness, a Physician was called, from the distance of sixty miles, and liberally paid by government. Were I here to pass unnoticed the attentions of the Rev. Mr. Stulker, Chaplain of the fort, I should think myself unpardonable, as they were equally kind and unremitting.

The preceding statement I have made, with the most scrupulous exactness, and publish with great pleasure, as a tribute justly due to the British ministry and the servants of the crown, with whom we were placed. In any circumstances such attention and liberality would have done them honor. But, with such

---

* How different this from the conduct of our own petty upstarts, during the preceding years! I am sorry I cannot produce a copy of these *original* instructions. I had such, but, some how or other, it has fallen aside.

representations and instructions from Ireland as gave rise to the orders transmitted to Fort-George, under which our confinement was, not only uninterrupted and solitary, but such as nearly precluded conversation, even during the few hours that our doors were unlocked, their conduct was more than honorable, and shall ever command my warmest praise. Nay, when I contrast it with what *I knew, witnessed,* and *felt,* during the preceding year, in what *was* "my *country",* but *now is,* or *yet may be, I know not what,* through the intrigues of an apostate, and the enormities of a faction, into whose hands God, in his displeasure, seems to have delivered it, I feel praise too cool for *their* merits, and language too feeble for the expression of *my* sensations.

On the morning after our arrival, we were visited by the king's messengers, who, according to promise, returned each of us the money given them at Greenock, or faithfully accounted for it. Major Hay also called on us, before he left the Fort. After some conversation, he asked me, as I believe he did the other prisoners, my name, my profession, the former place of my residence, my age, and the number of my family; the answers to all which questions he wrote in his pocket-book. On my asking the reason of this particularity, he told me that, "from our appearance and conduct, and the orders sent to the governor, he was convinced that we had been grossly misrepresented to the British government—that he wished, as far as he could, to do away with such misrepresentations—and that, on his arrival in London, he would state what he had seen, and what he thought, respecting us, to his Majesty's Ministers." This, I have every reason to believe, he did with *feeling,* and with *faithfulness.*

...

[The period at Fort-George is covered by fifty pages of the Narrative.
On December 30, 1801, the state-prisoners were informed that they were to be released.
On January 10, 1802, they were put on a ship at Greenock, and they landed near Hollywood on January 12. Dickson says that he was imprisoned for 3 years, 7 months, and 7 days and that "my liberation itself... demonstrates that evidence sufficient to satisfy either jury, or court-martial could not possibly be procured, or created, and carries, in its bosom, an acquittal as fair, full, and honourable, on the part of government, as ever man enjoyed" (Narrative p189).
During his confinement he had no knowledge of what had been said about him. About a year after his release, he managed to get a copy of the **Report Of The Secret Committee** of the House of Lords (a public document but, apparently, a rare one).
Between pages 192 and 237 of the Narrative, he reviews in detail the statements made to the Committee about him by John Hughes and Nicholas Magin.
In the next extract he takes issue with statements made by the Synod of Ulster.
The 1805 election, mentioned at the outset, was caused by Pitt's return as Prime Minister and Castlereagh's appointment to the Cabinet. It was then the practice that MPs, on being appointed to Government, resigned their seats and re-fought them. The popular interest in County Down, which in 1790 had sent Castlereagh to Parliament (as Robert Stewart, the Younger) now went into alliance with the Downshires against him. He lost his County Down seat, but got an English seat soon after.
The Downshires had been allied with the Londonderrys from 1795 to 1798, but the old antagonism revived when Hillsborough opposed the Act of Union. The confusion of the 1805 election, with the Downshire/Presbyterian alliance against Castlereagh, would need a book in itself to unravel and explain properly. That will be done in due course. Here I only mention the fact that it happened.]

During my confinement, many of my friends were alarmed for my life, and on the authority of whispers, and private letters from men, *who had access to people about the Castle,* these whispers, and alleged authorities, were frequently and warmly urged, for my signing the compact for self-exportation; and so fully were my friends convinced of their truth, that they charged me with *madness* in rejecting the proffered mercy, as it was then called. Even after my return to Ireland, I was frequently congratulated on my *fortunate* escape, and most earnestly solicited to avoid all interference in public affairs for the future. But, what is still more remarkable, the active part, I took, from beginning to end of the Down election in 1805, to assist the county in the vindication of its character by the rejection of lord Castlereagh; left some apparently unconvinced of the real situation in which I stood. Some of my particular friends even solicited me to leave the county, as I was certainly in his lordships power, *as they were well informed,* and my openness and activity would provoke his vengeance. I believed that I was not in his power, if justice enlightened by truth was to regulate that power, and acted accordingly. In fact, I would have proclaimed myself to the world, *as a villain,* if I had acted otherwise, let the consequence be what it might. In the year 1790, I had not only involved myself in debt, to bring Mr. Robert Stewart into parliament, on the faith of his repeated and solemn pledges, to be the advocate of a reform, embracing the interests of all the people. Hence I conceived it to be a duty to my character while living, and to my memory, if thought of, when dead, to oppose lord viscount Castlereagh as an apostate from the principles of Mr. Robert Stewart, the violater of his solemn engagement, and the unblushing betrayer of his country to a foreign *sanhedrin.*

In whatever light these circumstances may appear, when considered separately, I am sure, when viewed in connexion with the preceding Narrative, they will bring home the conviction to every unbiassed mind that no evidence of my being implicated "in seditious or treasonable practices" ever was, or now is in the possession of the Irish government or any of its servants. That the informations of Hughes and Magin contain no such evidence, I hope I have fully proved; and, had there been any other, there can be no doubt but it would have been produced.

Of all this my unsolicited release from confinement and exile, and subsequent transmission to my family at the expence of government, must ever stand as incontrovertible proofs. Hence it will naturally be supposed that no evidence of my treasonable practices was elsewhere treasured up, nor any self-created court presumptuously devising counsels, equally insulting to the government of the country, and ruinous to a brother; much less that such should be found in an assembly of men solemnly set apart to preside in the worship of the God of mercy, and preach the Gospel of the Prince of peace. Whether, and how far, this was the fact, in the present case, my readers will be enabled to judge, from the following detail.

That the court to which I allude, is the Synod of Ulster, or rather a little faction in that reverend body, whose influence in its proceedings has latterly been very great, and sometimes overwhelming, I mention with regret; and that I, who had enjoyed the privileges and exercised the rights of a member, for twenty-seven years, *blameless* and *uncensured*, should have ever become an object of obloquy, resentment, and persecution, has excited feelings the most painful that ever wrung my heart...

During my confinement in Ireland, for ten months, my Fathers and brethren kept at awful and loyal distance from my prisons. A very few, even of those with whom I had long lived in intimacy and friendship, *dared* to call on me; and a few more apologised for their inattention by pleading the *terror of the times*.

At their annual meeting, in 1798, no Presbyterial return was made to the Synod, respecting me or my congregation, though it was holden nearly three months after my arrest...

But, however trivial their minutes of this meeting may appear, so far as they respect individuals, with regard to the members constituting the body met, they will ever be viewed in a light truly interesting. Their address to Majesty, wherever read or heard, must ever command serious attention...

[Dickson here, on pages 242 to 245, gives the text of the Synod's Address To The King, dated 28 August, 1798. He takes issue with a paragraph in which the Synod beseeches the King: "deign to hearken to our solemn engagement to recall the deluded from their errors and crimes—to make a strict inquiry into the conduct of our delinquent members: and to withstand to the best of our abilities those pernicious foreign principles which threaten alike the temporal and eternal interests of mankind".]

Of legal processes I know nothing. But, to my understanding, it appears that duty, even as members of the state could extend no farther than the giving over such delinquents, as they might discover, to the government of the country to be dealt with as evidence might warrant, and justice require. In the principle part of these opinions I feel fully justified by notorious facts. The line of demarkation between ecclesiastical and civil jurisdiction is drawn with great precision, in every country of Europe, and the transgression of it has been guarded against with a jealous eye. Ecclesiastical inquisitors have never been suffered to interfere in matters of state; nor, even in crimes affecting the doctrine, worship, and discipline of the Church, were sentence and execution ever entrusted to ecclesiastical judges, but to the laws and judges of the state.

Some delicate minds, in theory, have exclaimed loudly against the present government of France, under which every religious denomination has equal freedom of access, not only to his God, but to the imperial throne, and the offices, honours, and emoluments of the state, because the Ministers of religion, on induction, are obliged to swear, not only to abstain from seditious practices and counsels, but to disclose to *government* all such as may come to their knowledge. How strange that these same delicate minds can enjoin "the several Presbyteries within their bounds to institute a solemn inquiry into state crimes

---

"the present government of France" —Dickson here refers to the Concordatist Catholic Church, which was made the established Church of France by Napoleon under an agreement with the Pope. I have described it in **The Veto Controversy** (Athol Books, 1985).

and to make a faithful report of their procedure (not to government, or the civil magistrate) but, to themselves, at the next meeting of Synod, *under penalty of severe censure"*.

Let the object of this injunction have been what it may, the several Presbyterians paid it due respect, by instituting inquiries, and reporting procedures, in June, 1799, at their annual meeting. At that meeting, the Presbytery of Bangor, of which I was a member, made the following report, equally modest, and correct: "The Rev. William Steel Dickson hath been, from the beginning of June, 1798, a state-prisoner, and is now such, at Fort George, in the Highlands of Scotland."

This report simply states a fact; a fact, too, with which the Synod of Ulster had no concern, except in their assumed character of inquisitors of state, as no application from my congregation, had been made to Presbytery, complaining of my absence, or charging me with crime. Their only application was to be supplied with preachers, each Lord's day, for whose services they punctually paid. While the Presbytery, therefore, reported my confinement, they wisely and candidly left the cause of that confinement even unhinted at. They acted on the knowledge that every man is, or ought to be, deemed innocent till convicted of crime; that no evidence to convict me of crime had ever been produced; that, if it had, they were not competent to judge, pronounce sentence, or inflict punishment, in cases of treason or sedition; that these powers were vested in government alone, in whose hands I then was, and whose willingness to detect treason, and punish traitors, could not be doubted. But, not so the General Synod. Under what influence, or on what authority, they judged and wrote, I do not say; but, be these what they might, they unequivocally, and without reserve, assign the causes of my confinement. Their minute, in their newly adopted Tyburn phraseology, runs thus: "It appears" (viz. from the reports of several Presbyteries) "that of the comparatively small number, who have *been implicated in treasonable and seditious practices*, two only, one a member, the other a probationer, have been executed; *two* are still in *confinement;* some have expressed their sincere contrition: others are no longer connected with the Synod; and the remainder have, either voluntarily, or by permission of government, removed from the kingdom".

...That all the persons alluded to in the preceding minute are unequivocally represented as having been actually *"implicated in treasonable and seditious practices"*, must be obvious to every eye; that the two of them then in confinement, *of which I was one*, were included in the number, cannot be denied; that I had neither been convicted, tried, or in any official manner charged with treason or sedition, is beyond a doubt... Yet, my rev. fathers and brethren have asserted my guilt, as "implicated in treason and sedition". Now, what is the plain English of this assertion, as addressed to the government of the country? Is it not, "your spies and your informers, who swarm over the land as locusts, not to devour the tender shoots of vegetating rebellion; but, pampered by your bounty, to destroy the innocent, have blinded your eyes and perverted your judgments. You see not the real traitors, and you sleep over your instruments of torture and of death. Our unworthy brother Dickson and his associates are feasting at the expence of his Majesty and the state, while their bodies should have been rotting in the earth, or suspended on gibbets, or sport for the winds, or food for birds of prey. To us IT APPEARS that they were "implicated in treasonable and seditious practices", and, on our apparitions and visions, we assert the fact, and, by our conduct, will maintain it."

...

...I assert... that unless the Synod of Ulster, in 1799, were in possession of clearer evidence of my criminality than government, though full of eyes within and without, could discover, or the committees of lords and commons pretend to have discovered, their statement that I was implicated in "treasonable and seditious practices" is a groundless and malicious calumny, in respect to them—that the man, who dictated it, dictated a falsehood—that the clerk who recorded it in their books, recorded a falsehood–that while it remains on the face of their books uncontradicted and uncancelled, they are the foster-fathers of a falsehood. To wipe off this imputation now lies with them; and this may be done, either by proving my guilt, or acknowledging their own error by cancelling their minute.

...

Note for Page 96:
D. B. Warden: David Bailie Warden of Greyabbey, Co. Down (1772-1845). Took degree at Glasgow University in 1797 and was licensed to preach by the Presbytery of Bangor the same year. United Irishman. Arrested and offered choice of trial or emigration. Emigrated. Taught natural philosophy (science) at various American colleges 1799/1804. Secretary to the US Ambassador in Paris 1804/8; Consul at Paris 1808/14. Settled in France. Translated **The Intellectual & Moral Faculties and Literature of Negroes** (1810) by HB. Gregoire, the Constitutional Bishop of Blois. Author of **The Origin Of Consular Establishments** (1813) and **A History Of The United States** (1819).

Chapter Six

"Retractions"

[Introductory Note

On his release from prison, Steel Dickson set about inquiring of the Synod of Ulster its grounds for asserting that he had engaged in treasonable or seditious practices, when he had not even been charged with such, still less convicted.

The Synod was then controlled by the Rev. Robert Black (a close friend and political colleague of Lord Castlereagh) and by his brother-in-law, the Rev. Thomas Cuming, who was Clerk of the Synod. The reign of Black and Cuming, which began in the terror of 1798 and continued for sixteen or seventeen years, is the one dishonourable period in the history of the Presbyterian Church in Ireland. It is perhaps understandable that a dark veil of forgetfulness should be cast over a period in which there is nothing to be proud of. But forgetting is not conducive to social well being, if only because the matter in question is never really forgotten. It becomes a suppressed memory: an inhibition at the back of the mind subverting thought.

Memory is a precondition of effective thought in social affairs. Society is not begun afresh every day. It exists, as Edmund Burke stressed, in an unbreakable continuity with the past. The present is always a product of actual history, even though the actual history which produced it may be unwritten.

Actual history, if unwritten, makes its effect on each new generation through the elliptical culture of the family, of the locality, and of the social shibboleth. It persists in constrictive forms. It is not material for progressive social reflection.

It is a cliche of media commentators, and all too often of academic commentators, that the Irish have long memories and that is their trouble. The implication is that the English have short memories and therefore evolve, while the Irish only revolve in ruts. But the truth of the matter is that the English have long and capacious memories, while the Irish, of either variety, have only shibboleths. All the chief literary materials of English history since the time of Elizabeth have been kept in print for each new generation to reflect upon, so that it might evolve. Writers of far less consequence in the history of England, than Steel Dickson is in the history of Ulster, have been kept constantly in print. And, if the conflict between Black and Dickson had occurred in an English context, there would have been a major review of it in each generation.

Robert Black dominated the affairs of the Synod in the period of reaction after 1798. In these ignorant times, it is customary to equate reaction with theological orthodoxy in Presbyterian affairs. But Black was not the leader of the orthodox. He was a liberal in theology, and was a close associate of the pioneer of Arian (Unitarian) theology, the Rev. William Bruce, headmaster of Belfast Royal Academy.

I have elsewhere attempted to explain why the association of unorthodox theology and progressive politics, which existed in England, did not exist in Ireland. (See article on John Paul in **A Belfast Magazine**, Vol 2, No 2.) The tendency of theological unorthodoxy in Ireland was towards a conservative or reactionary elitism, while popular reform movements tended to be theologically orthodox. Different social conditions in the two countries led to different alignments. And the crucial difference in conditions was in the social character of the philosophically 'enlightened' aristocracy. In England that aristocracy fostered reform: in Ireland it resisted reform, even to the extent of provoking insurrection.

Mountstewart, which slipped discreetly from Presbyterianism to Anglicanism as it entered the peerage, naturally became a sponsor of theological liberalism or indifferentism. (Londonderry made large donations to both the Presbyterian and Episcopalian Churches in Newtownards.) And, a few years later, it transfigured itself from a centre of political reform to a centre of political reaction. And, from that day to this, the equations between liberal theology and progressive politics on the one hand, and orthodox theology and political reaction on the other, which have had a loose validity in England, have had no validity in Ulster. Indeed, the terms of those equations can almost be reversed—almost, but not quite, because Steel Dickson and James Porter were theologically liberal. But they were political exceptions amongst the theological liberals. And furthermore they did not *preach* theological liberalism, as the political conservatives did. (This aspect of the matter is investigated further in the selection of James Porter's writings, which it is proposed to publish.)

When Steel Dickson, on release from prison, began to investigate the procedures of the Synod in 1798 and 1799, the line was held against him for some years by administrative stone-walling on the part of Dr. Black and his brother-in-law, the Rev. Cuming, Clerk of the Synod. He found difficulty in gaining access to Synod records. But, the more he was resisted, the more he pressed forward. Dr. Black obviously hoped that Dickson would come to be regarded as a crank, obsessed by something which all sensible men would see was only a point of pedantry. This approach, which is often adopted by powerful bureaucrats, is essentially an attempt to make the other person's mind give way. It was a dangerous game to play against Dickson, who was an enormously sane man. And, eventually, it was Dr. Black's own mind that gave way.

The pressure exerted on the Synod by Dickson increased instead of diminishing as the years passed. He accumulated evidence, gained access to records, wrote an account of his affairs insofar as they were of relevance to his imprisonment, wove all of these into the Narrative which he published in 1812, and dared anyone to refute any point of substance in the Narrative.

Hitherto, Dr. Black's best defence was silence, combined with administrative manipulation. But, in the face of the Narrative, silence would no longer do. At the Synod of 1812 (held in Cookstown), he launched an attack on the Narrative (which was at the same time a defence of his stewardship of the Synod), and he gave an Explanation of the motions of 1798 and 1799, which he hoped would explain them away. Though Dickson was present and spoke, the Synod supported Dr. Black on the strength of his Explanation.

According to the Belfast News Letter report (7 July, 1812): "The indignation of the Synod was so much excited, by the animadversions of Dr. Black, and other respectable Ministers, that it was proposed to expel him [Dickson] from the body. This, however, was commuted for a recantation and public apology, to be signed by Dr. Dickson."

A Committee was appointed, which drew up a Declaration for Dickson to sign, acknowledging that his Narrative "contains a number of misstatements and misrepresentations, (partly arising from misconceptions,) injurious to the characters of the Ministers of this body, and to the Presbyterian cause", and expressing regret.

Dickson declined to sign the Declaration. The Synod then adopted a motion suspending Dickson, until he made a public retraction of the Narrative. But the motion was not to take effect until the Synod of the following year, so that Dickson might have ample opportunity to consider the advisability of a retraction.

The Synod concluded the affair by adopting a resolution of thanks to Dr. Black, which had most unfortunate results for him, since it urged him "to publish his statement, in vindication of the Ministers of the Synod". This was *hubris* on the part of Dr. Black (on whose instructions the motion must be assumed to have been drafted).

Dr. Black polished up his Address to the Synod and published it under the title, **Substance Of Two Speeches Delivered In The General Synod Of Ulster At Its Annual Meting In 1812.** The Introduction is dated August 29, 1812.

Dickson responded with a pamphlet, bearing the following title page:

RETRACTIONS;

OR,

A REVIEW OF, AND REPLY TO, A PAMPHLET,

ENTITLED,

"SUBSTANCE OF TWO SPEECHES,

DELIVERED IN THE

GENERAL SYNOD OF ULSTER,

AT ITS ANNUAL MEETING, IN 1812,

BY THE REV. ROBERT BLACK, D.D.,

SENIOR PRESBYTERIAN MINISTER OF LONDONDERRY.

WITH

AN ACCOUNT," &c. &c.

" Great men are VANITY, and mean men are a LIE."—*Bible*
"When a man pretends to relate facts which involve the reputation of others, he
ought to adhere strictly to the line of truth, lest he be branded with the name of
calumniator, and expose himself to the reproach of propagating falsehood."
Dr. Black's Sub. p. 48.
"If I mistate, brand me as a candidate for disgraceful celebrity."
Dr. Black.

~~~~~~~~~

Belfast:
PRINTED BY JOSEPH SMYTH,
115, HIGH-STREET.
1813.

Black's pamphlet (his only published work) is pompous and empty, and its intellectual
content never rises above debating points. (But, unfortunately, it set the literary style for
future generations of the agnostic middle class with connections in high places.)

Dickson's reply, his Retractions, in which all is reasserted with increased force, is an
overwhelming combination of principle, logic, humour and contempt. In the mid-1970s
I received a letter congratulating me on a pamphlet I had published on the Northern Ireland
affairs of the time, and comparing its impact with that of Swift's **Conduct Of The
Allies**. I had read The Conduct Of The Allies without being able to understand why it
had been a success. Now, if I had been compared with Steel Dickson, I would really have
felt flattered. For sheer polemical power concentrated to a point, I would take Dickson in
preference to Swift any day. But, until now, Steel Dickson had only existed for my
private pleasure, the society which produced him having forgotten him.

The first extract from **Retractions** is about the meaning of the word *"implicated"*. The
following three documents are relevant to it:

SYNOD MINUTES, 1798
"The Synod reflecting with grief and indignation, on the conduct of some
members of this body, and of the licentiates under their care, who have been lately
implicated in seditious and treasonable practices, do hereby declare their most pointed
abhorrence of a deportment, so highly inconsistent with the character of a Minister
of religion. And they do strictly enjoin the several presbyteries within their bounds,
to institute a solemn inquiry into the conduct and conversation of their respective
members and probationers—to distinguish impartially between the innocent and the
guilty, that the Ministry may be blameless; and to make a faithful report of their
procedure, at next meeting of Synod, under penalty of severe censure."

SYNOD MINUTES 1799
"The several presbyteries having made their reports, according to the injunction
of last meeting, this Synod has the satisfaction of finding, that the general conduct
of its members and probationers has been conformable to order and good
government, in the late afflicting circumstances of the country. It appears, that of
the comparatively small numbers who have been implicated in treasonable or
seditious practices, two only, one a Minister, the other a Probationer, have been
executed; two are still in confinement—some have expressed their sincere
contrition—others are no longer connected with the Synod—and the remainder have,
either voluntarily, or by permission of Government, removed from the kingdom."

SYNOD EXPLANATION OF 1812
"On referring to the Synod's minutes of 1799, it was unanimously resolved, that
by the phrase, 'implicated in treasonable or seditious practices', the Synod did not
mean to express any thing more, than that Dr. Dickson and Mr. Smith, two of the
persons therein alluded to, had been confined by Government, under suspicion of
treason and sedition, and that this Synod now attaches no other meaning to that
expression; and if that expression has been otherwise understood or applied, the
meaning of the Synod has been misconceived."

Black prefaces the Substance of his speeches with an introductory narrative. It begins as follows:

"In the summer of 1798, during the progress of a rebellion, the object of which was to separate Ireland from Great Britain, and to establish a republican government under the protection of France, a few Ministers of the Synod were arrested, some on direct charges, and others on suspicion, of being engaged in this mad and criminal project. In this number was the Rev. Dr. Dickson... who is stated, in an Appendix to a Report published by the Committee of the House of Lords, to have held the rank of *Adjutant General of the Rebel Army in the County of Down*.

"...Until lately, the principles of a well regulated liberty, as remote from *licentiousness* as from *slavish submission to arbitrary power,* had distinguished *the Presbyterians of Ulster*. From their settlement in Ireland, in the reign of James I they had adopted the sentiments of the *English Puritans*, to whom, in the judgment of Mr. Hume, Great Britain is indebted for her present constitution, and their conduct, in the various struggles which marked the succeeding reigns, obtained for them the confidence and gratitude of the friends of *limited Monarchy*. During the five years which preceded the Rebellion, a mournful change had taken place with many, and in 1798, the Synod could no longer boast, that it did not contain a traitor." (p1/2.)

In fact, the Ulster Presbyterian outlook was so different from that of the English Puritans that the Belfast Presbytery in 1649 issued a denunciation of the Puritan Parliament in England, provoking a fierce reply from John Milton. Furthermore, the Puritan Constitution failed in England in 1660 and was certainly not revived in 1688. And, further still, the reason many Ulster Presbyterians became "traitors" in the 1790s was that their demand that the 1688 Constitution be made operative in Ireland was declared by Government to be seditious. Dr. Black's intellect is no more admirable than his heart. Nevertheless, his pamphlet played its part in history and ought to be in print.

In the remainder of his introductory narrative he lists the Synod meetings and motions of 1788 and 1789 and gives his version of events up to 1810.

In his first speech to the Synod of 1812, Black described Dickson's Narrative as "a mass of mistatement and misrepresentation", and "a disorderly and ill-arranged mass, (where every thing which is not mistated, is discoloured and perverted)". He "had hoped, that the events which unfortunately took place in our bounds, in the fatal year of 1798, would have been permitted to rest in forgetfulness; but the veil, with which they had been partly covered by the hand of time, has been rudely drawn aside."

He said he would confine his remarks to six points which he had discerned in the disorderly mass. These were charges against the Synod 1. with falsely branding Dickson a traitor in its minute of 1799; 2. with usurping the authority of the Crown over the Royal Bounty; 3. with injustice in distribution of the Bounty; 4. with injustice against the congregation of Keady because it had appointed Dickson its Minister; 5. with voting to suspend him from ministerial office in 1799 when he was a prisoner and unable to defend himself; and 6. with unjustly excluding his family from the benefits of the Widows' Fund to which he had subscribed for 27 years.

I have omitted points 2 to 6 in the extracts from Dickson. Most of Black's comment on point 1 is cited by Dickson when replying to it. I give the opening sentences here:

"1. At a distance of thirteen years, I have no recollection by whom the minute of 1799 was drawn, and as I was not an inactive spectator of the day, it is very probable I might have held the pen. But by whomsoever it was dictated or written, this I can with confidence affirm, that it was not offered to the Synod, nor adopted by that body, as conveying a *judicial* sentence of *guilty* against individuals. There were certain notorious proceedings in the province, which no man thought of explaining or questioning; the word *"implicated"* , was used in the common popular sense, well understood at the time, and neither conveyed, nor was meant to convey, any other idea than that some Members of the Synod lay under the imputation of having been concerned in the excesses of the preceding year. That it conveyed no other meaning to the Members present is evident from this, that it passed without observation or objection..." (p23).

Dickson's reply is prefaced with an address "To The Public" and a reprint of the News Letter report of the 1812 Synod. Reference is made in the address to the "Royal Bounty", the Regium Donum, or grant made by the Crown to help with the support of Presbyterian Ministers. Dr. Black became Agent for the Bounty, gained an increase in it, and used it to exert political pressure on Ministers and Congregations. The affair of the Bounty is complex. Since Dickson was not in principle opposed to it, but only criticised the purpose for which Black used it, I have not given an extract on the subject.]

*

To The Public

...

I feel that I ought to apologize for the liberty which I have taken, in teazing you with my petty doings and sufferings, and protracted persecutions, as I have done, and am now doing. But I will not insult you with apology. You will make my case your own. You will consider how a man ought to feel, after treading a *public* path, in a *public* character, under observant and sometimes *unfriendly* eyes, without blame and unrebuked for more than forty years, on being holden up to the world, by an *unbought* agent of Government for the distribution of Royal Bounty, as a Liar, Slanderer, and Traitor, "from whose society every *wise* and loyal man should shrink". Having considered these things, your own hearts will apologize for me.—Ye will think and judge for yourselves.—Having thought and judged, ye will treat me as I deserve.—That is all I wish.

[At this point the pamphlet includes a reprint of the News Letter report of Synod, giving the texts of the Explanation, the Declaration presented to Dickson for signing, and the motion congratulating Black and urging him to publish. It continues]

A Review of, and Reply to,
Substance Of Two Speeches

That the preceding report, and the minute subjoined, deserve some attention will be admitted by all who read them. That they refer to, or *implicate*, matters deserving the most serious attention of the Presbyterians of Ulster, appears to me equally obvious. And that they involve interests *dearer than life,* to every man pretending to truth and honour, and more especially to Ministers of the gospel, every mind alive to virtuous sensibility must feel. They contain in their body, and exhibit in their complexion, matter, which will leave a stain wherever it may fall, dark, deeply ingrained—perhaps indelible. Whether or no it may finally rest on my name, I shall not pretend to conjecture. From the late attempts of Dr. Black, approved by the *heartily* expressed *gratitude* of the Synod, for the *zeal* and ability with which they were made; justice requires, that every possible information should be given to the public, to enable them to judge fairly, where the brand of infamy should be impressed, under the sanction of their name...

To supply that information, which may enable the public to judge fairly in this matter, is my great object in the following pages. With this in view, I shall for a time, pass over the Doctor's introductory Narrative, notwithstanding the variety of matter which it contains, and confine myself to the "Six Points", which he has selected from a "disorderly and ill arranged mass, in which every thing which is not mistated, is discoloured and perverted" as the "parts most imperiously demanding the notice of the Synod."

The first of these points, the Doctor expresses thus:

"1. His charging the Synod with passing upon him a sentence of *guilty*, as a Traitor; and of Falsehood in its Minute of 1799."

That I have so charged the Synod, I freely admit. The words in which have I so done, are as follow:

"I assert farther still, that unless the Synod of Ulster were in possession of clearer evidence of my criminality than Government, though full of eyes within and without, could discover, or the Committees of Lords and Commons pretend to have discovered, their statement that I was implicated in treasonable and seditious practices, is a groundless and malicious calumny, in respect to them; that the man who dictated it, dictated a falsehood; that the clerk who recorded it, recorded a falsehood; and that, while it remains on the face of their books, uncontradicted and uncancelled, they are the foster-fathers of a falsehood."

The truth or falsehood of this charge, depends entirely on the meaning attached to the word "implicated" as applied to practices treasonable and seditious. I shall, therefore, from a sense of that duty which I owe to myself, to the Synod of Ulster, and to the public, endeavour to ascertain the real meaning of the word, that it may be seen whether the Rev. body or I have misconceived, misrepresented, and misused the phrase in question. That phrase, in the minute of 1798, is "seditious and treasonable practices"; in that of 1799, "treasonable or seditious practices".

From the first appearance of the latter minute, it was universally understood, as charging all to whom it was applied, with actual treason and sedition. In respect to me, it produced painful sensations, arising from unqualified censure, and virulent reproach. When combined with, and supported by, Dr. Black's declaration to Mr. Cuming, of Keady; *(see Nar.p.281,)* these were multiplied and invigorated, so as to extort memorials from my congregation and myself, requesting an explanation of the phrase used, &c. The repeated refusal of this finally obliged me to publish, in my own vindication, after suffering in silence for seven years. My publication extorted what has been called, an *"Explanation"*, in 1812, which may be seen in the minute prefixed. And that explanation has laid me under the necessity of making the following attempt.

To every intelligent mind, it must appear, that if the Synod's explanation be admitted, as giving the *real* and *approved* sense of the phrase in question, my charge, that the Rev. body "passed on me a sentence of *guilty*, as a traitor", is false and unfounded. It means no more, than that I had been suffering all the horrors of confinement, in a nasty black-hole, a loathsome prevost, a military barrack, a suffocating and chilling prison-ship; and that I was then suffering those of exile to, and confinement in, a foreign strong-hold; aggravated by a separation from my friends and family, the partial plunder of my property, and the *suspension* of all my little revenues, on which their support then principally depended; and all this, as the Synod asserts, under mere "*suspicion* of treason and sedition". Whether this suspicion may have been founded, or unfounded, the Synod have disclaimed the imputation of crime, or blame, to me. Their language is plain and unequivocal. The Synod did not *mean* ANY thing more, than that Dr. Dickson had been confined by GOVERNMENT, ON SUSPICION, &c." Does not this imply a translation of the charge from me, to the Government of 1798?—A charge, severe indeed—A charge, of inflicting all these pains and privations, not on evidence of guilt, but mere suspicion? It is true, considered merely as it respects *my* confinement, exile, and sufferings, it may be lightly thought of; but implicating, as it does, the inflictions upon others, particularly that of death, it must appear not only severe, but cruel. That it does so, must be obvious to ever one, who reads, understands, and compares, the preceding minutes. The former says: "It appears, that of the comparatively small number, implicated in treasonable or seditious practices, two only have been executed, two are still in confinement." And in the latter: "The Synod unanimously agreed, that by the phrase, 'implicated in treasonable or seditious practices', the Synod did not mean to express any thing more, than that Dr. Dickson and Mr. Smith, two of the persons therein alluded to, had been confined by Government, *under suspicion* of treason and sedition; and if that expression has been otherwise understood or applied, the meaning of the Synod has been misconceived."

From the phrase being prefixed to the classification of the executed, imprisoned, contrite, and emigrant members alluded to, in the minute of 1799, the explanation, in 1812, must embrace all the classes. Let us read the minute thus explained, as it applies to the "executed", who are placed in immediate contact with the phrase, "implicated, &c." It appears, that of the small number, "under suspicion of treason and sedition, two have been EXECUTED by GOVERNMENT." What? two Ministers of the gospel executed under mere suspicion! No—impossible—will be exclaimed by every man, acquainted with the constitution and Government of the country! Yet, that this charge has been made, *by the Synod of Ulster*, is evident, from the minutes which I have quoted.

But I have insinuated, under the disguise of a question, not only that this charge was severe, in respect to Government, but *dangerously bold* on the part of the Synod, and might have exposed them to more than *suspicion* of treason and sedition. It might have been conceived as wickedly and maliciously devised and published, not only to "injure the reputation" of Government, by "false and unfounded assertions and reflexions", but to weaken the People's attachment to, and shake their confidence in, it—Nay, probably, to goad them to, and implicate them in, treason, sedition, and open rebellion. At least, I may presume, that, if such a charge had issued from my lip or pen, Dr. Black and Committee would have deemed and pronounced it "confirmation sure, as proof of holy writ", that I was so deeply implicated, not in the suspicion, but in the guilt of treason and sedition, that my body should have been *suspended*, instead of my bounty.

Be this as it might, I shall now present to my readers a more astonishing instance of dauntless intrepidity in *Dr. Black and his Committee*, than that of incurring the suspicion, or vengeance, of Government exhibits. That is, their boldly incurring, and dragging down upon themselves, the SUSPICION, not only of gross ignorance, or STUDIED misrepresentation, of the phrases, which they use; but of the wanton and meretricious prostitution of words, whose chastity the learned, wise, and good, of all ages *laboured* to preserve spotless and inviolate.—Nay farther, of being "concerned in originating, fomenting, or fostering" seditious combinations, and openly committing acts of rebellion against the republic of letters—of undermining its constitutional principles, subverting its constituted authorities, trampling its established laws under foot, despising the decrees of its councils, and mistreating its legislators, the expositors of its laws, its judges in all cases of disputed or doubtful meanings, with all, who have submitted to their authority, or been directed by their wisdom, for thousands of years.

This charge is long and complicated. However it may be soon and easily understood, by attending to the words of a respectable judge; these are "Penes quem Arbitrium est, et jus, et Norma loquendi."

"The power, and privilege of forming, regulating, and explaining language, rest with the people, who use it." Hence it follows, that the meaning attached to words, by the most intelligent, learned and correct speakers and writers of any age or nation, and adopted by the people, is the true meaning. Happily for later ages, dictionaries, or word-books, showing *that* meaning, and grammars, containing rules for reading, speaking, and writing each language with propriety, long since have been, and still continue to be, written for the use of foreigners, of youth, and of future generations. In the foreign and dead languages, these are our only authorities and guides, with the assistance of the writings, termed *classical*, from which examples are to be taken; and in the modern we are well supplied with both. Now, as Greek, Latin, and English, are universally studied, and ought to be critically understood, by young men intended for the learned professions, it can hardly be supposed that any number of such men, much less that a numerous body of ministers of the gospel, not only considered as learned in these languages, but professing to explain the sacred books by virtue of their critical knowledge of the same, and some of them presidents in schools and academies—I say, it is hardly to be supposed that a body of such men should unanimously agree in the misconception, and *misrepresentation* of common words, or phrases, in any one of them.

Yet, that such agreement is not impossible, the Synod's minute of 1799 gives reason to suspect, in more than one instance. The third class of delinquents they there mention as "having expressed their sincere contrition". Sincere contrition for what? The Synod's *explanatory* minute of 1812 says, for being suspected, or being confined by government under suspicion, of treason and sedition.

Now it appears, and must appear, from the words of this minute fairly interpreted, that neither the suspicion, nor confinement under suspicion, rested with them: consequently, if either implied crime, that crime is chargeable, not to them, but to the government by which they were suspected, or confined under suspicion: and hence, the declaration, that they had "expressed their sincere contrition", would be deemed nonsense, coming from any other pen than that of a Synodical pen-holder. What is contrition? According to Lyttleton, it is a "severe sorrow for sins".* His explanation of "contrite" is still more determinate. "One who is greatly affected, grieved, or tormented by sorrow, for sins committed by himself.** The compilers of the British Encyclopædia, who are generally allowed to be tolerably good interpreters of words, define contrition still more strictly. "Contrition", say they, "is sorrow for *our* sins, arising from the reflexion of having offended goodness alone, without any regard to the punishment due to the offence; and attended with a sincere resolution to reform."

Here we see that, according to these definitions, the sins for which these delinquents "expressed their sincere contrition", must have been their own; whereas, according to the Synodical explanation, they were not their own. They were the sins of the Government—that very Government, which Dr. Black and his Committee have represented, as executing some, and confining others, members of the Rev. body, on mere suspicion of treason and sedition.

Though I might safely rest my charge of ignorance, perversion, and abuse of language, in this case, with every man of sense and learning; yet, I shall adduce another, which appears to give it substantiality, on a broader base. In the case mentioned, the ignorance and abuse extends only to one Latin-English word. In that to be mentioned, it implicates the Doctor and his Committee, in the suspicion of equal ignorance of the Greek, Latin, French, and English languages. As to the French, this is not strange, as it is not generally taught in our country schools; but as to the others, a competent knowledge of them is, at least, pre-supposed, on the admission of men to the Presbyterian Ministry. Hence, though a small minority may be deficient in that knowledge, it can scarcely be believed, that the whole body should be so grossly ignorant of Greek, Latin, and English, as "unanimously to agree" in misconceiving, and misapplying any one word—much less, that they should agree in the same misconception and misapplication. Yet, I feel myself called on to attempt showing, that this has been the case.

I feel particularly happy in the thought, that this will not require any affectation of learning, above the reach of a school-boy, or reference to any authority, to which he may not appeal. I mean the best dictionaries in the respective languages, to which necessity obliges the unlearned to apply, and in which the most learned confide, in respect to the meaning of words. In the

---

* Acerbus dolor, ex delictorum recordatione susceptus—Animi dolor ob Peccata. [A bitter sorrow derived from the memory of what one has done wrong—The sorrow of a soul on account of its sins." I am indebted to Niall Cusack for this translation: BC.]
** De Peccatis a se admissis multum dolens—Qui magno Peccatorum suorum dolore afficitur, vel cruciatur.

present case, there is not only a remarkable coincidence, but derivative relation, among these four languages, which has been preserved inviolate, from their respective reduction to a regular form, until the meeting of Synod, in 1812, as will appear on the following authorities. Greek, emplekomai; Latin, implico, irretior, innector, magnopere occupor, et extricare me non possum, vel magnopere incumbo in aliquod incœptum; French, etre impliquè; English, I am implicated, involved, entangled as in a net, interwoven, engaged so deeply, that I cannot extricate myself, eagerly intent upon some enterprise.*

To these authorities and examples, ancient and modern, all our compilers of English dictionaries give their unqualified sanction, without the slightest shade of difference in the meaning, by them attached to this *misrepresented, slandered, and persecuted* word. To prevent multiplicity of quotation, let Dr. Johnson be heard for the whole.

"To implicate, V.A. (impliquer, French; implico, Latin;) to entangle, to embarrass, to involve, to infold."

"Implication; involution, entanglement, inference not expressed, but tacitly inculcated."

Since the meeting of the Synod, I have paid particular attention to this word, wherever it has occurred in my contracted course of reading, and found it uniformly bearing the sense which the preceding authorities attach to it. Of this I shall give only one example, from the pen of a man, peculiarly remarkable for the correctness and precision of his language; and of whom it was never said, as Dr. Johnson said of a Rev. body, "that they had all got a MOUTHFUL, but none of them a BELLYFUL of learning." A man, on the contrary, and truly, said "to be not only *tinctured*, but *imbued* with learning." The man to whom I allude, is the late Mr. Fox. In his history of the Reign of James the 2d, speaking of Monmouth's Rebellion, he says: "I have mentioned Lord Devonshire, who was certainly not *implicated* in the enterprise, and was not even *suspected*."

Let us here pause, and contrast these authorities and examples, with the Synodical explanatory minute of 1812. The former uniformly agree, that *implicated* signifies "engaged, involved, or busily employed in"; the latter declares, that the Synod means no more by the word, than "being *confined*,

---

* The following examples are in strict conformity with these authorities, Greek; Arakhnè tous podas emplekhtheis, huptios ekremato: implicated or entangled by his feet, in a spider's web, he hung with his back downward.

En tosoutois kakois eisin empeplegmenoi. They have been implicated, or involved, in so many and great distresses.

Latin; implicantur contrahendis negotiis. They are deeply engaged in, or harried with, business.

Implicati Morbo; infected with disease, very sick.

Implicatus utraque Tyrannide Dionysiorum; entangled in both tyrannies of the Dionysii.

French; "S'impliquer dans quelque affaire; to entangle one's self in any business, or deeply engage in it.

executed, &c. under suspicion of having been so engaged, involved, and employed; and if any person understand or apply it otherwise, the meaning of the Synod is misconceived." Dr. Black says: "the word was used in the common popular sense, (in the minute of 1799,) well understood at the time, and neither conveyed, NOR WAS MEANT* to convey any other idea, than that some members of the Synod lay under the *imputation*** of having been concerned in the excesses of the preceding year." (*See Substance, page 23.*)

Admitting this, I have to regret, that the phrase, "implicated in treasonable and seditious practices", did not *convey* the idea of Doctor Black and his Committee, to the understanding of any man, whom I have heard speaking on the subject; but, on the contrary, that which has been uniformly attached to it, by the authorities and examples which I have mentioned. On these authorities, therefore—on these examples—on this uncompelled cloud of witnesses—this *honest* band of philological *informers*, who never shrunk from their information, nor disgraced themselves, by an attempt to *misrepresent* and falsify the words in which it is expressed, I rest my long and complicated charge, against the Rev. Doctor and his Committee, not only of being implicated in treasonable and seditious practices, but open rebellion, against the republic of letters, her constituted authorities, laws, lawyers, and judges, with all her lettered, loyal, and commonsensical subjects. On the same broad and solid base, I assert, that the same Rev. Doctor and his Committee, have insulted the understanding, and sported with the character, of the Synod of Ulster, by seducing, or overawing them into a conspiracy, to attach meaning to words, which the only legitimate arbiters of language never intended, or "thought of". I farther assert, on the same authorities, that I have not misconceived, or *misrepresented* the words of the minute of 1799, by alleging that they express a direct and unequivocal charge of treason and sedition, against the *few*, whom they, in their address to his Majesty, in 1798, call the "deluded, delinquent, and unworthy members" of the Synod of Ulster." Hence, instead of retracting, I avow every sentence in my Narrative, founded on the phrase, "implicated in treasonable or seditious practices"; and I repeat my charge, that "he who dictated the minute, in which it is contained, so far as I am concerned, dictated a falsehood; that the clerk who recorded it, recorded a falsehood; and that the Synod, while they retain it in their records, uncontradicted and uncancelled, are the fosterfathers of a falsehood."

...

Leaving this, to me disagreeable discussion, to the decision of the only competent tribunal, and universally acknowledged as such, I feel called upon to exculpate myself from the charge of *misusing* this same word "implicated", in which Dr. Black seems *modestly* confident that I have intangled myself. Though

---

* "Nor was meant." Let this phrase be remembered.
** "Imputation", not suspicion. Does the Doctor mean that this word has the same *meaning* as "implication" and "suspicion", which he and his Committee have treated as synonimous?—or of either? At this rate, *any* word may be used to dennote *all* things; and *all* words the *same* thing.

his words are numerous, from a sense of their importance, as exhibiting an instructive example of luminous criticism, I shall transcribe them all. "The word itself, is susceptible of different meanings. A writer of great name [Dr. Johnson, BC.], explains it by *embarrassed*; but that it does not necessarily denote a declaration of *guilty*, I will prove, and I trust, to the satisfaction of Dr. Dickson himself, on the authority of a writer, of whom, I know, he entertains a very high opinion, and whose taste, as a critic, and master of words, he will be unwilling to dispute. If he will have the goodness to turn to page 215, of his *own work*, he will find the obnoxious term which has given him so much torment, applied to 'examinations', in which he was *implicated*. I presume he means, named, or charged—for he will scarcely say, that he was *guilty* of *examinations*. But let him explain his own language, or that of his informant, as he may; I must protest for myself, and my brethren*, who composed the synod of 1799, against the application of a meaning which was never intended, and against a charge of having pronounced a ** *judicial* sentence without inquiry, and without evidence."

Another instance of the inoffensive sense in which this word may be used, will be found in Narrative, page 47, where the author complains of the "eagerness with which every word of his was laid hold of, which, even by *implication*, could possibly lead to his inculpation."

Thus Dr. Black has written, and I have no doubt, that presenting myself as a hypercritic, that is, "a critic of Dr. Black's criticism", may be deemed presumption. Yet, I feel myself called on to enter upon the office.

This I do with alarming apprehensions, as I feel myself obliged to dissent from him at the very outset. He says: "the word itself is susceptible of different meanings." I do not pretend to say, either what *words*, or those who use them, are susceptible, or *capable* of. Some of the latter seem *capable* of any thing. But this I say, that a word, *susceptible* of different meanings, is a very dangerous word, and ought to be avoided in speech and writing. It is true, a word, when combined with others, may convey ideas of very different objects. Thus we say, "a good Minister, a good horse, a good man", &c. Here ideas very different are presented to the mind: yet that difference does not arise from the *susceptibility* of the word *good*, but from the noun with which it is connected. In each, it signifies fitness for, willingness to discharge, and performance of, the offices for which it was intended. In like manner, the word "implicated", and every other word, except a noun, (name of a thing,) may, in a phrase, convey a different idea, while its own *meaning* continues the same.

On the same principle, which obliges me to differ from the *learned* Doctor here, I perfectly agree with him that the word "implicated" does not *necessarily*

* "Protest for his Brethren! For the meaning of their words too! Will Dr. Black protest that they did not pronounce an *injudicial* sentence, &c."
* Why "judicial" again? (see the preceding note.) And, how could I charge Dr. Black and his brethren with pronouncing a *judicial* sentence, in a case where I have denied that they had any right to sit in judgment?

denote a declaration of *guilty*, (perhaps the Dr. means, "does not imply guilt".) This was never alleged, or even *supposed* by any man, so far as I know. On this I presume to remark that I have not *misused* the word "implicated", in either of the cases which he has quoted. In the former, my words are, "On reading it to a friend, he asked whether I did not know of other *examinations*, before the Secret Committees, in which I was *implicated*. I answered in the negative. He then told me, that, though he had not seen their reports, he could assure me that they contained a long examination, &c. in which my NAME was *introduced*; adding, that if I passed it unnoticed, it might be concluded that it contained information against me, which I could not refute, and therefore dared not to meet."

Here my friend explained his own idea of implication, not as being *guilty of examinations*, but *charged with guilt*, in the information which they contained, and which, if not refuted, would leave the *stigma* of treason and sedition on my name. The propriety of this explanation, I presume, no man, the *critical* Doctor excepted, will deny. Nor do I suppose another would be found, who would maintain, that a charge of implication in practices treasonable and seditious, meant, that the persons implicated were guilty of making the charge, or any thing else than that they were charged with treason and sedition. In short, to be implicated in suspicion of guilt, is *to be suspected*—to be implicated in a charge, is *to be charged*—and to be implicated in the *practice* of any thing criminal, is to be *guilty* of the *crime*.

The second instance of my alleged misuse of the word, "implicated", taken notice of by the Rev. Critic, requires no vindication; yet is not unworthy of some notice. A military captain was sent from Newtownards to Portaferry, and afterwards to Downpatrick, to demand my authority for having said, that "a party of the black horse had gone over to the Insurgents", as this was distorted into an attempt to "originate or foment" sedition. This gave occasion to my words, quoted partially by Dr. Black; and, I presume, "proves with what eagerness every word of mine was laid hold of, which could possibly lead to my inculpation"; i.e. to charge me with being engaged in treasonable and seditious practices; and also, my having used the word properly, as signifying, *"interference not expressed, but tacitly inculcated".*

Notwithstanding all these, the Doctor affected to produce evidence, that the meaning attached to the phrase, "implicated, &c." in 1812, was the *common* popular meaning, &c. In "Substance", page 23, he writes thus:

> "That it conveyed no other meaning to the members present, is *evident* from this, that it passed without observation or objection; yet that meeting was attended by *four* Ministers, who had suffered a temporary imprisonment, but who felt no imputation cast upon them by the minute; (one of *them* had been tried on a capital charge, by a court martial, in Belfast, and acquitted.)"

Here is Dr. Black's *evidence*. Because these four did not object to the minute, and felt no imputation cast upon them, he asserts, that this makes it *evident*, that "implicated" conveyed no other meaning, than that some members of the Synod lay under the imputation of being concerned in the excesses of the preceding year. Let me intreat the impartial reader, to examine the Doctor's *evidence*—to inquire if these four Ministers are comprised in this minute. If they are not comprised in it, or in the slightest manner alluded to, then his *evidence* serves the purpose of convicting himself of *misrepresentation*. It appears, that the implicated members of Synod are described here, in five classes, placed at the time in different situations. 1st. "A Minister and Probationer, who had been executed." 2d. "Two still in confinement." These four are not alluded to in any of these classes. 3. "Some who have expressed their sincere contrition." But as these four did not express contrition, this cannot apply to them; and, if they had done so, they could not object to the minute, as contrition is an acknowledgement of guilt. But the *penitents*, whoever they may have been, should have objected to the word, if it had not conveyed the meaning of *actual guilt*; in that case, their expression of contrition was false.

The 4th class is, "Others no longer connected with the Synod". This could not include the four who *had* been prisoners in 1799, as they were then a component part of the Synod. The fifth class consists of those, who had voluntarily, or by permission of Government, removed from the kingdom. Therefore Dr. Black might as well have said, that when he wrote that minute in the Committee, he felt *no imputation* cast upon *himself*, and *did not object* to it, and this would have been as good *evidence* as that which he has produced. The words of the minute are, "that the comparatively small number *who have been* implicated", (that is, *confined and suspected*, according to Dr. Black.) Now is it not plain, that these four were a part of those who *had been* confined and suspected, yet no notice is taken of them—no mention of *some that are now liberated*, which would have made a sixth class. And when this class is omitted, the minute does not contain a true report of all those that *had been confined* and *suspected*; which is an additional proof that this never was the meaning attached to this phrase by Dr. B. and his Committee. If the words of the minute had been the small number who *are now* implicated, it might have afforded the Dr. a *pretext* for the meaning, which he has given to the phrase; but the sentence would have been absolute nonsense, to have connected those that had been executed with those that are *still confined* and suspected. And what puts it beyond all doubt, if any doubt should still remain, that those four were not included in the minute, is, that it is made out, in consequence of the reports of the several presbyteries. But the names of the four are *not reported* by their respective presbyteries, as may be seen by examining the Synod's records. So much for Dr. Black's *evidence*, that "implicated" in treasonable or seditious practices, did not mean engaged in, or *guilty* of, treason and sedition; for if it did, he, as *one of those who met and composed the minute in* 1799, *would not venture to seek society among men of honour.*

Here I take leave of this point, with a plain question, which the public will answer according to their own judgment: Is my charge against the Synod of Ulster, of "passing upon me a sentence of *guilty*, as a traitor; and (unless it had clearer evidence of my guilt than Government could procure) with falsehood in its minute of 1799", a groundless aspersion? Or is it not?

[Pages 3 to 16.]

*

...

Though the following passage is of little consequence to me, or any body else, I think it deserves some notice, merely as it shows this *good* Doctor's propensity, not only to hunt for *vile* motives, but, by "gross misrepresentation", to suggest their existence, where nobody else ever suspected them to be *concealed*.

Page 8. "In 1810, the Catholic question assumed an appearance of more than ordinary interest".——"It created much bustle among minor adventurers, who attached themselves to the Catholics, on the trading principle, 'of using them as a party.' At the close of this year, Dr. Dickson notified his intention of giving to the world, a history of his persecutions by Government and the Synod, to be published by SUBSCRIPTION; which, by particular *management*, to be noticed hereafter, made its appearance in May last."

That the Catholic question assumed an *appearance* of great interest in 1810, is very true. And, that it always possessed a *real intrinsic interest*, equally great, is not less true.—It is a question, in which, not only *Irish Catholics*, but every individual of the human kind, *even the Anti-Catholic petitioner*, has an equal interest.—A question, "of so great dignity, and such paramount importance," that the "ablest statesmen," and "minor adventurers," do equal honor to themselves, and justice to their common nature by "attaching themselves to the Catholics, and facilitating the attainment of the object of their pursuit."

That I am a *minor* adventurer in their cause, (though not as a hawker or auctioneer of mere professions,) I proudly acknowlege. That I am *only* a minor in abilities, I deeply regret. But, that my attachment and minor exertions commenced in 1810, I do not acknowledge. I had the honor to embark in the cause, four years before Dr. Black first distinguished himself, in 1782, at the memorable meeting in Dungannon, by a speech that excited the admiration, and commanded the esteem, of the most enlightened and liberal minds in Ireland; and particularly of her Volunteer patriots—the only protectors of her coasts, the guardians of *her* rights, and of Britain's safety; and what proved more useful to the Doctor, it procured him the ardent friendship of Robert Moore (the Doctor must remember him,) the *notice* of the Earl of Bristol, and, through them, the pastorship of the congregation of Londonderry. In my *minor* attempts to promote the Catholic claims, I was so animated by the *zeal* of imitating, not *emulating*, the Doctor, that I have hitherto persevered in my puny efforts; and all that I regret, is, that I was so far his inferior in abilities. In 1792, when the Doctor's zeal fell below ebullient heat, *my* heart retained its animating glow, my tongue continued to prate, and my pen to scribble, at the hazard of my liberty and of my life. I even *prostituted* my pulpit to "scripture politics," not by *three*, but by *ten times three* sermons, during that, and the succeeding year. In the last of the three sermons, published under the "quaint and irreverent" title of "Scripture politics," I pledged myself to "stand erect and firm, as

---

Scripture politics —Black commented that Dickson's congregation had been "accustomed to hear from the pulpit what has been quaintly and irreverently termed *scripture politics*, instead of the mild and peaceful doctrines of the gospel" (Substance, p30).

an iron pillar, or wall of brass, to declare the truths of the bible, and enforce my people's duty, while God shall vouchsafe me understanding to know, a heart to feel, and a tongue to express them." That pledge I have not yet forfeited. To preserve it safe, I have hitherto acted with uniformity, under various and threatening discouragements; and so long as I live, I shall continue to exert all the powers with which God, in his goodness, shall continue to favour me, for the same purpose.

[Pages 51/2.]

*

...

Page 39. "Doctor Dickson complains that he has been injured by the minutes of this Synod, which hold him out to the world as a Traitor and a Rebel. I will put his sincerity to the trial—Let him stand up in his place, and DECLARE SOLEMNLY, that he was not concerned in originating, fomenting, or fostering the rebellion of 1798, and I will move that his disavowal be recorded in your minutes."

Here the Doctor resigns the character of Vindicator of the Synod, and resumes that of *political inquisitor.* Several members were sensible of this at the time. One gentleman *asked* the Doctor, *if he was about to convert the Synod* into a *court of inquisition.* Others exclaimed that *no such question should be answered.* And one even dared to *irreverently* ask him, if he had never done any thing in his political career, which could be called "originating, fomenting, &c."* The Doctor gravely, and with some emotion, replied; "that he had not done any thing to *foster or foment,* &c." It was noticed, that he left out the word, "originate".—The Doctor sat down. But, even supposing the supreme ecclesiastical judicatory of the Presbyterian church, in Ulster, to have been transformed into a court of *political inquisition*, may I not presume to ask, to what purpose should I declare, whether I was concerned in the rebellion; and Dr. Black move that my disavowal be recorded in the Synod's

---

* What might be here alluded to, I dare not hazard a conjecture. Some may think, to his display of zeal and abilities, in 1782. Others suppose, to an *infamous* report, that he had been an active circulator of *Pain's Rights of Man.* And others still may suspect, that allusion might be intended to a *violent fama clamosa*, about a then patriotic captain of volunteers having preached in uniform, with the sword on the pulpit before him. Of these suspicions, the Doctor, no doubt, *"purged himself by a solemn disavowal".*

---

circulator of Pain's Rights Of Man —I have no independent evidence that Black was a Tom Paine enthusiast before swinging around to the opposite political extreme as part of the Mount Stewart entourage (see Introductory Note to Chapter 4), but even without Dickson's footnote I would have assumed that he was. In the Volunteer period he revelled in military display. He was a delegate to the Volunteer Conventions at Dungannon in 1782 and 1783. As Minister at Dromore he preached in regimental uniform, resting his Bible on a drumhead. His performance at the 1783 Volunteer Convention attracted the notice and the patronage of Frederick Augustus Hervey, Earl of Bristol and Bishop of Derry. Through the influence of the Earl Bishop he gained a ministerial position in Derry and a social position amongst the essentially agnostic Whig aristocracy.

minutes, if the minutes of Synod did not previously contain a sentence of guilty against me? None, that I can conceive. Or what purpose could the Synodical record of such disavowal serve? Dr. Black did not even insinuate that *he* would believe it. Perhaps some *hostile* spirit might have been tempted to hold it out to the world, as an addition to that burthen of falsehoods, with which he has attempted not only to load, but press me down.—I feel surprised at the Doctor's call for declaration, under such circumstances, and at such a time.—After every information which could be purchased by money, or extorted from fear, had been procured in vain; after Dr. Black had *studied* the reports of Lords and Commons; (by *mistake* so called,) after he had honored my "innocent, abominable" book, with two perusals; and, no doubt, been as zealously active, previous to the last meeting of Synod, as he was during his scientific and salutiferous tour to * Burncranagh, before the exposure of his Substance in public.—After all these efforts to collect and establish evidence of my guilt; and what is still more, after what I have called, and shall yet call, a sentence of *guilty* had been pronounced, and allowed to stand against me in the Synod's records, for *thirteen years*.—I say, after all these things, I was surprised, on being called upon to declare, whether I was *guilty*.—A question, I believe, never proposed in any court, after sentence passed and executed, as far as the court dared to usurp the power of inflicting punishment.

Surprised as I was, at the proposal of this declaration, it will not be wondered at, that I should be more than surprised, at the *solemn* manner in which it was to be made. A *solemn declaration* is all that a Presbyterian judicatory can demand, so far as I know, in place of what, in law, is called an *oath*; and, I trust, every Presbyterian considers it as equally binding.

The sequel of this paragraph is still more surprising. In it he seems to have fallen into a trance, or been ballooned into the regions of unembodied sound, and unsubstantial phantom. There he conceived himself vested with the office of *gaoler* or *executioner* in addition to those of *informer*, public accuser, Attorney-general, and supreme judge in matters of state; and must have seen, or imagined that he saw a spectre or spectres, about to rescue from his jaws the victim of his "zeal". The Doctor's words are strong and expressive. "Here Dr. Black paused, and *some voice said*," (not a respectable member of the Synod said, but a VOICE said,) "no man should be called on to *criminate* himself." Dr. Black resumed; "No, Moderator, *he shall not escape so.*" Escape from what? Not from punishment, or self-crimination, which might incur punishment—but from a *pressing invitation to declare his*

* During that time his inquiries in the County of Antrim were intrusted to a missionary. In Portaferry, he made them by letter; and, through the other parts of the County of Down, I do not know how, or by whom they were conducted. That they were made, I have no doubt, from what a friend wrote to me on the subject. He says that "great pains had been lately taken in that County, to collect information against me, for *political* offences, even before 98."

innocence. "I do not call on him," says the Doctor, "to *criminate* himself—I do not ask him to avow *guilt*—I invite him to declare his *innocence.*"*

Of my declining the Doctor's kind invitation, he writes thus: "Dr. Dickson said, in a low voice, and *without rising*, (disrespectful enough,) 'It was *unnecessary* to declare his innocence, as nobody could prove him guilty,' or to that effect."

There is a considerable *abbreviation* here, which may occasion a misconception of my words. These were, as nearly as I can recollect: "I am astonished at such a proposal. What end could such a declaration serve? Or to what purpose would it be recorded in your minutes? Even Dr. Black has not said that he would believe it. I will make no such declaration. If any man has a doubt of my innocence let him prove me guilty."

Here I feel impelled, once more, to ask: What had Dr. Black, his Committee, and *respectable young members* of the Synod, to do with this? Was the reputation of the body, in any way, affected by, or suffering under the *imputation* of, any treasonable expressions or practices, either proved or charged against me? Even if they were, where was, and whence came, their commission to hold a *political* inquest, usurp the seat of a court martial, pronounce a sentence of guilty, and

---

* "In Scotland, when there is a violent *fama clamosa* against a man—though there be no proof of guilt—he must purge himself by a solemn disavowal, before his is admitted to *communion.*" *Sub. p.*40.

The Doctor must certainly mean the "Church of Scotland", in this note. Does that church, in any of its judicatories, take cognizance of *clamorous reports* of treason and rebellion, or of other crimes against the state? has any court in Scotland, or any other country, ever called upon any man to purge himself, by a solemn declaration, either where there was or was not proof of guilt produced against him? No. The fact is, that when reports prevail of offences which disturb the peace of families, injure the character of individuals, or bring scandal on religion, but which do not generally admit of proof, being committed in secret, in order to restore peace, vindicate the character, and remove scandal, the church of Scotland requires such purgation; and as in such cases, the refusal is not only an acknowlegement of guilt, but an act of injustice to the persons injured, the accused is excommunicated. But where proof is supposed attainable, though not produced, no such purgation is required.

Even supposing this note to bear on me, it does not bear on me alone, in the Synod of Ulster. Many years ago, a majority of that Body were pronounced rebels, not only by individuals in their writings, but by the houses of Parliament; I mean those who were Colonels, Captains, and Chaplains in the Volunteer army, among whom Dr. Black was one of the most able and eloquent advocates for parliamentary reform, and Catholic emancipation. Did the Synod resolve that these men were implicated in treason and sedition? did they suspend their bounties because Government suspected them of, and Parliament charged them with, being so; or did Dr. Black and brother officers *purge* themselves by a solemn declaration? No. The Synod, it is true, *expelled* one of their members, for appearing in the house in military dress; but he no sooner returned in his proper habiliments, (having cast off the badges of his suspected treason in the inn where he lodged,) than, with a moderation becoming their character, they restored him to *communion.*

transmit it to the castle of the representatives of Majesty for confirmation? Such is not to be found, as far as I know, in the all-perfect MAGNA CHARTA of the christian constitution, or any existing code of ecclesiastical law—even in Spain or Portugal. And no special commission, by letter patent, or any other document under his Majesty's seal has yet been produced. Of consequence it must be implicated in the indefinite words, "his Majesty's service, and good of the kingdom;" or supposed to be agreed on by *secret treaty* in the protracted *negociations*, which preceded the *more wise* and liberal arrangement of bounty, in 1803. Be this as it may, the case is not only complicated, but nearly singular. The prosecution commenced in a court merely ecclesiastical, and confined itself to charges of misrepresenting and slandering the Ministers of the church. In a short time these were blended with allegations of political guilt, and implication in practices treasonable and seditious. These were transmitted to the Government, in language which conveyed the idea of a sentence of *guilty*; the prosecutors having usurped the character of judges. When these allegations were—or rather when *this sentence* was—transmitted, what member of Government—what man, whose *understanding was superior to that of an infant*, could suppose that Government would not attend to the information, and follow the example, of this ecclesiastico-political judicatory, by making a *strict inquiry into the conduct* of the persons condemned, and *distinguishing impartially between the innocent and the guilty*, as might *appear* just and wise upon *stricter* inquiry, and more mature deliberation? After these communications by *Dr. Black*, what man, except *Dr. Black*, could ask, "Will it be thought that the Government of this country would search the minutes of this Synod for directions how to treat their prisoners?"*
I ask further, what inveterate faction among men, except that of the Doctor and his Committee, could be supposed capable, not only of persevering in their charges, but hunting after new matter of charge,** against an individual, for many years after Government had fully and honorably acquitted him of the crimes imputed to him? These questions I leave every man to answer according to his own judgment.

...

[Pages 60-63.]

---

* *Sub. p.* 25.
** The Doctor candidly tells his readers that Government were not *uninformed* of my settlement; and hints that he could tell whether, and how far, my being Minister operated for or against the inclusion of the congregation of Keady, in the more wise and liberal arrangements of 1803. Why did he withhold information, on this point, from the Synod, in 1812? *Sub. p.* 31.

[Epilogue

At the 1813 meeting of the Synod, held at Cookstown on June 29th, it was resolved "that in the minute of 1799, the phrase 'implicated in treasonable or seditious practices', as applied to two of its members then in confinement, was inaccurately used, inasmuch as it appears to be liable to an unfavourable construction respecting them".

Though the Belfast News Letter had given a full report of the 1812 proceedings against Dickson, it did not report this vindication of Dickson's criticism of the 1899 Synod by the 1813 Synod. In fact, I have been able to discover no mention in the News Letter of the 1813 Synod. It seems that, rather than report what the Editor considered bad news, it preferred to carry no news at all.

It was also resolved by the Synod of 1813: "that this Synod regrets that the Synod of 1805 dismissed without an answer, a memorial presented to them by Dr. Dickson, requiring them to declare whether the expression 'implicated in treasonable or seditious practices' in the minute of 1799, alluded to him, & if so, what was the meaning attached to it."

(According to the minutes of the 1805 Synod: "A memorial from the Rev. William Steel Dickson, D.D., requiring the Synod to declare explicitely 'whether or no he is alluded to in a part of the minute of 1799, which has been construed into a reflexion on his character, as a man "implicated in treasonable or seditious practices", and if so, to explain what they then meaned by being implicated in "practices treasonable or seditious",' was presented to the Synod. It was unanimously resolved to dismiss this memorial.")

Following the adoption of these resolutions, this further motion was moved:

"Moved that a charge preferred at our last meeting, by Dr. Black & Mr. Thomson of Carnmoney against Dr. Dickson, of having grossly violated truth & decency, in an account given by him of a discussion which took place at a meeting of Synod in the year 1799 relative to the exclusion of Mrs. Porter from the Widows' fund, has not been substantiated.

"On this motion the previous question was put and carried.

"Against the previous question on this motion, Mr. Porter & others signified their intention to protest & to assign their reasons in due time.

"Moved that this Synod does not consider itself responsible for the Book published since our last by Dr. Black, entitled 'Substance etc.'

"Dr. Black rose and declared that he took the whole responsibility of that publication on himself, on which the motion was withdrawn".

At the concluding session the protest against the moving of the previous question was entered by twenty-two ministers, including Henry Montgomery, and ten Elders. The "Mrs. Porter" in question was the widow of the Rev. James Porter of Greyabbey, who was hanged in 1798. The matter of her pension will be dealt with in the selection of Porter's writings to be published as a companion to this volume.

(All quotations given above are from the official record, as printed in **Records Of The General Synod Of Ulster From 1691 To 1820**, published by the Presbyterian General Assembly in three volumes between 1890 and 1898.)

Dr. Black's influence over the Presbyterians declined sharply after 1813.

The moving spirits in the establishment of the Belfast Academical Institution were United Irish survivors. It was opened in 1814, despite the hostility of Dr. Black and his colleague, Dr. Bruce, the Arian headmaster of the Belfast Royal Academy. In 1815, when Black was absent from the Synod due to illness, it adopted a resolution approving Inst as a college for training Presbyterian Ministers. Though a Government grant made to the College was withdrawn (for "disloyalty"), in 1816, the Synod in 1816 and 1817 rejected motions by Black to cancel the 1815 resolution of approval. As consolation, a public dinner was given for him in Belfast in 1817, but it was not a success. On December 4th of that year he committed suicide by throwing himself off Derry Bridge into the River Foyle.]

Chapter Seven

Last Sermons

[Introduction

Steel Dickson's last publication was a book of Sermons issued in 1817:

SERMONS
BY
WILLIAM STEEL DICKSON, D.D.
Early in Life,
PRESBYTERIAN MINISTER OF BALLYHALBERT,
AND AFTERWARDS OF PORTAFERRY, IN THE COUNTY OF DOWN;
And latterly
OF KEADY, IN THE COUNTY OF ARMAGH.

———

BELFAST:
PRINTED BY JOSEPH SMYTH,
34, HIGH-STREET.

————

1817

These final sermons are not of the "Scripture Politics" kind. They are purely religious reflections, and are in the spirit which was prevalent in Glasgow University fifty years earlier when Dickson came under the influence of William Leechman, about whom a word would not be out of place here.

Leechman's father, a farmer of Lanarkshire, had in 1684 taken down the quartered body of Robert Bailie of Jerviswood from the Tollbooth of Lanark, where it had been put on display by orders of the Government, and given it to the Bailie family for burial. Bailie, who had opposed illegal arrests by the Government, was himself arrested in 1683 and accused of involvement in the Rye House Plot (which I have described in **Derry And The Boyne**). He was held for twenty months without trial, as no witnesses could be got to swear against him. On December 24th, 1684, when he was close to death after a long illness, he was tried for conspiracy against the life of the King (Charles II), convicted, hanged, beheaded, and quartered all in the course of an afternoon. He started to make a speech on the scaffold, but was cut off by drum rolls. His body was put on public display to impress the public with the power of Government, but was cut down by William Leechman, senior.

In return for this service, the Bailie family helped William Leechman, junior, to attend Edinburgh University. On graduating, Leechman worked for a while as private tutor in a family which spent part of the year in Glasgow. While in Glasgow, he attended the lectures given by Francis Hutcheson of Co. Down. Later he became Minister at Beith (Presbytery of Paisley).

In 1741, he preached to the Synod of "Glasgow and Air" on **The Temper, Character, And Duty Of A Minister Of The Gospel.** The sermon was issued as a pamphlet and became very popular in the "Scottish Enlightenment". I quote a passage from it as being entirely applicable to Steel Dickson:

> "...is it not matter of wonder and astonishment, how it should come about, that we, who believe, we who inculcate it upon others, that there is almighty Power, infinite wisdom and perfect goodness at the head of the Universe, perpetually presiding over it..., is it not, I say, very amazing, that by this belief our souls are not raised into a perpetual transport of joy and wonder...

"But let none conclude from what is said, that it is the duty of a minister of the gospel to devote his whole life to contemplation, to retire from the world and to maintain as little converse with mankind as an Hermit shut up in his cell. By no means. The most perfect character of a teacher of true religion is, that of one who lives among mankind, converses with them, and at the same time retains as much purity of mind, and discovers as entire disengagement of heart from the world, as if he were entirely separated from it. For such a man is fitted to moderate the desires of worldly things in the rest of mankind, to lower their high notions of the excellence and happiness which they imagine arise from the possession and enjoyment of them, and to display the superior worth and importance of these things which are spiritual and divine: That this is the proper character of a teacher of true religion,is very evident: for this was the character of Jesus" (pp16/18).

Leechman was elected Professor of Divinity at Glasgow University in 1743. But the Presbytery of Glasgow declined to enrol him because an allegation of heresy was raised against a sermon he preached on **The Nature, Reasonableness And Advantages Of Prayer**, which was also issued as a pamphlet.

Answering an objection to prayer as petition, on the ground that God, being omniscient, did not need to be told of the needs of an individual, Leechman said: "the design of prayer is not to inform God of things he did not know before. The real design of prayer is, in the first place, to express, under a lively impression of the presence of God, the sense we have of our dependence upon him" (p13). And, secondly, "to express, under an actual sense of the presence of God, our earnest desires of having all those sentiments and pious dispositions, which it is possible for us to entertain and cultivate, considered as dependent, reasonable, social and guilty creatures" (p15).

To the objection that God acts out of his own infinite wisdom and will not be caused to act by human importunity, Leechman replied: "Prayer only works its effect upon *us*; it contributes to change the temper of our minds" (p17).

In answering these philosophical objections to prayer, Leechman was felt by some, whose impulse was more simply theological, to be eroding the framework of Christianity. But the Synod of Glasgow and Ayr investigated the matter and judged that the sermon was not heretical, and this judgment was confirmed by the General Assembly. Leechman took up his post as Professor of Divinity, became Moderator of the General Assembly in 1757, and was Principal of the University from 1761 until his death in 1785.

The ground of Dickson's Christianity was formed in Glasgow under Leechman's influence, and Dickson's mind blossomed on that ground. Leechman was the innovator and educator, and that is why he is interesting. I looked through his own sermons, but nothing in them caught my eye. Leechman was the gardener: Dickson is the garden.

I imagine that Dickson had the Seceders in mind when composing Sermon XIII. An account of the rise of the Seceders will be found in the selection of writings of Thomas Ledlie Birch to be published shortly.]

Sermon I

The Goodnss, Mercy, And Truth Of God, The Foundations Of Public Praise And Thanksgiving

"Enter into his gates with thanksgiving, and into his courts with praise; be thankful unto him, and bless his name:
For the Lord is good; his mercy is everlasting, and his truth to all generations."
PSALM c. 4,5

...

...Matter is insensible and inactive. It is no more capable of self-direction, self-motion, or self-preservation, than of self creation. Hence the agency of divine power, and the direction of divine wisdom, by the operation of established laws, are as necessary to preserve and govern, as to give it being... It is by the unerring conduct of his hand, that the orbs of Heaven perform their revolutions; that the earth is balanced in her course, and returning seasons repeat their numerous gifts...

The same kind direction is equally observable through all the families of the brute creation. Every individual, as soon as produced to light, is guided by an unerring instinct to its proper food and residence; and, as soon as necessary, the use of the arms which nature has provided for its defence, or the annoyance of an enemy. In these respects, "the Lord is good to all: his tender mercies are over all his works: and his bounty is extended to every living thing."

Man is the only inhabitant of this world to which this unerring instinct is denied, and from which these means of safety are, in a great measure, witholden. He comes into the world the most helpless of creatures. For many years he depends on the care and protection of others. When left to himself, he hath no better guide than partial observation, precarious reasoning, or rash conjecture; and in the choice of his food, he is often obliged to follow the beasts of the field, and fowls of the air. Yet, even this long dependence and defect of instinct, with whatever immediate inconvenience they may be attended to him, serve many valuable purposes, and afford striking proofs of the divine goodness. The former gives birth to those kind affections between parents and children, brothers and sisters, which grow up with years and sweeten life; and to those social connexions which unite man to man, and family to family, in a compact body, whose combined powers enable him to repel individual attack, surmount difficulty, accomplish arduous enterprise with ease, and crown it with success. The latter renders the attention necessary for his support and safety as an animal, beneficial to him in his higher character of a rational being. It leads directly to studious inquiry, acute observation, rational discussion, correct judgment, and improvement of all the intellectual powers; and consequently, by a gradual enlargement and elevation of the mind, he becomes sensible of his own dignity, enters upon studies and pursuits worthy of his origin, and perseveres in them, till, by the knowledge of the "visible things" which God has made, he rises to that of "things invisible"; even his eternal power, the wisdom of his counsels, the goodness of his intentions, and happy effects of his gracious government. Hence he becomes sensible of his dependence and obligations, conscious of duties arising from them, and by the performance of them recovers his original likeness of God, in knowledge, righteousness, and true holiness; and the enjoyment of that inborn happiness, of which they are the source.

When we consider these as the effects of that temporary dependence, weakness, and defective instinct under which man struggles, we may see that their evils are compensated by the advantages arising from that attention which his safety and support jointly require, and the consequent exercise and improvement of his mind to which it leads. But judge of his as we may, he has no cause of murmur or complaint. "Goodness and mercy continually accompany him", and the same kind hand "which feeds the ravens, and leads the wild asses to streams of water in the wilderness", supports in him the tender principles of youthful being; supplies his wants; conducts him in safety, amidst dangers, difficulties and snares, to full maturity; and thence upholds his declining age under all its infirmities, till death extinguishes the lamp of life.

That the spacious field which I have thus faintly sketched, teems with the bounties of heaven, and liberally supplies the means of support and happiness to every order of animated beings which inhabits it, and consequently affords matter of praise to every spirit endowed with understanding to perceive, and reason to trace, characters of excellence, cannot be doubted; and when we attend to the superior advantages which man derives from the arrangement and government of the whole, and the happiness for which he is indebted to them, we can as little doubt, that on a due consideration of them, he would perceive and feel, from the constitution of his nature, not only an obligation, but a sentimental impulse, to expressions of gratitude.

Yet, however spacious this field may be—however richly stored with the bounties of Heaven, which contribute to the support and happiness of a fleeting life—and however solid the foundation which they lay for the expression of praise and thanksgiving—it teems with blessings equally conspicuous and infinitely greater to us, as intelligent, rational, religious, and immortal beings. While we are employed in the pursuit, or blessed with the enjoyment of temporary good, mind is called into exercise, and by that exercise it becomes sensible of its own powers and capacities of improvement. Yet, all the records of antiquity which have reached us, lead to the painful conviction, that though, by the exercise of these powers, and the improvement of these capacities—or, perhaps by an original impression, that "every effect presupposes a cause," they concurred in the belief of a God, or gods, by the word of whose power the system of nature was commanded into being, and by whose counsels it is governed, they never attained such a correct and comprehensive knowledge of his works, the end for which they were created, their mutual dependance, the harmonious consent with which they move and act, and the laws by which they are governed, as to form just conceptions of his character, or even the idea of his unity: much less, though all derived and dependent beings owe duty and respect to the Author of their existence, and Dispenser of the blessings in which they rejoice, did they clearly discover what that duty was, or the means by which they might attain and secure his approbation. Hence the candid acknowledgment of the prince of ancient poets, who spoke the language of nature, "that" in respect to these, "the clouds of ignorance and error could never be dispelled from the minds of men, but by the interposition of a divine teacher."

In this acknowledgment, the necessity of a divine revelation is fully admitted, in order to enlighten and expand the human understanding; to unveil the perfections and government of the ONE only living and true God; ascertain the duties of life, by the performance of which his will is done and his favour secured; and unfold prospects of present good and future advantage, for the support and comfort of frail humanity, amidst the temptations, difficulties and dangers through which it must pass, in the pursuit of religious knowledge, the practice of religious virtue, and the path to an happy immortality.

Thanks! eternal thanks to God our Father! who in the exuberance of his goodness, has richly supplied us with revelations of his will, and our duty, "as lights to our feet, and lamps to our path", in or weary wanderings through this wilderness of error, absurdity, vanity, and corruption. I say, "Revelations"; for, in compassion to our weakness, and fatherly attention to our improving powers, and growing capacities of receiving instruction, appreciating its worth, and profiting by it, he hath been graciously pleased, through a long succession of ages, to interpose in our behalf "at sundry times and in different manners", by the ministration of prophets, the mission of angels, and lastly, by those of the early and often predicted Messiah, justly denominated "the Son of his love". The first of these revelations, like a morning dawn shed a faint but cheering light over a part of the intellectual and moral world, enveloped as it was in darkness, and involved in confusion. A brighter and gradually increasing lustre was shed by those who succeeded, till in the "fulness of time" the sun of righteousness arose in mild majesty and unclouded splendor, dissipated the clouds of ignorance, delusion, and blind-led superstition, presented heaven-born truth in her native beauties, clothed righteousness with her lawful authority, and diffused the seeds of live and peace, and joy, over a regenerated world.

Such were the gracious interpositions of Heaven—such the order in which they took place—such the end which they proposed—and such their happy effects in favour of a race wandering in ignorance, misled by error, enslaved by corruption, and laden with sins.

Yet, numerous as these interpositions were, and inestimable the benefits of which they were productive, to those among whom prophets were raised up, to whom angels ministered, or who heard the "words of eternal life, which are able to make wise to salvation those who believe", from the lips of Christ and his apostles, there is something farther to be attended to by us, equally expressive of the goodness of God, and demonstrative of our obligation to "enter his gates with thanksgiving, and his courts with praise". Had these words been recorded only on the tablet of human memory, they would long since have been forgotten, and their gladdening sound would never have reached the ears of us, on whom the latter ages of the world have come; or, if remembered and conveyed to us through the polluted channel of human tradition, they would have been so tainted by the breath of folly, intermingled with the fables of pious ignorance, and misrepresented by the tongue of presumption, impudently pretending to correct and amend them, that their spirit would have been lost, their power broken, and their end defeated. This, however, hath been happily prevented by the provident kindness of our gracious Lord. The words of life, pure as they flowed from the lip of inspiration, were faithfully committed to writing, and transfused into the languages of many nations. By the same kindness they have been preserved entire, and, notwithstanding the ravages of time, handed down to us in safety. In the bible, which we revere as the repository of the oracles of God, and statute-book of Heaven, prophets, the Saviour of the world, and his inspired apostles, though long dead, still live, and speak to us in a style plain, expressive, and affecting, the words of unerring wisdom and of life eternal. In it, too, religious services are prescribed, which directly tend to expand the thoughts, elevate the sentiments, and attach the hearts of men to things divine. By the reading and exposition of its contents they are taught the good and acceptable will of God, and the necessity of ding it, that they may enjoy his favour, in which alone they can be happy here or hereafter; and, by the devotional services with which they are accompanied, they are formed to the temper, raised to the dignity, and prepared for the society and joys of Heaven's first-born, the spirits of the just made perfect, and the angels of God.

...

Sermon V

Duty Of Preachers To Declare, Fully And Fairly, The Truths Of God, Etc.

"And Micaiah said, As the Lord liveth, what the Lord saith unto me, that will I speak."   I KINGS XXII, 14

...

...More or less of the leaven of prejudice taints every mind; and some favourite opinion will be carried along from system to system, and claim admission in every stage of intellectual improvement. And when nothing else can be offered for its support, it will claim respect for its antiquity, plead its obscurity as its defence, or even rest its certainty on the impossibility of being defined.

This observation is unhappily confirmed from the records of all ages. The dregs of Judaism and heathen philosophy were early poured into the fountain of Christian truth, corrupted its waters, and have run down in its streams even to these remote ages. With these the mind of man has been so shamefully intoxicated, as to mistake the rage of bigotry for zeal, to substitute the opinions of men in place of the wisdom of God, to fortify the faith of the church with fines, prisons, and racks, instead of evidence, argument, and sound reasoning; and, on almost every occasion, to decide religious controversy by the arm of flesh, though no weapon could be fairly admitted, but "the sword of the Spirit, which is the word of God."

When we look through the history of the Christian church, we see a continued succession of scenes marked with blood, devastation, and horror; and the meek, forbearing, and gentle spirit of the gospel, prostrate under the feet of obstinate prejudice, and intemperate zeal. Every seeming innovation, in matter of opinion, alarmed the prevailing sect, and was considered as precluding all claim to lenity, forbearance, and charity.

In such situations as these, we can hardly fail to perceive the painful state of a mind animated with the love of truth, and desirous of promoting its interests. To restrain such a mind from inquiry, is the most irksome tyranny; to indulge it, doubly dangerous. If any thing new, however important, is discovered, if inconsistent with popular prejudice, it must either be published at the risk of poverty and persecution, or concealed, at the expence of a good conscience, and the favour of God. While this is the case, the progress of religious knowledge must be, at best, extremely slow. The base, degenerate, and selfish, will seek only to please by flattering opinion at the expence of truth; the indolent will go smoothly on in the beaten track, rather than submit to the fatigue of inquiry—and the remaining few will be able to do but little, from the popular cry which is always excited by those whose "trade is endangered", by the breaking in of truth; and who are always ready to take shelter behind excommunications, penal statutes, or the sword of magistracy, which hath been so often drawn to "do God service" by oppression and murder.

Should it be said that these shocking scenes are the exhibitions of other times; and that a milder spirit hath gone forth, than that under whose influence they were acted; we shall readily acknowledge the truth of the observation. That God, we have been long free from the scourge of direct persecution; and, if we may judge from some late instances of national liberality, the day is fast approaching when the public modes and expression of religion will be as free from the restraints of human laws, as the sentiments of the heart, from which they proceed.

But, taking it for granted that all this was fully accomplished; are we to imagine that all opposition to truth and reformation would be at an end, and that the world would act as under the influence of wisdom, and judge of doctrines merely from the evidence adduced to support them? If we indulge such thoughts, we will certainly be mistaken. Experience uniformly declares that such a part has never been acted; and probability intimates that it never will. Though men have ever encouraged public teachers, and supported them at considerable expence, they seem willing to allow that they have neither prejudice to remove, error to correct, nor vice to reform. All they wish for, in general, or will bear with patience, is to hear a continual change of old words, endless genealogies, and unfathomable mysteries, rung in their ears. The man who teaches what has been long believed, and deals in general descriptions of virtue and happiness, which every one is ready to apply to himself, or of vice and misery, which never fails to suit a neighbour or acquaintance; or who paints human nature in such gloomy colours and ungainly attitude, that when the piece is produced as a standard of truth, the most abandoned finds himself an angel of light, upon comparison, seldom fails of popular applause. But he who brings forth from the treasures of knowledge "things new as well as old"—who opposes the current of established opinion, however erroneous, and boldly attacks vice in its almost impregnable strongholds, often finds his best endeavours to inform to inform the understanding attributed to impertinence, and his reforming zeal to pride or depravity of heart.

From these facts, which even at this day, are but too notorious, we may easily see, how difficult it is to serve the world faithfully, in its most important concerns; and we may see, also, that the difficulties generally arise from the very quarter, from which every possible encouragement should be derived. "The

Prophets not only prophesy falsely, but the people love to have it so."

It must be allowed, indeed, that among us, the horrors of persecution are greatly softened; but, while ever a man is in danger of suffering in his reputation or circumstances, on account of mere opinion, his proneness to inquiry will be checked, and the activity of his mind greatly abated; and even the knowledge which he hath attained, will be communicated with much hesitation, lest he forfeit the means of his support, or the favour of those from whom they are derived. How much, then, must he be enfeebled in his resolution that "what the Lord saith unto him, that will he speak!" and, as his efforts abate, ignorance will gradually thicken, like the evening shades, till the gloom of night shall envelop all; and the people of God will be poisoned with absurdity, or left to wander in the gloom of mental darkness, and "perish thro' lack of knowledge."

From all these things taken together, it is evident that the difficulties attending the discharge of ministerial duties, are great and many, even now, notwithstanding their importance, and the general concern which men have in them.

It is true, they are not so great or many, but that they may be overcome. It is true, also, that the ministers of the gospel should always "obey god rather than man"; and "speak the truth with all boldness". But is it not equally true, that those to whom they minister should be ever ready to hear "what the Lord hath spoken", and to encourage them freely to declare the whole counsel of God"? To this they are justly entitled, "for their work's sake", independent of every other consideration.   And it is this alone, amidst the weakness of humanity, of which all partake, that can crown with pleasure, what a sense of duty clothes with authority.

Sermon XII

Mystery Not Unintelligible
"In which are some things hard to be understood,which they,
who are unlearned and unstable, wrest, as they do the other scriptures,
to their own destruction."   2 PETER, iii.16.

That a revelation from God, for the declared purpose of instructing mankind, and regulating their conduct should be level to their understanding, is a self evident proposition. So far, therefore, as any thing pretending to be a revelation, is involved in impenetrable obscurity, or rises above comprehension, it forfeits, at once, its claim and character.

However, we are not hence to imagine that all revealed truths are so plain as to be perceived intuitively, or ascertained without inquiry and exercise of the understanding.   This would be a notion as vain and groundless, as the presumption that they rise above the reach of intellect, and exceed the widest grasp of human comprehension.

These two extremes are equally inconsistent with the character of a revelation made for the improvement of reasonable beings; and equally foreign from that of Christianity. While its precepts are plain and easy to be understood, and their propriety and obligation admit of the clearest proof, yet the force of that proof depends on previous apprehensions of God, of our own nature, and the relations in which we are placed. But with such apprehensions, and a very moderate attention, the whole may be understood and adopted, on principles of soundest knowledge.

The same may be said of the doctrines expressing the unchangeable truths, on which these precepts rest, and from which their obligations are deduced. Though it would be presumptuous to pronounce them all *self-evident*, they are reducible to principles, on which our minds repose with the greatest certainty.

In many instances, however, this is not so easy as to preclude the danger of mistake, or prevent the possibility of misrepresentation. But, if the difficulty be not insurmountable—nay, if a moderate share of penetration, knowledge, and honesty, be sufficient to remove it, the intelligibility and reasonableness of Christianity are not affected by it.

The words of our text fairly admit that there are "things hard to be understood, in the writings of Paul, as well as in the other scriptures", and that these were perverted, from their true meaning, "by ignorant and unstable men, to their own destruction".

The use, which hath been made of this acknowledgment, affords a striking instance of its truth. The difficulty, which the apostle admits hath been magnified into an impossibility; and ignorant men have founded a doctrines upon it, that the distinguishing doctrines of the gospel, and the principles on which they rest, are altogether unintelligible. And, as Christ and his apostles have used the word "MYSTERY" they have laid hold of it, affixed to it the idea of something incomprehensible, and held it up as a thick veil, behind which (if we believe them,) divine truth lies hid in impenetrable darkness.

This, however, is an obvious perversion of the apostle's words, by which they are wrested from their plain meaning, and forced to express one totally different. For, though he acknowledges that there are some things "*hard* to be understood", in the writings of Paul, and in the other scriptures, he doth not insinuate, even in the most distant manner, that any of these were so obscure that they *could not possibly be understood*. Nor can such a conclusion be fairly deduced from the facts which he admits.

Were every truth absolutely unintelligible, the discovery or due understanding of which is attended with difficulty, our knowledge would be limited for ever, to those things which are immediately discerned by our external senses, or so evident, that understanding perceives and comprehends them at the first glance. But, we know that this is not the case. We are conscious that we clearly comprehend many things dark, and hard to be understood, to the knowledge of which we have traced our way, by studious application, and laborious inquiry, aided by the instructions of others, who had trodden the same path before us. We know that this is the case, in respect to all the arts, which contribute to the support, comfort, and happiness, of human life, and of all the principles on which they have been cultivated. The practice of the one, and the knowledge of the other, is attained with difficulty, and requires time, thought, and diligent application. Yet, great as these difficulties often are, we never consider the arts as unattainable, or their principles as rising superior to human understanding. The reason is obvious. We know, that though few have studied them, all who possess the ordinary abilities of men, and enjoy the opportunities of instruction, are capable of understanding them.

Of this, a very slight attention to one common case supplies a satisfactory example. Suppose that ye had never seen the letters of the alphabet, or the characters used in arithmetic. Suppose them, for the first time, laid before ye, could ye comprehend, how all the thoughts of the human mind, and all the sentiments of the heart, could be communicated from man to man by the varied combination and arrangements of the former, and that, by the latter, numbers could be calculated, with correctness and precision, almost to infinity? Would not this appear to you a mystery—nay, an absolute impossibility? Yet, ye all know by experience, that a short time, with moderate application, aided by plain instruction, is sufficient to teach men—nay, children—to read, write, and calculate numbers—by reading, to learn what others have known, thought, felt, and done—by writing, to communicate their own ideas and sentiments to the world—and, by the calculation of numbers, to transact business with regularity, extend science, and improve the arts. In these, and all such cases, we clearly distinguish between a thing not understood, or the knowledge of which may be acquired with difficulty, and a thing which rises superior to all knowledge, and all understanding. And, if we thus distinguish in respect of every other subject, why do we exclude the distinction in that of religion? Why argue, that because there are some things in scripture, "hard to be understood", they rise superior to all understanding? This is as unfair in reasoning, as the conclusion, which it is intended to establish, is unfounded in fact.

That revelation contains "mysteries", or, as it is expressed in our text, "things hard to be understood", cannot be denied, without denying the *truth of revelation*. But, that these are not things which cannot be understood—nay, that they are things which may be, and are understood and known, from the information which revelation itself supplies, I shall endeavour to prove.

The first thing to be done, in order to this, is to settle the meaning of the word "mystery", and the sense, in which it is used in scripture. Till this be determined, all reasonings concerning it would be foolish and unmeaning.

Its proper and original meaning may be easily settled, by an attention to the language from which we have borrowed it, and the occasions on which it was used. In that language, it was originally confined to religious matters; and the word, from which it is derived, signifies "to initiate, to instruct in, or introduce to the participation of, religious rites". In these, the heathens observed the greatest secrecy. Every god had his priests, temples, and forms of worship, peculiar to himself. To the common sacrifices, every worshipper was admitted; but there were rites and doctrines, which were confined to a few select votaries, and these generally of the priestly order. In these, so great secrecy was observed, that their celebration was preceded by a solemn proclamation to all those who were not regularly initiated, to keep at a distance. And the intrusion of a profane person, i.e. a person not regularly initiated, was accounted so heinous a crime, that it was punished with instant death, when discovered. That this secrecy might be the less liable to violation, a kind of obscure language was frequently affected; and in some instances, the records of religion were written in characters unknown to the multitude.

But as the persons who were entrusted with these secrets, were subject to mortality, it often became necessary to fill up the places of those removed by death, by the choice and introduction of others. This introduction to the knowledge and participation of these secret rites, belonged to the priests; and hence, from the original word, which signifies "to instruct in, or initiate into, the secrets of religion", they were called "mystae", and the rites themselves "mysteries", or religious secrets.

This is the true origin of the word; and from this it appears, that it signifies a thing unknown, or not understood; but that the ignorance of it does not arise from its being incomprehensible, but from its being kept secret, or unexplained; and of consequence, that, if published or explained, it becomes an object of knowledge and understanding.

Now, as this is the proper sense of the word, let us inquire whether Christ and his apostles used it in this sense. That they did so, is very probable, from a plain, but important observation. The use of language is, to convey the ideas of the speaker to the person spoken to. Hence, every word must have a determinate sense, else this end cannot be answered. Whatever language, then, a teacher adopts, he must use its words in the same sense in which they are commonly understood, or the persons whom he pretends to instruct, will unavoidably mistake his meaning. As the evangelists and apostles, therefore, have recorded the history of Christ and his religion in the Greek language, it follows, that they must use it in the same sense in which the Greeks used it, or lead those who understood it into perpetual errors. The use of words which admit of double meaning, *may* lead men astray; but a departure from the sense in which they are generally used, *must* do so; and wherever this takes place, it can be for no other purpose but that of deceit and imposture; a purpose with which, I am sure, none of us would dare to charge the blessed Jesus or his apostles.

But, whatever force there may be in this argument, or with whatever probability it might establish a general principle, we have no occasion to rest upon it here. The cases, to which Christ and his apostles applied the word "mystery", will lead us more clearly to the sense in which they used it, than all the abstract arguments in the world. Let us therefore examine the passages in which these are recorded, as they lie before us.

In the gospel by John, the word is not used at all; and it occurs only once in each of the other evangelists. In them, too, we meet with it as used by Jesus himself, and one one occasion only, which they have severally recorded. If, therefore, we can determine the sense in which he used it on that occasion, we may safely hold it as the only sense which it can bear in his religion.

When he delivered the parable of the sower, neither the disciples nor the multitude understood it. But when he was alone, the disciples came to him, and asked both an explanation of it, and the reason why he spake to the multitude in parables. "And he said, unto you it is given to *know* the *mysteries* of the kingdom of God; but to others in parables, that seeing they might not see, and hearing they might not understand. Now, the parable is this: Behold, a sower went forth to sow; and when he sowed, some seeds fell by the way-side; and the fowls came and devoured them. Some fell upon stony places, where they had not much earth; and forthwith they sprung up, because they had no deepness of earth: and when they sun was up, they were scorched; and because they had no root, they withered. And some fell among thorns; and the thorns sprung up and choked them. But others fell into good ground, and brought forth fruit, some thirty, some sixty, and some an hundred fold. He who hath ears to hear, let him hear."

Here the parable, as originally proposed, was a mystery, because not understood. To the multitude it contained a mystery, because left unexplained. But to the disciples it was given to *know* these *mysteries*, because their master explained them to *them*. And, so soon as the explanation was given, the parable became so plain, that the dullest apprehension may perceive, and the narrowest understanding comprehend its meaning. But, read the explanation, and judge for yourselves. "The seed is the word of God. Those by the way side, are they who hear; then cometh the deceiver, and taketh away the word out of their hearts, lest they should believe, and be saved. They on the rock, are they who, when they hear, receive the word with joy; and they have no root, who for a while believe, but afterward, when affliction, or persecution for the word's sake, ariseth, they are offended, and fall away. That which fell among thorns, are such as hear the word; and the cares of this world, the deceitfulness of riches, and the lusts of other things, entering in, choke the word, and render it unfruitful. And these are they, who are sown on good ground: such as hear the word, and receive it, and bring forth fruit, some thirty fold, some sixty, and some an hundred."

In this instance, then—the only one in which the word "mystery" is mentioned, as used by our Saviour,—it evidently appears in its original and primary sense; and the whole passage shows, that it does not signify "any thing unintelligible, or that a man cannot possibly understand"; for "to you" saith he, "it is given, to know the mysteries of the kingdom of God"; a declaration, which would have been only solemn mockery, if mysteries cannot be known and understood.

...

Sermon XIII

Faith Dependent On The Information And Exercise Of The Understanding

"Faith cometh by hearing"   ROM. x. 17

...

The understanding, in man, is the power by which he perceives and judges of whatever is presented to the mind. In its greatest extent, it comprehends all his powers of thought, reasoning, and reflexion. Hence, as a principle of perception, it has been called with great propriety "the eye of the mind", and knowledge "the light", by which it discovers the truth or falsehood, the fitness or impropriety, of what is presented to it. And as knowledge is the light of life, and derives its principal importance from its necessity and usefulness in directing the conduct, it is justly styled, in the emphatical language of scripture, "the candle of the Lord".

However, as subjects infinitely various are presented to the understanding, so they appear with degrees of evidence equally various. Some are so plain, and carry their evidence so fully with them, that they appear in their true colours and dimensions, independent of all reasoning. Others, though less evident, may be traced so directly to self evident principles, that they exclude all doubt or uncertainty. To the convictions, of which these are the objects, we give the name of "knowledge".

But there are others, which appear in a shape more questionable, and whose evidences admit of controversy;   consequently, the convictions of the understanding, which respect them, differ in their strength, in proportion to the proof by which they are supported. These we properly denominate "opinions".

Other propositions depend on testimony, and their truth is measured by the character, competence, and credibility of the witnesses by whom they are attested. It is the reliance on such testimony, which is expressed by the term "belief", or "faith". And it is this faith, or belief of truth resting on credible testimony, which, as the apostle asserts, "comes by hearing", in respect to the gospel.

The difference of circumstances, in our situation, from those of the persons to whom the apostle addressed himself, may give this expression an air of peculiarity; but its propriety is very obvious. Before the invention of writing, which represents sounds in a visible form, all information was communicated by the ear; and even afterwards, while books were multiplied by hand-writing only, the situation of the multitude continued the same. From the time and labour which were necessary, copies were so few, and the expense so great, that few were able, and fewer perhaps disposed, to purchase. Hence books, and the information which they supply, were confined to the rich or curious; and the great mass of the people depended on conversation, testimony, or public discourses, for all their information. And on this information, and the exercise of their own understandings concerning what they heard, their faith necessarily depended.

This ascertains the meaning of the apostle's language, and at the same time justifies its propriety. The justness of the conclusion which it expresses, is evident from the whole argument, as stated in the preceding verses. "Whosoever shall call on the name of the Lord, shall be saved. How then shall they call upon him in whom they have not believed? and how shall they believe in him of whom they have not heard? and how shall they hear, without a preacher?"

These enquiries directly lead to, and fully establish, the general principle on which the conclusion rests; that is, that faith arises from the information and exercise of the understanding, and from them alone; and of consequence, that men cannot believe what they have never been informed of, or what they do not understand.

The illustration of this would be altogether unnecessary, would men consider themselves in their distinguishing character of intelligent beings, and attend to the structure and organization of their own minds. Its truth seems so obvious, that it is hardly possible to overlook or reject it. And the contrary leads so directly into absurdity, that we cannot follow it a single step, without feeling ourselves involved in it. If we admit that a man can believe what he has never heard, or enjoyed any means of becoming acquainted with, it directly follows that he may believe all the truths which have ever been known, and all the facts which have taken place from eternity, in the boundless universe, though he is only the creature of a day, and his knowledge and information confined to a spot in the immensity of space. Or if we allow that he can believe what he does not understand, we must allow also, that children, idiots, and even the beasts of the field, may believe as much, and as firmly, as the most enlightened of men, or of the angels of God. In the former case, the enquiry of the apostle, "How can they believe in him, of whom they have never heard?" would be foolish and impertinent: in the latter, "the candle of the Lord" would be extinguished, an important character of humanity blotted out, and all the intellectual and reasoning powers reduced to an empty name, or useless incumbrance.

Farther, if faith be independent of the understanding, a consequence of a more awful nature directly follows. God, whose wisdom is boundless and unerring, is chargeable with folly. In that case, the revelations of his will are useless; The ministrations of angels were unnecessary; and the blood of the prophets was shed in vain. The mission of Jesus was a mockery of reason; his doctrines an unmeaning disclosure of divine truth; the declaration that he was sent as "a light to enlighten the nations", and denominating him "the Sun of righteousness", from the parity and extent of the knowledge which he diffused, are mere pomp of words. All the revelations, by them are only new information to the understanding of men: and therefore, if faith be independent of the understanding, they are all vain, and every effort to extend the knowledge of them if foolish and extravagant.

A very slight attention to these consequences must be sufficient to expose the absurdity of the principles on which they rest, and excite some degree of surprise that they have ever been adopted among men. And this surprise must be greatly heightened, by considering the numbers who have adopted them—who have boldly condemned the interference of reason in the concerns of religion, and pronounced the understanding "a blind guide". But it is more surprising still, that they have not rested satisfied with divorcing reason from religion, and understanding from faith. As if this had been insufficient, they have set them in direct opposition to each other; so that, if they judge right, a man can believe, not only what he has never heard, or what he cannot understand, but what is directly contrary to every perception of the understanding, and every principle of reason and common sense. So far has this been carried, that an ancient father of mystery declared that an opposition to these was the very foundation of his faith. "I believe", said he, "because it is impossible".

This was abandoning the region of understanding all at once, and launching boldly into the depths of absurdity, even beyond the reach of Omnipotence itself. To attempt following such an adventurer in the sober path of reason, would be vain indeed. Fancy, even in her most daring flights, must despair of overtaking him. Yet, many have been his followers, and many follow still. Leaving them, however, let us pursue the path marked out by the apostle, as leading to the source of faith, with sober steady pace, as the eye of the understanding, enlightened by the word of God, can trace it out.

Here however, it may not be impertinent, first, to trace this faith, which disclaims understanding as its parent and guardian, towards its pretended source, and take notice of some of its eccentric wanderings.

If we may trust its own declarations, this source is truly elevated. It boldly resolves itself into an immediate and extraordinary infusion of the Spirit of God. Were this its real origin, it must bear the resemblance of that Spirit. Now, God is perfect reason, and unclouded understanding; and therefore, the faith which proceeds from him, must be rational, intelligible, and consistent. And, as he is unchangeable, it must be steady, uniform, and equal in its operations.

Besides, understanding is the candle of the Lord, lighted within us for the noblest purposes. If God, therefore, by immediate inspiration, infuses faith into the souls of men, it must be conformable with the perceptions of the understanding; else, he is chargeable with inconsistency, the destruction of his own gifts, and the counteraction of his own laws. But, none of these features of divinity can be traced in it. Indeed, nothing rational or intelligible can be expected, where reason and intelligence are disclaimed. And to steadiness and uniformity it has no pretensions. Sometimes it swells into confidence, rises superior to hope, and clasps in its arms the throne of God; and sometimes it trembles on the brink of perdition, and is ready to plunge into the gulf of despair. Sometimes its eye is dazzled with beams of glory, to which it looks up as its sure portion; and sometimes a dark cloud arises, overshadows the heavenly prospect, and clothes it with gloomy horror. This moment, it raises its possessor above the possibility of sinning; and the next, sinks him into iniquity beneath the reach of mercy itself. In a word, nothing can be so unequal, changeable, and extravagant—nothing so passionate, and inconsistent—and therefore, nothing so unlike the operation of the Spirit of God—nothing more inconsistent with that pure intelligence which dwells in him.

But if the tree may be known by its fruit, we may safely ascribe it to the flights of imagination, unrestrained by reason—to the sallies of unbridled passion—or perhaps, in many cases, to the influence of bodily disease. This last, indeed, seems to be the true parent, whose sickly dreams fancy moulds into realities, and imposes upon the heart as revelations from God. What pity! that hearts all alive to the sentiments of religion, should disclaim the guidance of understanding, which alone could enable them to distinguish its genial warmth, which fosters all the virtues of the soul, from these devouring flames, which convulse the heart and agitate the frame, till, self-exhausted, they die away, and leave all behind in dark and melancholic gloom.

These characters of a faith which disclaims all relation to the understanding, the distresses into which it leads, and the absurdities which we have mentioned as flowing from it, afford a strong presumption, that we must return to the principle laid down by the apostle, and seek for a solid, satisfactory, and rational faith, in the due information and exercise of the understanding, and in this alone.

That this is the only source from which it can be derived, is obvious from a very moderate attention to our own minds. As faith is the *conviction* of the understanding, it must imply the *exercise* of the understanding. And the terms in which any fact is related, or doctrine proposed to the mind, must have certain ideas affixed to them, or in other words, "they must be understood", before we can believe it either true or false...

...

Chapter Eight

In Place Of A Conclusion

Steel Dickson died on December 27th, 1824. His death was marked by the following editorial in the Northern Whig.

"We record with pain, the death of the Rev. *Wm. Steele Dickson*, D.D. in the 79th year of his age, a Presbyterian divine, who, during half a century, was ranked deservedly high as a scholar of the first order; and whose life was rendered more painfully conspicuous, by the eventful scenes through which it was his fortune to pass.

"He was born in the parish of Carnmoney, in the County of Antrim, on the 25th of December, O.S. [Old Style, ie, before the reform of the calendar, BC], 1744; and was, of course, within a few days of his 80th year. After the usual routine of school education, he went to the University of Glasgow, in November, 1761. Here he had an opportunity of studying under the celebrated Dr. Adam Smith, who was then Professor of Moral Philosophy in that University. Here, also, he became, at once the pupil and friend of the celebrated Mr. John Millar, Professor at Law. By him, he was initiated in the principles of jurisprudence and civil government. From this period, he became attached to political speculations; and to this cause, most of his subsequent misfortunes may be traced. He went through the whole of his College course, with such distinguished success, as to attract the notice, and call forth the warmest encomiums of the different Professors. They afterwards conveyed to him a strong proof of their esteem and approbation, by conferring on him, without solicitation, the degree of Doctor of Divinity. After finishing his College curriculum, he was received on trial by the Presbytery of Templepatrick, and was licensed by that venerable body to preach the Gospel, in March, 1767. In the year 1771, he was ordained to the pastoral charge of the Presbyterian Congregation of Ballyhalbert, in the County of Down, from which he was removed to Portaferry, in the year 1780. At this period, the Volunteer system was in the meridian of its glory. Dr. Dickson was then in the vigour of manhood; and, both from natural temperament and early associations, was ardent, impetuous, and enthusiastic in the cause of civil and religious liberty.   His conduct was, in consequence, exactly what might naturally be expected from such a man, at such an era. He took a conspicuous part in the different measures which grew out of the Volunteer system; and, in several of the popular movements which subsequently took place, in rapid succession, in the North of Ireland. He was an ostensible delegate at the celebrated Convention at Dungannon—a distinguished speaker at the town-meeting of Belfast, on the subject of Catholic Emancipation, in 1792—and an active and influential agent in the various contested elections, which were produced, in the County of Down, by the rival houses of Hill and Stewart.

"In all these various public transactions, he invariably took his stand on the side which was considered at the time, to be *the most liberal*. In Erin's evil day, at the period of the insurrection of 1798, he fell under the suspicion of the government. He was in consequence arrested, and, after being kept in confinement for more than three years, the principal part of which was spent at Fort George in Scotland, he was set at liberty by the government of the day. After his return to his native country, he obtained a call to undertake the pastoral charge of the Presbyterian congregation of Keady, in the County of Armagh. Here he continued for 12 years. Obliged, at length, by age and infirmity, to relinquish the duties of the ministry, he came, some years ago, to the neighbourhood of this town. Here he lived in that state of pecuniary embarrassment and poverty, which the events detailed might be expected to produce, and, on the 27th instant, he closed his long and eventful pilgrimage.

"Abstracted from the political contentions, in which he conceived it his duty to take a part, we know not the man for whose genuine philanthropy, kindness of heart, and ardent desire to promote the progress of moral and intellectual knowledge, we entertained a higher opinion. We have met him in public, and bear willing attestation to the deep conviction which he felt of the purity and patriotism of every principle which he advocated. He had a single heartedness of mind, which rendered the advocacy of the cause of civil and religious liberty, the paramount principle of his life. In prosperity—in exile, shall we write it?—in poverty—he never changed. He was a man of the most unbending integrity; but we loved him most, when turning from the thorny path of political controversy, we entered with him into the field of moral discussion, theological inquiry, and ecclesiastical research. We differed from him in theology: but we bear willing attestation to this fact, that not studious man sat in his society, without admiration of his genius; or left it unimproved by the morality of his advice. He felt an interest, almost of a paternal nature, in the weal and welfare of every candidate for the Presbyterian Ministry.

"He was the private and personal friend of Leechman, that mildest and most amiable of men; and to him he owed his recommendation to the highest Collegiate honours.

"For ourselves, let us say, that we never met him, without encreasing respect for the purity of his mind, and the profoundness of his researches into the elements of language, and the principles of morals. We write these lines with a deep consciousness, that his literary acquirements were too little prized, and his religious constancy too lightly estimated, by his contemporaries.

"His remains were accompanied to the grave, by a considerable number of the most respectable inhabitants of Belfast. An impressive and eloquent address was delivered to those present, by the Rev. W.D.H. M'Ewen.

[Northern Whig, 30.12.1824.]

The Northern Whig, the most effective Unionist newspaper of the 19th century and the first half of the twentieth century, was a sort of posthumous offspring of the United Irish movement. Its founder, F.D. Finlay (1793-1857) was the son of a Newtownards farmer who was apprenticed to a Belfast printer. He came to the notice of some eminent United Irish survivors when working on the magazine which they published between 1808 and 1814, and he acquired his substantial liberal outlook through personal contact with them at a moment when liberal politics was in severe recession.

Then,

"in the year 1824 he entered on the bold and hazardous experiment of establishing *The Northern Whig*. I say bold and hazardous; for the sad scenes of the suppressed

Rebellion of 1798 had nearly extinguished the patriotic spirit of the North. Confident, however, in a good cause, full of youthful ardour, and sustained by honest convictions, he steadily persevered; and in a few years, by the firm, yet moderate, advocacy of sound principles, and the employment of the best literary talent within his reach, he placed his paper, not only at the head of the Provincial journals of Ulster, but on a fair equality with those of the Metropolis [i.e. London, BC]. That high position *The Northern Whig* has proudly maintained during the last thirty years, with a regularly-increasing reputation and influence. In fact, it has led the van in all great reforms since the year 1829, and is, at this moment, viewed, in all parts of the British Empire, as the leading organ of Liberal sentiments in Ireland."

I quote from the Rev. Henry Montgomery's obituary on Finlay in the Northern Whig in 1857. Montgomery, whose first action in the public sphere was a defence of Dickson against Black at the 1813 meeting of the Synod of Ulster, was one of the chief contributors to the Northern Whig in its early years. The Rev. M'Ewen, who delivered Dickson's funeral oration, was acting editor of the Whig at the start. And the paper was established with the support of William Drennan and Hamilton Rowan, gentlemen who had played a part in the United Irish movement.

If, in the months before his death, Steel Dickson gave any thought to the probability of leaving behind him an enduring literary reputation—which I doubt—he would have had grounds for supposing that his future fame was assured. The resurgent liberalism of the 1820s had numerous connections with the United Irish liberalism of the 1790s. And, if he had lived another eight years, he would have seen the triumph of both the causes to which he dedicated his political life—Catholic Emancipation and Parliamentary reform.

If this book you hold in your hand had been published in 1825—as it ought to have been—it would have concluded with a certainty that Steel Dickson was one of the literary immortals. It would have found it inconceivable that such a combination of thought, articulacy, spirit, character, and action should fail to leave a lasting impression on the world. But since there has been a delay of 166 years in its publication, this book must contrive to find a different way of ending.

*

James Seaton Reid's **History Of The Presbyterian Church In Ireland** was written in the mid-19th century and was published in three volumes. Though last issued in 1867, it remains the most ambitious attempt at a comprehensive history of Presbyterianism in Ireland. Its authoritative status is not diminished by the fact that it is unavailable to the public in Belfast. (I could not get a copy of Volume 3 to read in either the Central Reference Library or the Linenhall Library, but found one in London.) It is authoritative because it is known to exist and because nothing else like it exists.

Seaton Reid deals with Steel Dickson as follows:

"unhappily for himself, as well as for his Church, he became better known as a political demagogue than as a sober, pious, and edifying pastor. When the Society of

United Irishmen was established, he warmly espoused its cause, and, in 1798, proved so unmindful of what he owed to his own character as a minister of the Prince of Peace, that he permitted himself to be appointed commander of the rebels for the count y of Down.*" (Volume 3, p397.)

The asterisk indicates the following footnote:

""'In 1812, Dr. Dickson published 'A Narrative of his Confinement and Exile', in which he disingenuously attempts to deny this statement, but its truth is now admitted on all hands (See Teeling's 'Personal Narrative', pp226,228 and Madden's 'United Irishmen', second series, vol.ii, p.431)."

The description of Steel Dickson as a "political demagogue" is about as accurate as would be a description of John Locke and Edmund Burke as political demagogues. He was, like them, a political philosopher who was led be philosophical reflection into political action. And it would be more in accordance with historical fact to say that the United Irishmen espoused his cause than that he espoused theirs.

Seaton Reid's charge of disingenuousness against Dickson for his "attempts to deny" that he "permitted himself to be appointed commander of the rebels for the county of Down" is itself "disingenuous" in the extreme. Dickson never denied it. He neither denied it nor confirmed it. He was arrested and imprisoned by the Government, without due process of law, on an accusation of being a rebel General. The Government, despite the vast resources at its disposal, and the powers of punishment and advancement which it could bring to bear on individuals, was unable to assemble evidence in order to bring its accusation against Dickson to law. He was released uncharged after three years of arbitrary imprisonment. Being released uncharged, there was no case for him to answer, and he had no occasion to plead either guilty or not guilty. On his release, he demanded that the Synod of Ulster should review its proceedings of 1799 in the light of this fact. After some hesitation, the Synod eventually admitted to having acted rashly in 1799.

Britain prides itself on being a state based on *"the rule of law"*, the law in question being the English common law, and until very recently it frankly regarded all other peoples who had not been subjected to the British Empire as *"lesser breeds without the law"*. It is not actually the case that the British state was based on the rule of law—the sovereignty first of the Crown and later of Parliament was clearly located beyond and above the law. And I am of the opinion that the virtues of the English common law have been wildly exaggerated. But it is indisputable that Steel Dickson acted entirely in the spirit of the common law by declining to plead when no charge had been brought against him, and his attitude towards his arbitrary imprisonment indicated a stronger belief in the pretensions of the British state to be based on the rule of law than did Seaton Reid's view that, though uncharged at law, he should have admitted that he was guilty.

If this affair had happened in England, Dickson would have been regarded as having strengthened the law by his attitude to it. Though the common law is far from being all it purports to be, it must be admitted that, insofar as it operates, England lives in accordance with it.

English common law has no concern with truth. A legal concern with truth is the hallmark of lesser breeds without. Dickson was imprisoned without trial for over three years and was then arbitrarily released uncharged. The Government had failed utterly in the game of law, and therefore, on English attitudes, Dickson was not only innocent, but was injured. Whether he was actually a rebel general then becomes an utterly obscure question lost on the other side of his arrest. It becomes a meaningless question, even a bad mannered one.

There is much to be said for "inquisitorial" law—for law which is concerned with truth. It is much more appropriate to democratic social conditions than the common law—which is essentially law for the gentry. And it is much more in tune with the historic culture of Presbyterian Ulster, with its roots in Scotland, than the common law is. But the English common law is what has existed in Ireland for close on four centuries, and when Presbyterian Ulster achieved a degree of autonomy in 1921 and established a separate jurisdiction it adopted the common law unquestioningly and never contemplated a shift to Scottish law. And yet today, not less than in Seaton Reid's time, the spirit of Protestant Ulster remains half-heartedly committed to the moral implications of adversarial law in which the law is indifferent to truth. It cannot live its law, as England does, because the common law is concentrated Jesuitry, and because the forthright spirit of the Covenanters still flourishes beside the official English apparatus of social life in Ulster and in contradiction of it.

That is the most charitable construction I can put on Seaton Reid's comment on Steel Dickson.

Reid went behind the law—or the abrogation of law by Government—to the superseded question of whether Dickson was in fact a United Irish General. And he refers to Teeling and Madden in proof that he was, but does not present those proofs to the reader.

Teeling wrote:

"In the absence of Russell another leader had been appointed, the Rev. William Steele Dickson... He had been the early asserter of Ireland's independence, the eloquent advocate of his Catholic countrymen for the full enjoyment of their civil rights, and had on some occasions to encounter a torrent of bigotry which required no ordinary nerve to resist. Sacrificing personal interest at the shrine of national right, he was refused any participation in the *Regium Donum* which was extended to several members of his Communion in the synod of Ulster; but he preferred poverty with virtue to the allurements of fortune with a compromise of principle...

"Dickson repaired to his post, but was arrested with two of his staff; the others having been apprised of his misfortune, eluded the vigilance of those into whose hands he had fallen. Down was now without a first in command, the centre of unity was broken, and the more subordinate chiefs were either dispersed, or over-awed by the prompt and decisive measures which followed.

"Antrim had determined to act in conjunction with Down, and by dividing the attention of the enemy, these counties would have been an overmatch for the British troops which garrissoned both. The period of action had been previously arranged, and the respective duties assigned; but Antrim being prepared for the field, could not be induced to wait the appointment of a new commander for Down. To supply the place of Dickson was not an easy task... Down urged the necessity of delay, but Antrim was resolved—was already committed. Her military chiefs had assembled in council; numbers had quitted their homes for the field... All waited orders from the first in command, when, to their inexpressible astonishment, his formal resignation was announced.

"There was now no safety in return, no encouraging hope in advance; the secession of the chief communicated doubt and alarm... Flight secured the safety of those who wanted nerve for the field, while in this moment of consternation the attention of the bolder spirits was directed to the man on whose firmness all could rely; this was the gallant M'Cracken, in whose breast no timid counsel ever found utterance." (Charles Hamilton Teeling: **Personal Narrative Of The Irish Rebellion Of 1798**, London, 1828, pp226/7).

I cannot see that Teeling does any more than repeat what was freely alleged about Dickson by the Irish Government in 1798. Considered as evidence, it is mere hearsay. And the Narrative as a whole is remarkably short on specific detail. (And the reader will see that Teeling's statement of what happened to the Generalship of Down on Dickson's arrest conflicts with Madden's statement, which is given below.)

Charles Hamilton Teeling (1778-1850) belonged to one of the few families of Catholic gentry in the North. His father, a member of a Co. Louth family of Norman descent, set up as a linen merchant in Lisburn and was active in the reform movement of the 1780s and 1790s. Charles Hamilton was arrested in September 1796, at the age of 18, on a suspicion of treason. The arrest was made personally by Lord Castlereagh, "who was a personal friend of my father".

Teeling's account of his affairs from 1796 to 1798 was written twenty years after the event. In the interim, he had been a successful newspaper owner and editor. His Personal Narrative is an interesting reflection on the times, but its title is a misnomer. The book is for the most part a history of events of which he could not have had personal experience, and I found it impossible to extract his personal history from it.

He gives the date of his arrest (September 16th, 1796) but few dates are given thereafter. He was taken to Dublin and held in prison for an unspecified period. In his account of the Battle of Antrim he says he knew Henry Joy McCracken well as he "was my fellow prisoner for twelve months, often the companion of my cell". So he was in prison until mid-September 1797 at least. Then he fell seriously ill and was released for nursing to the widow of a British Army Captain on bonded security of £4,000. He says that his recovery was slow. At a certain time he presented himself at Dublin Castle to redeem the bond. He met Under-Secretary Cooke who suggested that it would do his health no good to return to prison. He said that a return to his native mountains would do his health great good, but Cooke disagreed. Teeling therefore remained at liberty, on parole not to go North. Some time later, however, he did go Northwards, though he gives no dates and few other details. In the summer of 1798 he was named as a proscribed person. He was living in Dublin at the house of a gentleman. He drew up a memorial in which he offered to surrender on condition of being sent for trial without delay. He accosted the Viceroy (Cornwallis) while he was out riding and tried to present this memorial to him. Cornwallis seemed willing to accept it, but an aide insisted that such things must go through official channels. The gentleman with whom Teeling was staying took the memorial to Dublin Castle. The Government replied that it could not agree to Teeling's condition of a trial, but that if he surrendered he would be allowed to emigrate. Teeling then went into hiding, but found that he was not being hunted—though his elder brother, Bartholomew, who had gone to France in 1796 and returned with Humbert's Army to Mayo in 1798 was executed by Courtmartial that September. In 1802 he set up in the linen business in Dundalk, declined to get involved in the 1803 rebellion, and soon after began his career in publishing.

What I cannot see is when he might have had authoritative knowledge that Dickson replaced Russell as General for Co. Down. He was arrested the same day as Russell, spent the following year in prison and an unspecified time after that seriously ill, and from then until the rising the course of his career is submerged in obscurity so far as his Narrative goes.

Seaton Reid must have seen that Teeling's evidence was mere hearsay. He must also have seen that his remarks about the Regium Donum did not indicate sound information about Steel Dickson's affairs. By 1828 O'Connell's insidious influence on Catholic affairs was well established, and it had become virtually impossible even for Catholics who were well-disposed towards Presbyterians to understand Presbyterian affairs. The corrupting effect of the Regium Donum had become a catch-all explanation for resistance to O'Connell even by Presbyterians who continued to support Catholic emancipation. Teeling's remarks seem to be in tune with this new order of thought. But they are basically misleading in that they suggest that Dickson never received the Bounty, being excluded from it by Presbyterian bigotry. In fact, Dickson approved of the Regium Donum and was in full receipt of it during the 1780s and 1790s. He was denied it at Keady, after his release from prison, due to the influence of Robert Black and Castlereagh.

Seaton Reid understood these things very well, and therefore he must have known that his witness was unreliable.

Seaton Reid's second witness against Dickson is the chief historian of the United Irishmen, R.R. Madden. The passage in question is as follows:

"Thomas Russell was appointed by the Colonels of Down, in 1796; his arrest in the winter of that year occasioned the appointment of another adjutant-general, and the Rev. Dr. Steele Dickson was then appointed. Dr. Dickson, in his narrative, has taken a vast deal of trouble to disprove the statements of Maginn and Hughes, with respect to the military appointment conferred upon him, but he takes care to avoid any explicit denial of the fact. The attempt, however, to encumber the statement of it with reasonings on its improbability, and arguments against its credibility was an unworthy effort at deception, where there was no plea of necessity arising from legal proceedings for the endeavour to disprove a statement which could not be denied with truth.

"The late Mr. John Gunning, one of the Colonels of the United system in 1798, (then Mr. Byers,) informed us that on Dickson's arrest, Mr. George Sinclair, who had formerly served in the army, was appointed adjutant-general of the County Down, and that Government through some channel (he named Maginn) was in possession of all their proceedings and appointments from 1796. Dickson was arrested on the 4th of June, 1798, three days before the time appointed for the outbreak of the Ulster insurrection."

Madden's work is entitled: **The United Irishmen: Their Lives And Times**. It was published in three groups of volumes: the First Series (2 volumes) in London in 1842; the Second Series (2 volumes) in London in 1843; and the Third Series (3 volumes) in Dublin in 1846—seven large volumes in all. It was issued in a second edition between 1858 and 1860, and has never been reprinted since then to my knowledge. The second edition was issued in Four Series, each Series being one volume. The second edition varies considerably from the first. It took me many years to find my way around this confusion. I think I have now seen all that Madden published under the title, **The United Irishmen**, but I am not certain that I have.

The work is not a coherent history of the United Irish movement—and no such history has ever been attempted. It is a series of independent biographies. In the seven volumes of the first edition, there are nineteen individual biographies, and three groups of biographies (of the Wexford, Wicklow, and Mayo, United Irish). There is no biography of Steel Dickson—or of Thomas Ledlie Birch, or of Sinclare Kelburn.

Madden's comment on Dickson referred to by Seaton Reid is from the biography of Henry Joy M'Cracken. M'Cracken, who emerged as the daring man of action in June 1798, is comprehensible to Madden, but he has no insight into the philosophical and political character of the movement as it developed in Ulster during the preceding six years.

He frankly admits that he cannot understand how the Northern Star could have become a popular newspaper (see 1st Series, Vol 2, p54).

Madden was born into the Catholic middle class in Dublin in 1798. The house where he was born was searched by the notorious Major Sirr on the day he was born. But the national disposition of his mind was of a kind which enabled him to be a British diplomat in the 1830s and 1840s. His object in undertaking to "elucidate this period of Irish, or rather British History" was to assimilate the history of the United Irishmen into British political culture, as the history of the 1745 Rebellion in Scotland had been assimilated (Preface to Vol. I of First Series):

"Little do the people of England know the class of persons who were driven into rebellion. Englishmen may probably have heard that a number of obscure, ill-disposed and reckless men, had engaged in an unnatural and unprovoked rebellion... As such persons read this work, they will find that a great portion of these unfortunate persons, were gentlemen by birth, education and profession: many of them celebrated their talents, respected for their private worth; several of them scholars who had distinguished themselves in the University of Dublin [ie, Trinity College, the exclusive University of the Ascendancy, BC]; the majority of them members of the Presbyterian Church; some of them Presbyterian ministers; few, if any, of them who did not exert more or less influence over their countrymen" (ibid).

*

Moderate and responsible men were driven to rebellion by systematically perverse government to which there seemed to be no other remedy. But the rebellion, though it failed, secured a remedy. Cornwallis was sent to Ireland both to suppress the rebellion and to eradicate its cause. The Ascendancy was subverted by the Act of Union. And, once the rebellion was put down, the rebels were granted *oblivion* for their actions. Irish affairs started afresh with the new century. Ireland in the 18th and the 19th centuries might be different countries for all the historical continuity there is between the two centuries.

That is the best approach to an understanding of three provinces (or three and a half), but it does not meet the case in eastern Ulster. In Antrim and Down there is substantial continuity of social life across the Act of Union. The elements were not dissolved. A new society was not forged in the 19th century, as was the case in the south. There could be oblivion in the south because both society and Government started afresh. In three and a half provinces a new Ireland began because the old Ireland, the Ireland of Grattan's Parliament could not continue. But Ulster continued.

Madden's contention that perverse government drove the property and intelligence of the country into rebellion is even more true of Ulster than of the rest of the country. Dickson and his colleagues were people of a more sober disposition than were the southern United Irish Protestants; they were more rooted in a viable society; and their wealth, though less spectacular, was self-generated and economically functional.

During the regime of Lord Camden, many wealthy southern gentlemen became acutely aware that they were members of an elite caste which was stretched precariously over a seething mass of people with which it had no organic connection. They sensed that Armageddon was at hand and they became rebels in a desperate effort to ward it off. The Government had sowed the wind and they attempted to ride the whirlwind. The events in Wexford in May/June 1798 brought home to them the impossibility of what they had attempted, though they had had no honourable choice but to attempt it. When the new Government of Cornwallis instituted a new regime and offered them the Treaty under which the Rebellion would be dealt with by a sort of gentlemen's agreement without recourse to law, they had no good reason to refuse that offer. And the great body of Catholics certainly had no reason to wish for continuity on the basis of law whose chief object had been to outlaw them.

In three provinces the disconnected elements of a social jumble were driven frantic by the regime of Lord Londonderry's brother-in-law, Lord Camden. It was in Ulster that an orderly and industrious society was driven to rebellion by prolonged state terrorism. And it was in Ulster that the Government was required by those whom it had at its mercy to act through the law, and that the offer of a Treaty of amnesty in return for voluntary admissions was spurned.

Madden, a product of the new society which began after 1798, has no insight into the old society in Ulster, whose continuity of social experience stretched back more than a century, and was not broken by either Rebellion or the Union.

Having been imprisoned without charge, Dickson refused to plead, and having been released still without charge, he still refused to plead, and he insisted that the Synod of Ulster take account of these gross facts of the matter in the way that is appropriate in a state which purports to be a rule of law, that law being the common law of England. Madden has no patience with that. I think it was not the least admirable of the many admirable things done by Steel Dickson.

*

But this is not an argument with Madden. It is an argument with Seaton Reid. For Madden, Dickson was one of a welter of United Irishmen. But Seaton Reid was the historian of the Church in which Dickson had been eminent. And what is of concern today is not so much the stupid injustice of Reid's way of dealing with Dickson as the effect which that stupidity has had on the political culture of the Presbyterian community.

It was the behaviour of the Presbyterian community in the mass which produced the United Irish movement in the early 1790s, and it was the catastrophic behaviour of the Government from 1795 onwards which drove that movement for constitutional reform into military conspiracy. But Seaton Reid depicts Presbyterian involvement in the United Irish movement as marginal, and Government behaviour as reasonable. And, whereas the entry on Dickson in the Matriculation Albums of Glasgow University indicates pride in having contributed to his development, for Reid, Dickson is only an embarrassment.

There is no doubt that Dickson, in the 1780s and 1790s, was known as "a sober, pious, and edifying pastor". His political influence was directly connected with his reputation for sober and edifying piety. He could be a successful "political demagogue" only because he was highly respected as a pastor. His last work of 'political demagoguery' was published in the spring of 1793—Scripture Politics. A few months later he was elected Moderator of the Synod of Ulster. And the Synod of 1793 adopted, with only one dissentient, an Address to the King on the lines of the United Irish programme.

*

Dickson's two great enemies in Ulster—his former political colleague, the Rev. Robert Black, and his former pupil and admirer, Robert Stewart, Lord Castlereagh—both died before him, and both died by their own hands. Black flung himself off Derry Bridge in 1817 and Castlereagh cut his throat in 1822. If Dickson had been the one who committed suicide, Seaton Reid would no doubt have found an instructive moral lesson in that fact. But since Dickson was the one who did *not* commit suicide, Reid finds no moral in the fact. Indeed, he leaves his readers to discover from other sources that Black was a suicide. He only informs them that Black "died under melancholy circumstances" (Vol 3, p435).

The death of Castlereagh in disgraceful circumstances removed a burden—a nightmare—from Unionist political life in Antrim and Down. The close association of the House of Londonderry with the Act of Union inhibited the growth of positive Unionist sentiment amongst the popular, or "independent", interest. And right-wing sentiment was against the Union. (The News Letter published no statement in support of a Union during Castlereagh's long struggle to carry the Act in the Irish Parliament in 1799 and 1800.) This state of affairs led to Castlereagh losing his seat in the County Down election of 1805, through an alliance against him of those who had secured his election in 1790 with the Downshire interest.

Mountstewart had defected from the popular cause in 1795 and had subsequently acted with malicious brutality against those who continued to espouse that cause. That was something which could not readily be forgotten. Castlereagh's prominence in accomplishing the Union was therefore a factor inhibiting the development of popular Unionist sentiment. The man and the cause were too intimately associated to allow the cause to be viewed independently of the man. The man overshadowed the cause.

I do not share Dickson's view of Castlereagh. But I can understand why strong popular feeling against him persisted for a generation in the community in which he grew up and which sent him to Parliament. The mere fact that he was the Londonderry heir was sufficient reason for his rejection by County Down and for Dickson's venomous references to him as the man who sold his country. Neither of these things indicated an earnest opposition to the accomplished fact of the Union. The behaviour of Antrim and Down at the time of Emmet's Rebellion in 1803 demonstrates that they had already taken the Union for granted then, but the growth of exuberant Unionist sentiment could not occur until the House of Londonderry was overcome by misfortune.

It was the proper business of Seaton Reid to unravel these complexities of the real life of Ulster and to assimilate the culture of the United Irish phase of Presbyterian history into the Unionist phase. Instead of doing that, he sought Victorian respectability by blotting out the United Irish phase.

I commented in a biography of Thomas Moore: "The weeding out of Moore was a major act of cultural vandalism... A nation which does such things to itself needs no external oppressive force to make it culturally poor" (**Life & Poems Of Thomas Moore**, Athol Books, 1984, p32). But the weeding out of Moore was a very minor act of vandalism in the life of nationalist Ireland, compared with the weeding out of Steel Dickson in the life of Unionist Ulster. And I cannot see how Unionist Ulster can regain its political health while that act of vandalism stands.

What one is capable of in the present depends on what one supposes has happened in the past.

BIBLIOGRAPHY

A. By Dickson

1. **Sermons On The Following Subjects**   Belfast, 1778 (see p39 for further details)
2. **A Sermon On the Propriety And Advantages Of Acquiring The Knowledge And The Use Of Arms**   Belfast, 1779 (see p52)
3. **Funeral Sermon For James Armstrong**   Belfast, 1780. (This is listed in the Dictionary of National Biography (DNB). I have not seen it. Armstrong was Dickson's predecessor as minister at Portaferry)
4. **Psalmody**   Belfast, 1792. (Listed in the DNB. I have not seen it. DNB describes it as "an address to Presbyterians issued with the approval of nine Presbyteries)
5. **Three Sermons On The Subject Of Scripture Politics**   Belfast, 1793 (see p60)
6. **Stromata Theologica, Historica, & Prohpetica; Or, Theological, Historical, And Prophetical Pieces Of Patchwork: For The Amusement Of The Curious, Instruction Of The Ignorant, And Benefit Of All. Patch 1.**   London, 1805

   (There is a handwritten note on the British Museum copy of this booklet: *"said to be written by Steel Dickson a presbyterian Minister in the Co. of Down, Ireland—who was arrested in 1798 on suspicion of being concerned in the Rebellion"*. In the days before it became the British Library, the Reading Room of the British Museum took great care with the cataloguing of its books, and I have found its attribution of the authorship of anonymous publications reliable.

   This purports to be a translation of an old manuscript found in " the lower parts of Germany", and describes the decline of early Christianity into idolatry and tyranny as the Papacy established itself.)
7. **Speech At A Catholic Dinner In Dublin, 9 May 1811**   Dublin, 1811 (Listed in DNB. I have not seen it)
8. **A Narrative Of The Confinement And Exile Of William Steel Dickson D.D.**   Dublin, 1812 (see p10. Includes account of assault on Dickson after he attended a Catholic meeting in Armagh, and a reprint of "Scripture Politics" in an Appendix)
9. **Speech Of The Rev. Dr. Dickson At The Armagh Catholic Meeting**   In Walter Cox's **Irish Magazine,** Dublin, June 1812
10. **Letter** to Belfast Monthly Magazine, containing **Preface** to be included in 2nd edition of the "Narrative Of Confinement And Exile".   Belfast Montly Magazine, Belfast, August 1812
11. **A Narrative Of Confinement And Exile.**   2nd edition (with added Preface of 15 pages reporting and commenting on the1812 meeting of the Synod of Ulster. Belfast, 1812

    (According to the DNB, both editions of the Narrative were published by subscription, and the 2nd edition was of two thousand copies and sold at a guinea)
12. **Retractions**   Belfast, 1813 (see p110)
13. **Sermons**   Belfast 1817, (see p129)

B. About Dickson

   The entry in the Dictionary Of National Biography, London, written by the Rev. Alexander Gordon, is the main item published about Dickson between his death and the present day. It was published about a century ago. It gives the following family details: Dickson married Isabella Gamble in 1771. She died in July 1819. They had two daughters and four sons. The eldest son, a surgeon in the navy, died in 1798. Another son went into business, and a third was an apothecary.

   Gordon, who I believe was English, ends with the indisputable statement that "Dickson was a man of genius".

INDEX

Athol Books Publications *1991*

A Story Of The Armada
> by Captain Francisco De Cuellar, Joe Keenan and others *£3.50*

The Constitutional History Of Eire/Ireland
> by Angela Clifford *£15*

Northern Ireland And The Algerian Analogy: A Suitable Case For Gaullism?
> by Hugh Roberts *£3*

The Dubliner: The Lives, Times And Writings Of James Clarence Mangan
> by Brendan Clifford *£7.50*

Thomas Russell And Belfast (A biography of "the man from God knows
> where", the Munster Soldier who was central to the social life of Belfast
> in the United Irish phase, and was executed for his part inEmmet's
> Rebellion by Brendan Clifford *£5*

The Veto Controversy, including Thomas Moore's
> **A Letter To The Roman Catholics Of Dublin** (1810)
> by Brendan Clifford *£10*

The Life And Poems Of Thomas Moore
> edited by Brendan Clifford *£5*

Farm Labourers: Irish Struggle 1900—1976
> by Dan Bradley *£5*

The O'Neill Years, Unionist Politics 1963-1969
> by David Gordon *£7.50*

From Civil Rights To National War, Northern Ireland Catholic Politics
> 1964-1974 by Pat Walsh *£7.50*

Available (mail order only) from:
Athol Books,
10 Athol Street,
Belfast, BT12 4GX.

"Scripture Politics" is the title of one of the most influential books ever published in Belfast. Written by a Presbyterian minister, it was the manifesto of the movement of the United Irishmen in Antrim and Down in the 1790s. Today, many would see the two words of this title as a contradiction in terms—some because they deplore politics, and others because they deplore religion. But the United Irishmen saw them as inseparable.

Three Presbyterian clergymen were at the heart of United Irish activity: the Revs. Steel Dickson, James Porter and Ledlie Birch. They fought for representative government and Catholic Emancipation. Dickson was imprisoned without trial, Porter was hanged, and Birch was exiled. But, though their writings and political actions were of the greatest consequence in the North of Ireland in the years leading up to the Union, they have been written out of history by those who try to portray the 1798 rebellion as something it was not.

Brendan Clifford has embarked on a project to re-integrate Northern Ireland's present with its past by publishing selections from the writings of Dickson, Porter and Birch, and other works. This book is a vital link in that grand project. Apart from the editorial material about those exciting times, it contains Steel Dickson's views about the American War of Independence, his Sermon on the Advantages of Acquiring the Knowledge of Arms, his reflections about a Christian's political duty, as well as extracts from his autobiography which he published during his campaign to revive in the Synod of Ulster the independent spirit which had declined in the years of 1798.

ISBN 0 85034 044 6

ATHOL BOOKS 1991